From Now to Now

Marlis Jermutus

pelorian digital

pelorian digital
One Front Street
Leeds, Massachusetts
01053 USA
www.pelorian.com

1st Edition 2011
2nd Edition 2015

Book and Cover design by
Richard Rasa and Marlis Jermutus
Cover graphic:
Teilchen und Welle (Particle and Wave)
Ink on Paper, 1974, by Marlis Jermutus

Back cover photos:
Photo of Marlis by Rasa
Photo of Marlis & Lisa by Bastian
Family photographs by the family

Library of Congress Number: 2011922544

ISBN-13: 978-0615448930
ISBN-10: 0615448933

From Now to Now

by Marlis Jermutus

Translated by Richard Rasa

Dedication

This book is dedicated to
my parents and my children.

Acknowledgments

Love and gratitude
to Julianne Murray
for her editorial assistance,

and to Dr. Zaida Rivene
for her compassion and insight
expressed so beautifully in the Foreword.

Contents

Preface

I want to thank Rasa who sat with me for hours and hours brilliantly translating my German and my peculiar English into a poetic narrative. Through the process of writing this book, echoes of the emotions I experienced during my life washed across me. Sometimes I was overwhelmed by those intense memories. In moments of imbalance, Rasa always held me with compassion, helping me through to the next chapter. As I wrote about the obstacles on my path, I thought about the advice to parents from Kahlil Gibran in his book *The Prophet*.

> *Your children are not your children.*
> *They are the sons and daughters of Life's longing for itself.*
> *They come through you but not from you,*
> *And though they are with you yet they belong not to you.*

I was already a mother when I first read these words, but I was also a child who desperately needed freedom from the world my parent's generation created. For me, The Prophet had a double message, and so my writing tells the story of how I was a child and an adult - and in some ways always both.

Philosophers say that to make an accurate map of the world, it would have to be the same size as the world. An accurate account of one's life might take as many years to tell as there are years in the story. I am grateful to have learned something from every person and experience in my life. There are many people and experiences that I have left out of this story, but they are not gone from my memory and my heart.

The experiences I describe - the events, my feelings, my thoughts, my reactions - I present them all as I remember them, fully knowing that this presentation arrises from my own perceptions and interpretations. The people in my life have their own perceptions, as all people have their own unique perspectives on their lives. I cannot say that another's perspective is necessarily false if it differs from mine. My perspective is not supreme, it is simply mine.

Preface to the 2nd Edition

There are a small number of minor edits in the 2nd edition. Some readers who found themselves as part of the narrative corrected a few minor facts, and I am happy those small edits bring some greater accuracy. Some edits arose from a desire to change a few words in order to add more clarity to some of the philosophical concepts. Many thanks to those people whose conversations about these concepts brought many hours of joyful and productive thought and introspection.

Foreword

This is a woman's story for women, told with such sincerity, compassion, and deep intimate truths that my cells cringe with emotional anxiety when reading such an honest and unabridged description of Marlis' deeply personal weaving of her first completed cycle of sixty-eight chronological years. This is the spiritual artist emerging from womb-time in war torn Germany to this present now, truthfully disclosing a life journey of her spiritual quest, unravelling cultural and customary tribal beliefs, of facing the deepest fears and false assumptions, of dismantling the egotistical mind and giving birth to her highest self awareness, therefore, awakening to a life lived exactly how she desires it to be.

Marlis' book is also a story for men. Look at all the men in this book, as the fathers, brothers, lovers, husbands, the sons, the teachers, the abusers, the friends, and the supporters - Marlis teaches us that all the men in a woman's life are to be honoured and held in full gratitude and light for their contribution to the growth and clarity of our spirit and the resonating vibration to our souls.

Living a life exactly how we want it to be, grounded in the virtues of joy, love, compassionate detachment, justice and mercy, intention and integrity is humanity's common denominator. Marlis guides us through each chapter, reminding us to recall our inner power to be greater than any challenge and experience that confronts our orbit of living.

This book awakens a deeper thirst to spend more time in what matters in our lives. To surround ourselves with the qualities of spirit, by prayer and meditation, by the practice of cleansing breaths and water purification, by being quiet and doing nothing. Marlis gently encourages us to give ourselves permission to dance freely like the fire flames, to get in touch with our inner alchemist's transmutational power, and especially to be gentle with ourselves.

Dr. Zaida Rivene
Swellendam, South Africa
February 15, 2011

From Now to Now

Chapter 1

Born into World War II

It is in the inherent nature of human beings
to yearn for freedom, equality and dignity.
Brute force, no matter how strongly applied,
can never subdue the basic desire for freedom and dignity.
- His Holiness The 14th Dalai Lama

That familiar round-faced alarm clock with two small bells on its head sat on the night table next to the bed where my mother and the midwife helped me into the world. Illuminated by the morning sun, the clock read ten minutes before seven. The messenger of the Gods, Mercury, was on the ascendant in Gemini. It was Friday, May 14, 1942, and my hometown was Wesel, some kilometers from the border with Holland, but three years away from liberation by Allied soldiers crossing into Germany over the River Rhein. In those three years, with Europe at war, my first impressions of life were colored by hunger and horror, despair and desperate efforts at survival.

Today is Monday, the fifth day of February, 2007. I am sitting on a floor chair in our tower in an old Victorian mansion in Northampton, Massachusetts. The four tower walls are nearly all windows with a glass door entering onto a rooftop deck. The view in three hundred and sixty degrees around me waves in the winter wind with green needles of evergreen trees and the naked branches of maple trees. In a light pearl blue sky, puffy white clouds move quickly from west to east. They pass over the Berkshire Mountains on one side of the tower, and follow one another to the Holyoke range in the east.

After my morning meditation, I am drinking a nice cup of organic Sumatran coffee with organic soy creamer. These mornings on the East Coast, my studio two floors below, I enjoy some time for myself, drinking my coffee, dreaming my daydreams, looking out the windows, listening to music, or reading my books.

This morning I am sitting in the tower and thinking about my life. In three months I will celebrate my sixty-fifth birthday. I am thinking about what I have made out of my life so far. Sixty-five years seems like a very short time to me when I feel the speed and energy of my life. I feel as if I have the same timeless spirit in me now as when I was a small child picking flowers, unmindful of the war around me. Between then and now could be an evening's dream. But as I examine the details, when I go beyond the reflections on the surface my mind first recalls, when I really look from now to now, I realize this being has experienced a great transformation. The consciousness now composing these words is not that little child picking flowers. It is that little child, and the girl that came later, and then the adult she became moment after moment as she navigated the events of a life over sixty-five years. That little girl could have remained in a small town in Germany, growing old with tragic memories slowly turning into the leathery habits of conformity. She could have been that normal girl, trying like so many others to find an island of security. She could have, but she wasn't. She chose another path.

My parents, Walter and Susanna Jermutus lived on the second floor in a small two story row house on Sandstrasse. I came into their lives when my brother Walter was five years old, and my brother Günter was three. Walter was the classic older brother, mature, even when he wasn't, and Günter was more quiet, though thoughtful and sensitive. When my mother became pregnant with me, they had hoped my brothers would one day have a sister. My mother told me years later that my father had especially wanted a daughter. She said my brothers would sing the first line of an old nursery rhyme,

"Klapperstorch du Bester, bring mir eine Schwester!"

They were singing to the stork to deliver a baby sister.

My mother delivered me on the bed in my parent's bedroom. It was a very plain room, with clean wooden floors, but no carpeting. The furniture was simple and the room's one window brought in the morning light. A coal oven in the room gave warmth and hot water for the midwife, but also always the faint odor of burnt coal.

The midwife had delivered babies for over thirty years. Her name was Hildegard, a strong name for a strong woman whose long experience gave her both commanding confidence as well as an understanding kindness. Everything was clean and well prepared - towels, hot water, the instruments to cut the umbilical cord. My father, as was typical, was not allowed to be in the room, and so he sat in the hallway outside the bedroom door reading a newspaper while waiting for my arrival. My parents had agreed to name me Marie Louise, the same name as the Austrian princess who became the wife of Napoleon, and Empress of France. But my father, excited in the hallway, saw the name Marlis in the newspaper. I think in the name Marlis he saw a simpler version of Marie and Louise. In any case, he decided just then to change my parent's agreement.

May fourteenth was warm with the promise of spring flowers. My mother laid only thirty minutes in labour before I was born. She told me I was an easy baby to bring into the world. I was seven pounds with tiny golden locks of hair on my head. The midwife cut the umbilical cord and then turned me upside down and gave me a slap on my bottom. My first breath of air carried the fresh smells of the season, but also the harsh smoky particles of coal dust I would learn to live with for years to come.

My father was delighted when he was finally allowed into the room. He had the daughter he had wished for. He looked down on wife and daughter and told us about the new name he found. My mother liked the name Marlis immediately. It could be my parents were smiling and laughing at this precious moment in their lives, but I know they were also feeling a deep emptiness growing in their beings at the same time. In two days my father must leave for the Russian front to fight for the insane dreams of the Führer.

At that time in his life, my father was a mechanical drawing technician for the Krupp corporation, the giant company that headed munitions production for the German war machine. He traveled by train about forty kilometers from Wesel to the city of Essen where he spent every day drawing the intricate details of all kinds of weapons.

My father was not in the Nazi party. He did not believe in racism and war, but in Hitler's Third Reich these feelings had to be a secret. My father tried not to talk about politics at work, but one of his colleagues discovered that he was not a member of the party. Especially at Krupp, proudly supporting the war effort, this was not following the company ethic. The next morning my father was called into his boss's office. He was asked why he was not a member of the party. It was a short and fearful conversation that I'm sure my father had known may come anytime. I can sometimes imagine that conversation. It was only some hours later my father was told his contract with Krupp was terminated. In addition, his boss told him that within the next couple of days he would be in uniform and sent to the Russian Front. He came home to tell his wife this news, just as she was about to call for the midwife. I would arrive in the world just in time to see my father go off to war.

My father was listening to forbidden underground radio broadcasts. He knew that Germany could not sustain this war and would one day be defeated. As he came home that last day at work, his thoughts were shifting from the horror of visions of his coming part in the war, and the tormenting thoughts of his wife, two sons and new baby daughter living on a poor government salary, and with no father.

On the day of my birth the city of Wesel was relatively calm, but after three years of war, every facet of life was touched by fear and insecurity. I look back now and feel as if I was born into an atmosphere of death. My father was a thoughtful man. He was a great lover of books. I'm not sure if he enjoyed reading the stories of tragic heroes, but he easily could have been thinking he was one. To reassure my mother, he told her that he would come home in some months, when he had an opportunity for a short leave. In truth, he could not know what might happen. It was over a year later when he met my mother, my brothers and me again. He met us in Vienna where my mother was waiting for a government relocation. The national relocation was the party's plan to maximize the productivity of all citizens. Soldier's wives who had no children usually worked in factories or offices, while women with children were sent to work on farms. On a farm there was more food available to feed the children, and so Hitler's young soldiers of the future would be cared for as well as possible.

When my mother was seventeen she sat often with her friends in a favorite cafe. They would drink real coffee, instead of the grain substitute coffees most people would frugally drink at home. From one corner of the cafe my mother noticed an interesting young man who was often looking her way. When Walter Jermutus would introduce himself, no German speaker would recognize the Macedonian origin of the name Jermutus. Jermutus has a pleasant sound in German, but definitely unfamiliar and foreign. In English you might describe the pronunciation as something like "Year-moo-toos." The three syllables move the mouth first into a small smile, and then moves the lips into two small kisses. After four generations living in Germany, the Jermutus family had become completely German, but perhaps the unusual name gave Walter an exotic aura. I can guess what attracted my father to my mother on that day. He saw a tall elegantly dressed woman with a round face and dark brown eyes. She had the long legs and good figure of a movie idol like Marlene Dietrich. Her short black hair was combed down over her forehead and cut straight above her eyebrows - what was in that time a very modern style.

As Walter Jermutus was about to leave the cafe, he stopped next to my mother's table and introduced himself. He wondered if she would like to meet him the next day at that same cafe. My father was twenty-three, six years older than my mother, and I have a single impression of what he looked like from that time through a precious photograph of the two of them that survived the war. My mother sits with perfect posture, her hands relaxed in her lap, her angelic face tilted upwards, glowing with a Mona Lisa smile. My father leans forward, perhaps reaching for something out of the picture, a slight look of concern on his face. They had no photographs from their wedding. They had nearly nothing left from their lives before the war. I was fortunate to be with my brothers and my mother away from Wesel in February of 1945 when the British Royal Air Force destroyed any wedding photos my parents had, along with almost all of the rest of Wesel. Ninety-seven percent of the city was turned into rubble. The population of Wesel when my parents met in that cafe was about twenty-five thousand. By the end of the war, with evacuations, and especially after three days of bombing, less than two thousand people remained.

These scenes in my mind of my parents in Wesel before the city was destroyed come from my mother's descriptions of those years, and my own vivid impressions of returning to Wesel as a young child a few years after the war ended. I've seen paintings of Wesel by medieval artists - a picturesque walled city along the river Rhein with many towers and church domes. My parents fell in love in a Wesel where many of those buildings still existed.

After a short time my mother became pregnant with my brother Walter, and for as long as she could she tried to hide that reality from her parents. When that became no longer possible, she was forced to confess to her mother and stepfather. Their reaction was swift and harsh. They told her she had to leave their home immediately. At first, she couldn't even think of where she could go. She had only Walter for support. He took her home to his parents house where he lived. To my mother's great relief, Walter's parents agreed to let them live in an upstairs room in their house. Soon they were married and eager to find their own home. My grandparents were generous, but my father's mother was not very kind to her new daughter-in-law. About two years later they were able to move to their own home.

By the beginning of the war my mother had two children. My parents felt lucky that my father was not immediately forced into joining the military. Both of my parents were from liberal working class families. They considered themselves members of the SPD, the German Workers Party, even though the party was banned in 1933 when they were the only political group to vote against the Nazi government's Enabling Act. The Enabling Act took power from the Reichtag, the parliament, and gave it to Hitler's cabinet.

In the days immediately after my birth, my father was sent to the Russian Front, and my mother was informed by the state that as a wife of a soldier, she must take her children to wherever the Third Reich needed a working body. If my brother Walter had been two years older he would not have gone with us. Children seven years and older were sent to live in training camps where they became the HJD, the Hitler Jugend Deutschland, the Hitler German Youth. They attended all the normal school classes while also experiencing a full program of physical and mental programming. Girls and boys were separated. The boys learned rigorous outdoor training skills in preparation for their future service. The girls were educated in being perfect German mothers and housewives, meaning they knew how to clean a home perfectly, and how to keep their homes and families healthy with the latest ideas about proper hygiene. Both boys and girls were taught to be physically fit. All the children daily did the exercise program of Turn Vater Jahn, the early nineteenth century health innovator whose philosophy of exercise brought health consciousness to the whole nation. Boys and girls were also both taught the motto "Obedience, Cleanliness and Duty," and that they should be brave and aware that they were Aryans, a special race of people above all others.

At first, my family was sent to a farm in the Black Forest in the small village of Göttelfingen. There in the South, most of the neighbors were supporters of the Reich. The feeling for my mother was dark, and the work on the farm was hard. She grew up in a small city, but she was still a city girl and not used to farm labor. The local people had mixed feelings about her. They were curious about her sophisticated manners, but not put off. She was always very open and friendly and the local small community appreciated that. On the other side, she was from that liberal politically conscious part of society that did not entirely support their belief system. They liked that her husband was fighting for their beliefs on the war front, but my mother was cautious enough to never discuss her personal thoughts about politics.

My mother came to Göttelfingen not knowing how to milk a cow or harvest potatoes, but she quickly and painfully learned. She worked all the day with her bare knees on the ground pulling potatoes out of the earth, piling them in baskets and carrying the heavy loads through what seemed like endless rows of ploughed fields. At the end of a long day she would come back to the farm house to give her attention to her children. She went to sleep every night thinking her work was endless.

In August of 1943 she was given train tickets and all the other proper forms, and was told to take her family to Vienna, Austria. For about six months we lived with many other women and children in a large hotel. This was a meeting place for women in transit. There was a lot of work in cleaning the hotel and cooking and looking after the children. All the time, families came and went.

Before we moved from the Black Forest to Vienna, we went back to Wesel for a short while. Everyday my mother would walk to the post office and look on the bulletin board to see if my father's name was listed in the latest war casualties.

After a couple of months in Vienna, and after my father had served for fifteen months on the Russian Front, my father sent a letter saying that he would be able to meet the family for five days. My mother was extremely happy. My father too was in joy to see his family again, but his mind and heart were burdened with the knowledge he brought back from the front. This was August of 1943 and he told my mother that the war was lost. To say something like this, even just to his wife, was considered the worst kind of treason. My father said that everything my mother had heard about the war was a lie. It was all Goebbel's propaganda. He told my mother that he was certain that he would not return again from the front. My mother heard these words, and she said that in the months that followed she was mostly unhappy and sometimes desperate with grief, but she had faith that somehow change would come, and somehow life would get better. Before my father left that last time he took my brother Walter in his arms and told him that he had to look after his mother and younger brother and sister. Walter, named after his father, would now be the man of the family. My brother was six years old and he took that message to heart. He gave his promise to his father, and for his entire life afterwards he always carried a strong sense of responsibility for his family.

Not long after my father returned to his regiment in Russia, my mother realized she was pregnant again. In September 1943 she received orders from the Department for Children's Welfare to return to Wesel. The Department issued her travel papers, gave her tickets for the train, and notified the corresponding offices in Wesel who provided her with money for rent and ration stamps for food. The Third Reich had everything under control, meaning they had everyone under control. My mother said she never felt at ease. Even in the most normal comfortable setting in her own apartment there was always at least a slight feeling of fear. Many years later when I first thought deeply about what her life was like, I simply cried. I felt a great emptiness in my being as if some part of our humanity had been stolen. In time I came to understand our lives and the paths we take with wider understanding, and I came to compassion. I realized that compassion is not the sympathy one has for another person, but the love and care one has for all beings.

It is of course a dilemma for a German to write sympathetically about another German's suffering during World War Two when it was the German war machine that so ruthlessly obliterated so many others. I certainly feel the fear that so many experienced within and well beyond Germany's borders. I grew up in a nation so traumatized by its own hideous behavior that our parents appeared to have erased all memory of the war after it ended. There was a guilty silence from my parent's generation. My generation grew up knowing our history, but always reminded by the shame, or sometimes just the silence and denial of our parent's generation, that if we did not want to share that national guilt, then we must prove to ourselves and others that we were different.

As I describe these experiences, I find myself in this uncomfortable position of being an adult trying to put myself back into the world I lived in as a child. For the two year old me, my picture of the world was primarily illuminated by my mother and the love and security I needed as a child.

While back in Wesel again my mother continued to make her regular walks to the post office, always hoping for good news but always fearing the worst. In the early spring of 1944 my mother received the news that my father was missing in Stalingrad. Women usually received from the state the thin metal identity tags from their dead husbands. Many soldiers would never be identified in the brutal carnage of the Russian Front. I have one photograph of my father standing together with several other soldiers. They are simply standing, looking at the camera, an earthen mound, earth from their foxhole, piled up in back of them - a photograph my mother received in a letter and carried with her through the war.

My mother had written to my father, telling him about her pregnancy, but she never received a reply. I was a little too young to understand the grief my mother felt, but I could feel her feelings, and in the way of a two year old I experienced a nameless insecurity.

On May 22, 1944 my sister Rita was born. She was a fragile child. We had so little to eat, and we never had enough calcium and vitamin D. Rita was especially vulnerable as an infant. All the cities had severe shortages of every necessity. We were fortunate that my mother only stayed, at that time, for a year in Wesel. The following November the family was again relocated by that government office responsible for managing our affairs - "for the good of the Fatherland."

Chapter 2

Life in Lüderitz

Come away, O human child!
To the waters and the wild
With a faery hand in hand,
For the world's more full of weeping
than you can understand.

- William Butler Yeats

In October of 1944 we left Wesel and traveled by train to the little farm village of Lüderitz near Stendal in Eastern Germany. We arrived at the horse farm of Herr and Frau Wilke, and the five of us were given two rooms in the upper part of the farm house. There was a bedroom and a kitchen. On the same floor of the house was one other room for the other worker at the farm, a Polish refugee named Wladislaw Kendra. Herr Wilke raised racing horses, but during the war years his horses were used by the military. Wladislaw was primarily responsible for looking after the horses but really took care of the whole farm. My mother was brought to the farm to help with all manner of chores. We were all fortunate to be on a farm where we could regularly have fresh milk and bread, and also meat and vegetables that had been nearly impossible to find in the cities.

Wladislaw had lived on the farm for five years. In 1939, Germany invaded Poland, and Wladislaw escaped the desperate situation in his native land, ironically fleeing to Germany. He grew up on a large farm near Krakow, and said it was not easy for him to leave his family. He walked all the way to Eastern Germany, sleeping in barns and taking some charity from local farmers. When he arrived at the horse farm in Lüderitz, he asked Herr Wilke for work.

Herr Wilke agreed, and that arrangement gave Wladislaw food and housing throughout the entire war.

My mother worked on every part of the farm. There were grain fields, a vegetable garden, pigs, cows, doves, chickens and geese - all needed tending. In the house she cleaned and cooked. She worked for many hours in the day, and through all this time she held the knowledge that her husband was most likely gone, but because she had no real evidence, because there was no metal ID tag in her hand, there was always the slim chance that he might one day simply knock on the door. Of course every day that passed took her farther away from that slender dream.

My mother, myself and my daughter - we all have within us a spirit that can not be broken. Sometimes, in very low times, we may really struggle, but all three of us always look for a positive outcome. We trust something will come that will help any bad situation, or we know that we are resourceful enough to make a change for the better ourselves. Even when in her deepest sadness, my mother always could lift her spirits, and the spirits of those around her. I learned this from her at a very young age, and I realize now that a lot of that education came from song. My mother had a wonderful voice. She sang often when she worked. Sometimes these were church hymns or folk songs, other times simply little melodies she made up.

I heard my mother sing so often that I learned to sing at the same time I learned to talk. When my mother sang, her heart would open, and that good energy filled the hearts of all of us. The melodies wrapped themselves around us children like we were snug and safe in bed under our blankets.

The chaos of the war imprinted itself on my consciousness in every moment of the first years of my life, but even with all that drama, I was still a happy and confident child. I first walked when I was eight months old. When I first talked I had very good pronunciation, no slurring of words, or mistaking consonant sounds. Perhaps because I sang so much, my ear was well tuned for language. I was always singing as a child, often as much as my mother. Even when I was only two, I know there was a part of me that felt my mother's sadness. I responded with that positive attitude I saw in her so often. I was never shy as a young child. The first day we arrived in Lüderitz, we were meeting the Wilkes for the first time. My mother had my sister Rita in her arms. My brother Günther stood cautiously behind my mother, while my older brother Walter, seven years old, stood well-mannered next to my mother. I came skipping through the whole scene. I stood in front of the Wilkes and simply began to sing a sweet melody.

Kommt ein Vogel geflogen
setzt sich nieder auf mein' Fuss
Hat ein Brieflein im Schnabel
von der Mutter einen Gruss.

In the song, a bird has flown to me. He sat himself on my foot. In his mouth he had a little letter - mother sends her greetings. My mother didn't let me sing too long just then, not wanting me to get in the way, but I guess the Wilkes enjoyed my little concert. That opening of a little heart in song speaks to everyone. With my spontaneous concert and my mother's good-humored slight embarrassment, the Wilkes could only smile, feeling their own hearts opening.

The village of Lüderitz became my home for the next five years. I recently looked at Lüderitz from above with Google's earth viewing program. The village is still tiny, though maybe twice as large as it was back then. When we arrived in 1944, Lüderitz had only about thirty families, but with just enough diversity of occupations that the village was relatively self-sufficient. There was a baker, a blacksmith, a shoemaker, a church, a small school, a general store, a doctor and a dentist. The rest was mostly farmland and farm families. Lüderitz was militarily insignificant and so relatively insulated from the worst aspects of the war. Even so, as a little girl, even an outgoing and friendly little girl, I always felt some uneasiness, as if

I was never completely secure or free from danger.

When we first arrived in Lüderitz, Wladislaw Kendra gave me a tour of the whole farm, introducing me to all the animals, and where they lived. I have always had a very sensitive sense of smell, and I have to say that after seeing the whole farm, I was far happier to be in what became my favorite place for a private retreat. When Wladislaw Kendra brought me up the simple steps in the barn to the grain storage, my nose filled with the most wonderfully sweet smell of freshly threshed grains of wheat, rye, oats and barley. There were many times later on when I was a little older when I would secretly run up those steps, open the grain storage door and fall back onto the piles of grain, breathing deeply. As much as I enjoyed this place as a favorite haven in Lüderitz, I still always felt some unease. I always felt as if someone might at any time come up behind me.

One of my favorite days on the farm, really everyone's favorite day, was when we cooked Zuckerrübenkraut. After harvesting the big white sugar beets, full with leaves, the leaves go to the animals, while the beets are cut up in a powerful grating machine. In a large copper kettle, the beets are cooked for hours and hours, while constantly being stirred with very long handled wooden ladles. It slowly becomes a very thick, very sweet dark brown syrup. Soon after the cooking begins, the sweet smell of the hot syrup fills the entire farm house.

My mother dressed us children as fashionably as possible given the difficulty of finding anything nice during the war. She made knitted sweaters for my brothers, and dresses for my sister and me in all different colors. I especially liked light blue and white. In my mind, I always felt like I was dressed like a princess, especially when I was playing in the meadows. I felt like a princess, but I was a very curious and often mischievous tiny monarch. I was not a malicious kind of mischievous child. I was more often imperiling just myself as I so often went skating on thin ice. That is a metaphor, but based in reality as well. Out of sheer foolish and bold curiosity, I fell two times as a child into icy water while trying to test the limits of nature by seeing how far I could skate on thin ice.

I had several dresses but only two pairs of shoes. Shoes were especially hard to get during the war. Throughout most of the year, I was only allowed to wear my good black patent leather shoes on Sundays. My other shoes were so old, worn out, and too small for my feet, that I never liked to wear them. Over the week I always went barefoot, which I liked, even in the cold winter months when there wasn't yet frost or snow. I really preferred to not wear shoes, a habit I still often have. Sometimes when I am in New England, people look at me strangely because I am walking through snowy cold streets with only a pair of light sandals. As a teenager I started to wear pointy-toed high heeled shoes, extremely uncomfortable creations designed to make women's legs look longer and their hips sway more seductively, which I liked at that time. My high heeled period lasted fifteen years before I discovered shoes that still could be said to look good, but were made with the idea of comfort and support.

One time when I was the princess playing in the meadow I decided secretly to wear my good shoes, as I believed a princess should, but when I got to the meadow I just took them off as I was playing. I didn't even realize I didn't have them on until I got home and my mother immediately asked me where my shoes were. She was very aware of everything and noticed that my shoes were not in the house, and then not on my feet. When I told her that I forgot the shoes in the meadow, she went to get a leather belt. I immediately ran and hid under the kitchen table. She quickly found me and hit me with the belt while I yelled and yelled. My brother Walter, who was watching over me in the meadow, also felt the sting of that belt. Afterwards my mother told him to go to the meadow, now in the dark, and find my shoes. Luckily it was a small meadow, and he soon returned with those precious shoes - shoes I really didn't like wearing at all.

I have always loved the smell of flowers, trees and meadows. I loved that small meadow in Lüderitz. One Christmas I received a doll and doll house from the Christkind. I had clothes for the doll and I loved to play with her, but mostly, when I had the chance,

I loved to play outside in the meadow. I loved to be in nature. I only had to walk five minutes down the main street, passing all the houses, and then into a little forest fresh with the succulent smell of grass and flowers. I would sing my songs, pick flowers and make crowns and jewelry out of them, dressing up for my make-believe kingdom. In the summertime, I would walk to the little lake and walk around in the shallow edges. Around the lake grew light blue forget-me-nots, bright yellow buttercups, and clover flowers in red and white. For me this was pure color therapy. I know now that color vibrates at different frequencies, and our bodies, minds and souls respond to these visions. As a child after the war, with Russian soldiers everywhere, I was far enough from the center of the village that I could not hear the sound of trucks and tanks and soldiers marching. I was in my meadow, princess of the flowers, for a while away and free from worry - one small kingdom at peace in a world at war.

I loved fairy tales. When my mother had time, she would read stories to all of us. Over time we heard most of the stories from the Brothers Grimm. My favorite tale was called Sternen-Taler. A little girl whose parents have died finds herself without a home and only a piece of bread and the clothes she wears. As she walks through the village she meets a poor hungry man and she gives him her bread. Then she meets other children with even less than her. To each one she gives a piece of her clothing until at last in the dark of night she gives away her dress to a naked child younger than herself. She thinks that in the dark no one will see her in her thin little shirt, so why not give away her dress? And then when she has nothing left, stars begin to fall from the sky. She holds out the edges of her shirt, and as the stars collect in her garment they turn into golden coins. And she lived happily ever after. This story touched me deeply as a child. In the simple way of a child I didn't think about the meaning - the generosity, the compassion, the wondrous drama - I didn't think, I felt simply the goodness of the little girl's heart.

In that small meadow I played out many of these fairy tales. Hiding in the hollow of old trees, weaving my jewelry from the flowers, taking on the roles of fairyland characters. When I wasn't playing in the meadow, I was often in the old garden in the church yard. Two rows of palm-like bushes, whose fronds were used on Palm Sunday, led to a gazebo at the end of the garden. I would pick flowers and fill up a small basket I carried. As I walked up and down the pathway I would hand out my flowers to all the angels who had assembled there.

When I was five years old, I began to attend kindergarten. On the way to kindergarten every day I would pass the office of the dentist Doctor Bernstein. He was a friendly man with a broad warm smile. Almost every morning before kindergarten I would stop into his office to say hello. I missed my father so much that I was often open-hearted to men who appeared to me to be kind and non-threatening.

One day he examined my teeth, and he found he had some work to do. I trusted the friendly Dr. Bernstein, and so I was sitting in the chair relaxed and only a little excited, not really knowing what happens in a dentist's office. Suddenly his two assistants came into the room. They stood on either end of me. One held my head and the other held my body while Dr. Bernstein began to work. No one explained to me that I would have a tooth removed, simply pulled from my head, without any anesthetic. When I realized how much pain I felt, I started crying, yelling and moving around, but the two assistants kept me pinned down, though squirming in the chair. The pain was nearly unbearable. At one point I kicked my foot out and hit the doctor right in his belly. He had been leaning over me, very concentrated on my teeth. He didn't expect to suddenly have his breath taken away. In that second he became very angry. He looked at me cooly and explained that he had to continue for some short time longer. I think I was almost as afraid of Dr. Bernstein at that moment as I was of the pliers in his hand. That was one of the most painful experiences of my life. After that day, and for quite a while longer, I didn't always walk directly by Dr. Bernstein's house on the way to kindergarten.

I did like to go to the kindergarden, but I didn't like to stay there.

I would often come into the room, and then after a while I would simply walk out and wander off into nature to play by myself. I sometimes played with other kids, but I was often playing alone, exploring the forest or sitting by a lake. One lake in Lüderitz was the site of one of my near drowning encounters. I was testing the strength of the ice when I broke completely through and could not for the longest time grab anything solid. All the ice was too slippery and the water was deeper than I could stand. I don't know how long I struggled, but I finally pulled myself onto the icy shore. While in the water I really thought I was drowning. I was frightened and frozen as I walked home, and my clothes smelled horribly from the standing lake water. When I came in the house my mother did not immediately take me in her arms and comfort me, and as she cleaned me up I was sad inside that she was angry with me instead of happy to see me safe at home. It was only many years later that I saw myself soaking wet and smelly walking through the house, and coming up to my mother, and seeing from her perspective one more unnecessary chore added on to all her other responsibilities. My mother knew well my appetite for getting into trouble.

I was not a trouble maker, it was more that my adventurousness led me into more than I could handle in the moment. I know now that I was never really at ease as a child, responding to fear by letting my curiosity distract me. I didn't worry a lot, and even with the ever-present war, I was still that optimistic child who loved to sing, and make myself and others happy. At night I would tell stories to my sister Rita and my brother Günther. My stories had something borrowed from the Grimms. I often told stories about very poor children who faced some dangerous deceiver. At the end of every story an angel would always appear to the poor children to give them hope and love.

In the spring of 1945, a month before my third birthday, the war in Europe was finally over. I began to have an uneasy feeling different from the general feeling of fear I was accustomed to during those first three years of my life. The adults were talking a lot about *die Amis* (pronounced *ah-mees*) and *die Ruskis*. They had a very different feeling towards these two groups. There were already stories about Russian soldiers, themselves ravaged by years at war, suddenly taking out their release of aggression on the civilian populations. Years later now we know that Russian soldiers raped even Russian women who had been held in German concentration camps. After the Russians swept through Berlin they slowly headed west. Lüderitz was only one hundred kilometers away, but it took them a while to get there. Rumors were traveling far faster than the Russian troops.

When the Russians arrived, I was very excited. In my first years of life experience I had only been conscious of trains and horse-drawn carts. Now every day, cars, trucks, and tanks were coming through the village, and lots of strange soldiers were in the street. From my perspective, having already explored all of Lüderitz and all the surrounding woods and meadows, this sudden invasion of activity was marvelous.

For a time a group of soldiers camped in one of my favorite meadows. Often I walked to the camp to visit them. They were very friendly to me, and it is generally true that even the people in the village saw that the Russians were very nice to children. There was one soldier in particular who always liked to talk to me. I don't remember if he was speaking German, or I just replied in German when he spoke Russian. In either case, I think we both received a lot of well-needed compassion from one another. I had a good feeling from a lot of the soldiers. Even though now I realize how traumatized they must have been, I see too that they were elated at having survived the end of the war. I think what they saw in me was what they saw in all children, perhaps what all the fighting soldiers see in children - the hope for an innocent time without war.

When the Americans came into Germany as liberators, they had chocolate, swing music and Hollywood. By comparison, the Russians had nothing. When the Russians first came to Lüderitz they searched from house to house looking for food and Nazis soldiers, but even in little Lüderitz there were many cases of rape and looting. When the soldiers came to Wilke's farm everyone was very frightened, but Wladislav stood in front of the house as the soldiers arrived holding a pitchfork to his side. He spoke to them in Russian and told them that there was no reason for them to come inside the house. There were only women and children. Perhaps because of his manner, or more likely because he was Polish and the Russians were looking for Germans, miraculously the soldiers left without protest. There was a feeling from all the adults, and even in my older brother, that Wladislav's bravery that day certainly changed their lives.

Chapter 3

Crossing a Divided Germany

One never reaches home,
but wherever friendly paths intersect
the whole world looks like home for a time.
- Hermann Hesse

*I*n the chaos in the early years after the war it was very difficult for women to travel unaccompanied, but my mother very much wanted to meet with her sister Karola. She decided to make a short trip to Wesel. I had to stay in Lüderitz with my sister Rita at a neighbor's house. My brothers stayed at the farm and helped Wladislaw with the farm work.

Karola had been living with Gussi, my mother's youngest sister, in Wesel since the city began to repopulate after its near total destruction. The aerial photographs of Wesel after the bombing show a landscape that looks more like a horrid moonscape where the craters are all the same size and lay in long orderly rows surrounded by rubble. It is amazing to see the steeple of the Willibrordi Cathedral still intact, while nothing around it remains. But the people quickly moved away the rubble, literally turning it into the foundation of a new city. Karola and Gussi lived in a brick house that had survived the bombs mostly intact. Karola and Gussi lived in the upper floor, while the owners lived in the rooms below. Gussi had a great lust for life, and so it was probably not too surprising for Karola to find that Gussi had fallen in love with an American soldier. At some point Gussi's passionate affair spiraled out of control, and one night as Gussi stood in their landlord's hallway behind the locked door of the house, the soldier enraged, demanded to be let in. Gussi refused, and the soldier shot his gun at the door. Gussi dropped to the floor dead.

My mother was devastated by this news. She was one of eleven children. One brother had died before the war from a lung infection. During the war her seven remaining brothers had been killed on the battlefield, and her mother died in the bombing of Aachen. Now her youngest sister had been killed.

My mother wanted to see Karola, but she also wanted to see Wesel. She wanted to find some way to bring her children safely back to the West, and she needed to know if the family could survive in Wesel. After being gone two weeks, she came back to Lüderitz sad and exhausted.

In those two weeks with my mother in the West, I stayed with the neighbors, the Schulzes, who lived across the street from the farm house. On one Saturday afternoon I was instructed to take a bath in a large tin tub in the kitchen. The neighbor's friend, the director of the village school, came into the house and saw me in the tub. It is hard to describe now my feelings in that moment. I was not simply embarrassed, but a mixture of shame and fear held me, and I refused to come out of the tub while he was there. I was used to being naked in my own house, but suddenly I felt a terribly strange and uncomfortable emotion, perhaps triggered by a memory I held hidden even from myself. Something made me terribly afraid. Frau Schulze told me I should not be so ashamed, but I didn't want to be naked in front of this man. I was already nervous about starting school for the first time the following week. My nervousness turned to panic and tears with the head of the school watching me take a bath. I can't say I got a bad feeling from him. I only know that something felt terribly wrong in that moment. When school started that week, all the children were standing in a line and were told to say their name and birthday. When it came to my turn I was so embarrassed I couldn't speak. When I saw the director of the school looking at me again, I began to cry again. My mother didn't know why I cried, and I never tried to tell her about the experience. I was simply too confused by all the fearful feelings and too young to know how to explain.

About a half a year before my mother's trip to Wesel, she began a sexual affair with Wladislaw. As the time passed in Lüderitz she never fully gave up hope that my father might somehow still be alive, but I think the reality of her situation was not hidden from her, and she felt she should move on in her life. In April of 1948 my brother Klaus was born, son of Susanna and Wladislaw. Perhaps just trying to hold onto something meaningful from the past, my mother didn't marry Wladislaw until 1953.

One day in the summer of 1949 my mother came to me and told me that I had to give away my doll, all her clothes, and the doll house to my former kindergarten. I certainly didn't like this idea, even if my mother was clever enough to sweeten the request. "You are certainly getting older," she said encouragingly. I liked the way that sounded. Then she added, "certainly too old to be playing with dolls." Regretfully I went with my mother to the kindergarten - my mother holding the doll house, and me holding my doll. The children, of course, were delighted with the gift. As I watched them playing, laughing and immediately making up games for my doll to play, I remember a smile coming to my face as well. As I was walking home I started thinking, and I became sad at the thought that the small children would not take care of my doll and dollhouse as I had done. Even so, this was a strong print for me - to consciously give away even a precious possession. Since then I have always given away my possessions, consciously, but freely. Several times in my life I have given nearly everything I owned away.

One night soon after that, my mother woke me up and quietly told me I should dress myself, including shoes, because we were going to take a walk. We did take a walk, although after walking one hundred and thirty-six kilometers, we were happy to trade a very valuable slab of bacon for a ride most of the rest of the way to We-

sel in the back of a produce truck. For me, even the last twenty-five
kilometers we had to walk after the truck dropped us off seemed
like a thousand. The first part of the journey was mostly a nightmare. We slept in the woods by day and walked only by night. We
avoided in any way possible any encounters with Russian soldiers.
We actually avoided everyone we could, just so we wouldn't call attention to ourselves. We were, altogether, ten people - three adults
and seven children. Along with my mother and Wladislaw, we traveled with Hilde, a friend of my mother's, and Hilde's three children,
Ilka, Ute and Peter. My mother met Hilde when we were in Vienna,
surprised to learn that she too was from Wesel. The social welfare
department had later arranged for the two Wesel soldier's families
to be assigned to the same farm town in the East.

I don't remember a lot of the details of our escape from East to
West Germany. I was friends with Hilde's children Ilka and Ute,
and so I was happy to be with them. I remember once we came to
a beautiful long sloping hill in a meadow. All the kids jumped to
the ground, laid on their sides, and rolled and rolled all the way to
the bottom. Another time I remember sneaking by a railroad station, crowded with Russians. All of us children were told to not say
anything at all, and move as quietly as possible. They couldn't see
us, but we could see the whole train through the bushes and trees,
equipment piled high, and soldiers hanging onto the sides of cars.
We were really frightened. We walked from Lüderitz to Hanover,
before we risked stopping a truck for a fortunate ride to Oberhau-
sen, only twenty-five kilometers from Wesel.

When we arrived in Wesel, all was in transition - one of many
transitions in the city's long history. When the Earl Arnold of Cleve
married Ida of Niederlotharingen, he received the city of Wesel as a
dowery. That was in 1115. Some three hundred years before that, a
large manor and church was built in the settlement by the soldiers
of Charlemagne. Seventy years after the birth of Jesus, the Romans
built a watchtower on the east side of the Rhine, just across from
the future site of Wesel, to keep an eye on the tribes from this region the Romans called Germania. Artifacts from an ancient burial

ground were found in Wesel that dates early settlements to around 700 BC. Over a period of four days in February of 1945, the Allies did not bomb Wesel back to the stone age, but it looked that way.

We came to a Wesel four years after the destruction. My mother was wise in waiting in the East as long as she did. Everything in Wesel had been broken by the bombing, most importantly supply lines of food. Nothing moved for four years as the people struggled to turn rubble into a city again. 1949 is the year the city historian counts as the year Wesel came back to life. New buildings were being constructed from the bricks of the old, and everywhere something was being built or repaired. We moved into a house that was one of the few that survived the bombing, but it just survived. Not everything worked perfectly, especially under the stress of four families sharing the house.

We moved in with my Aunt Karola and her six children. We were eleven children and three adults sharing two rooms. One room was used as a kitchen and living room, with a small place for my mother and Wladislaw to sleep. Aunt Karola slept with the eleven children in the other room. There was one bathroom, our only source of water, used by all four families in the house, and I think it was the part of our house the Allies were aiming at. There was almost always water on the floor, and I so clearly remember, that because of some broken line in the house's electrical wiring, whenever we stood on the wet floor and touched the sink's faucet we would get a small shock. I hated living in that house. There was never a quiet moment, and even to be alone in the bathroom was little bit frightening. The only thing I liked about that house was leaving it. We were on the edge of the city, and I could walk out the front door and be immediately surrounded by forest and farmland.

I loved being outside in nature. In tiny Lüderitz I created my own play world, mostly by myself. In busy Wesel, and in that very busy house, I was always with other children, and I began to enjoy making friends, learning their games, and introducing them to the kind of games I created for myself out of the trees and flowers.

There were often the echoes of fairy tales in my imagination as I played in nature, but I was not in the forest and meadows to play the part of a fairy tale character. I realize now that during the first year of my life my entire being was centered around survival. This was pure reaction of the first chakra, that energy center in the body that grounds us to our most basic instincts. In the plants and water and the earth itself I found the security that seemed missing everywhere else.

I was too young to understand the war when I was living through it. For that first year in Wesel, I don't believe I understood the reconstruction of the real world around me. I didn't pay very much attention to what the adults were busy doing when I didn't have to. My mother's life that first year in Wesel was completely in the real world, and I think she didn't have a lot of patience for me when she so often had to call me out of the world I lived in to participate in the real world.

We were in Wesel for about a year before my mother felt the crowded situation in the house was no longer bearable. She made the difficult decision to send two of her children away for some time until she could better manage our lives. She sent my brother Günther to live with his Godparents who lived some fifty kilometers away. She sent me to live with my Godparents, who lived in Göttelfingen. I was only days old when the state sent my mother to the village of Göttelfingen, three hundred and sixty kilometers to the south. My mother was Catholic, my father, Protestant, and when my mother arrived with a new baby in this very small farm village, I immediately found Godparents helping in my baptism. My Godparents, Onkel Albert and Tante Mina, the owners of the farm my mother had worked on, would now be my guardians for the next year.

As a baby, Göttelfingen was only important to me as it was the location of my mother. I had no memories of the village or the people. Now, at eight years old, I was aware of my surroundings. I was also a city girl from the West in a southern village of farmers who had a fascination with the sophistication of the city but usually expressed their feelings with disapproval.

Every part of Germany has its own regional dialect or accent. In Wesel most everyone spoke *Weselaner Platt*, although my mother was more exact in her language, almost speaking what we call *Hochdeutsch*, or Proper German. I grew up easily understanding Weselaner Platt and Hochdeutsch, but when I arrived in Göttelfingen, I discovered an accent that seemed nearly incomprehensible. For most of my year there I hardly understood anyone. I did learn some words, of course, but I was so often teased by both children and adults, after a while I really didn't want to talk to anyone. I made no friends in Göttelfingen. I spent all of my free time by myself. My Godparents were nice to me, but even they were amused by my lack of what you can call the *farmer's sophistication*. I was always shocked and afraid when animals were slaughtered. Everyone in that village had grown up watching the slaughter of animals, and had been thankful for the meat when much of the country had none. Even at age 8, if I had had the ability to explain my feelings, I still didn't know how to speak the language. Most of my time in Göttelfingen I looked for meadows and forests where I fully understood the language, and I could be alone with nature.

I attended school from the beginning of my stay in the Black Forest, but because I had so much trouble understanding the teacher, my grades were only good in two activities - acting in the school theater and singing in the chorus. When I was very young in Lüderitz I acted in school plays, and I continued to act in most of the schools I attended. Perhaps my early training in exercising my imagination in meadows and forests prepared me for success in school plays. In any case, I almost always had the lead roll, and I always could feel the essence of the character in me as I acted. Over time, I began to learn more and more of the local dialect, but most everyone still thought of me as an amusing outsider. When the time came for the harvest, I received no consideration for my inexperience with hard farm labor. I was slim and not very muscular. In the evenings I was exhausted from a day of harvesting hay in the hot summer sun. At night many times I would cry in my bed. I missed my family, but especially my sister Rita. I was not always the sweetest older sister. Reacting from my insecurities, I would often tease Rita. Even so, I really loved her. She was often ill as a child, and I felt very protective of her. My mother sent me a photograph of Rita looking very ill in her hospital bed. I cried many times while holding that photograph. In this strange village so far away from my family, I felt like I was the small one in need of comfort. That feeling often made me think of Rita.

During that year, my mother came one time to visit me, near to Christmas. I was so excited to see her, watching her walk off the bus, but I was also embarrassed to see how nice she looked in her elegant dress. She wore stockings and high-heeled shoes, appropriate for Wesel, but in Göttelfingen at that time of year the snow was so high you sometimes couldn't see out of the windows. I was afraid the villagers would ridicule her in the same way they acted towards me. My mother didn't care what the villagers were thinking about her. She cared more what the villagers were feeling. The bus stopped right in front of the farm house, which in this tiny village was also the village's guest house. There were probably no more than three hundred people in the whole village, and since everyone knew everyone, my mother's arrival was an opportunity for a community gathering. She walked off the bus, tall and slim, confident and warm. She always got along well with people, and the villagers were very open to her honest heart.

Eight months later when my mother came to take me home, I felt so happy, standing with her waiting for the bus to come. I had once before escaped and fled to Wesel with her, and I was really too young to understand the reason why. This time I was not much older, but some part of me felt as if I was no longer the little girl who left her doll and doll house in Lüderitz.

When I returned to Wesel I found our living situation had changed, in both good and bad ways from my perspective. We were living in the same apartment, but my aunt and my six cousins had moved to their own apartment. We had not a lot of room, but it was now only for my immediate family. My immediate family, however, had also changed. While I was in Göttelfingen, my mother had married Wladislav. I had known him for seven years as Wladislav, my friend. Now I was expected to call him father. I was not prepared for that, but I did learn to call him Vatter, the Weselaner Platt, which always felt a little more familiar, a less formal way of pronouncing the proper word for father. A strange twist appears in this story, although I don't think I really thought of it at the time. Several months before he married my mother, Wladislav had received citizenship from the German government. In the process, he translated his Polish first name into its German equivalent. Wladislav was now Walter, the same as my real father's name.

I still had the meadows and forest nearby, but I also had to go to school. I was often shy in school. I was so often the new girl, and I felt for most of my life insecure at home, wherever my home happened to be from now to now. It took some time for me to adjust to being from Wesel, and then actually living there. Everything was a bit too new for me. Everything was new for everyone in Germany at that time. The country was being rebuilt, but in the early fifties the economy had still not recovered. Walter, my new father, had always been very dedicated to whatever work he had. In Wesel he worked as a carpenter, a profession much in demand at the time, but still he was not able to make a lot of money, and almost everything he made went to pay for rent and food. For several years, until I was about twelve years old, I never felt like we had enough food. We would always eat a simple dinner when my stepfather came home from work, but there was never much else to eat in the house. It was like that throughout Germany for working class families. I remember being so happy to find some bread when I came home from school. I would eat bread and margarine, and if I was really lucky, we would have some sugar beet syrup to spread on top. Every Sunday we would eat a big lunch with meat, potatoes and vegetables. On holidays we would have semolina pudding sweetened with sugar.

Sunday mornings we would walk to church, leaving the house at eight in the morning. It took an hour to walk to church. I didn't listen closely to the sermons, but I did love to sing and pray in church. Silently, to myself, I made up my own prayers when everyone was reciting the church prayers. I always asked God for forgiveness, protection, and that we always have enough to eat. We would be in church for an hour, and then we would walk an hour back home. My mother would serve our Sunday lunch, and then later in the afternoon we would set off again for the hour walk to church to attend late afternoon Mass. Eventually, I went four times every week to church. We had a Thursday night Mass, and on Mondays I went to practice with the chorus. As a young teen I traveled with my church chorus to sing at events in different cities in the Ruhrgebiet, the large urban industrial area just south from Wesel, in the area known as North Rhine-Westphalia. Often we sang with other choruses, and sometimes in very large halls with one thousand chorus members all singing together. I always liked going to church, even on Thursday evenings with my mother when I didn't have to go. I was mostly bored with the talking, but I loved to sing, and silently talk to God in my prayers.

Chapter 4

My little Soul abused

Father, forgive them, for they know not what they do.
- Luke 23:34

When I returned to Wesel from Göttelfingen, at nine years old, I began what could have been the first stable part of my life. I had spent most of my life away from my hometown. I never experienced the stability of growing up as a native, comfortable with a common accent, knowing all the neighbors thought of me as one of them. We were foreigners in the small farm towns of Lüderitz and in Göttelfingen. Of course, I was not conscious of my insecurities. I lived my life in the moment, perhaps because during the war there really was only the moment. The future was so uncertain. I didn't consciously know the future was uncertain, but I was always observant and sensitive to feelings. I grew up with uncertainty as the normal state of my environment, but even though I always felt that strange undercurrent of unease, I was a child. I liked to play. I loved to find joy in simple things.

Perhaps because thinking about my situation would be too painful, I mostly didn't think a lot as a child. Outwardly I was very friendly. With strangers I was always at first shy, but with my family and friends, I could easily be the adventurous and open hearted girl who never appeared to have a dark thought. Once living in Wesel for a while, I began to make friends, and with singing in church, and playing as often as possible in the meadows and forests, most of my time was entirely in the now. The past was gone. It was easy not to be reminded of the past, as most of Germany was trying to forget the past. I had been unconsciously trained not to think about an uncertain future filled with war, and so even after the war I had retained the habit of hiding my fears and doubts, and simply enjoying whatever came in each moment. I lived as if I had no past, and had no future.

From the beginning of my age of reason, when young children traditionally start to put the pieces together and form a view of the world, I never really thought about how things worked. I remember sitting often, and thinking nothing. It sounds strange to describe this, as normally children are always busy *putting it all together*, playing, thinking things out. Maybe because I never thought about the future, I didn't think about how to get there. As I grew up I would easily rely on making decisions by feeling, rather than thinking. In some ways this was a profound gift disguised in the form of war time desperation and poverty. I had developed my intuition without my rational mind interfering. On the other side, in strange situations, my inner self was so deep into its own world of fear and denial, also a gift from the war, that sometimes I could even block out reality totally. Sometimes, for a small, innocent and vulnerable young girl, blocking out reality seemed like the only sensible choice.

I loved walking to church every Sunday. We had to walk nearly around the whole city as the church was on the opposite side of Wesel. One very hot Sunday, I was happy to hear that an older relative had offered to take me for a ride on his bicycle into nature. We had a blanket with us, and when we came to a beautiful meadow surrounded by trees and bushes, he laid the blanket onto the grass. We both laid down on our backs on the blanket, enjoying the sound of a nearby stream. I closed my eyes and just smiled in that wonderful moment of relaxing into the sensations of nature. Suddenly I smelled his strong male breath. I opened my eyes but looked at nothing as I felt him kissing me, and then pulling on my clothes. His body looked enormous over me. I felt paralyzed. I was used to trusting this man, but now I was frozen with fear. He tried to put his penis into my vagina, and as he pushed I felt as if my skin was tearing. I cried out, but he just kept trying. I cried and cried, but no one heard me. After a while, without success, he finally stopped. As we rode home I was still sobbing. The experience of breathing in his heavy breath and his heavy body crushing down on me would stay with me for life. He stopped the bike before we got home. He turned to me and with a very threatening manner demanded that I not say anything to my mother. And so I didn't.

Living in the now, I should immediately put that experience behind me, and let it disappear into the invisible past. That had been my habit and my ability. Hunger, the sound of a bomb exploding, the loss of family - all these things I had always let go of in the worlds I created out of each moment. My life, from now to now, always moved forward with my heart's intuition as my guide. I was that joyful little child who brought a smile to the face of a Russian soldier. Now I was riding on the back of a bicycle behind a man from my own family who had just abused me. And I promised not to say anything. Maybe if I had not made that promise I could have let go of the experience somehow. I could have returned to the now. But I had to return home and act like nothing happened. Until that day, I always felt like I was the one who created each new moment. Those bad experiences I put behind me in each new moment seemed to stay safely in the past. This experience was different. This fear affected every part of my being. I thought of nothing as I rode on the back of the bicycle. I only sobbed and shook in fear, but turning in me was the uncontrollable reality. I really didn't even know what had just happened to me, but I was in pain and terrified by my sudden horrifying vulnerability. Over the coming days I handled my fear by acting unafraid. I was always a good actor, but part of my strength as a child actor came from the security of knowing my mother would protect me. Suddenly, now, my mother could not protect me. For the next eight years, until I left my parent's house, I was a very good actor.

In describing this experience of abuse, and in those that follow, I have purposely hidden the exact identities of the men involved. I have also not mentioned many other incidences. It is not my intention to punish or embarrass anyone. As society evolves, as humanity becomes more humane, I believe it is important to see what needs to change, or nothing will change. We open the window to bring fresh air.

I know my mother noticed that something was wrong in my manner when I came back to the house that Sunday afternoon, but in the press of daily life she didn't reflect deeply on her nine year old's passing mood. Almost immediately after I was told to not say anything, the event began to enter my subconscious. I wasn't allowed to talk about it, so the subject disappeared from my personal world, at least that part of my world that the outside world could see. In the coming days I acted normal, the *normal* my family was used to.

This was the beginning of a pattern, a pattern burned into my consciousness and only healed decades later after years of serious effort. Before I was old enough to leave home, I suffered the abuse that I think must be common in all the male-dominated cultures on the planet. After I was on my own, I was still not free of the pattern as I continued to let misguided men abuse me. For the longest time I remained silent. For the longest time I was unable to even understand that part of my psychology. Then the work began. Now I am finally free of that old part of me. Now I can see it clearly. Now I can describe my experience.

I first felt fear and physical pain, and then mental anguish. Then I carried the secret. This was a secret that only two people shared. In my trauma, I began to unconsciously feel that I was part of a shameful conspiracy. I began to feel guilty. I didn't think about this. I felt it. I was too young to understand the psychological trap, but my subconscious mind knew only that I agreed to the horrible secret, so I must be guilty.

Shortly after that experience, my mother sent me to live with my step-grandfather, who lived on the other side of Wesel. It could be that my mother smelled something wrong in the air, but the spoken reason I went was the same reason a lot of kids were passed from home to home at that time. There was just not enough food to go around. My mother had to feed five kids. My stepgrandfather Toni lived with my aunt Leni, whose husband was killed in the war.

With them I would have enough to eat for dinner every night. Every day at school I was reminded of how poor we were. I was nearly ten years old, and with all the poor children in school, I waited in a line to receive a lunch container from the Red Cross. That first day I didn't want to be one of the poor kids in line, so I didn't eat any lunch. My aunt asked me later how my food was at school, and I told her that I didn't take the food. She was very angry with me and demanded that I not refuse the next day. So I stood in the Red Cross line. Every day I had their simple lunch - usually soup, or vegetables and potatoes. On Fridays we had fish or eggs. I remember I was always excited about Fridays. I loved that on some Fridays we got a roll with hot chocolate. I would dip the bread into the chocolate, letting it fill like a sponge. Every bite was like pudding.

My grandfather, my mother's father, died when my mother was only two years old - the same age I was when my father was lost in Russia. My grandmother remarried some three years later, and when the war started she moved to the nearby city of Aachen where her husband Toni, my step-grandfather, was sent as a customs officer at the border with Holland. Toni was a strict conservative German. I don't know if he eagerly served as a member of the Nazi party, but I imagine he must have been loyal to have been assigned such a sensitive position. He was certainly mercilessly strict with me. He demanded absolute obedience. He was especially concerned about my clothes never getting dirty, certainly hard on a young girl who so loved nature. One time I came home with some mud on my shoes. He flew into a rage and slapped my face. My head hit the brick wall of the house. I think even he was a little shocked to see me hit the wall so hard, and so he stopped, but then simply walked back into the house. I was very afraid of him. I tried as often as possible to simply stay out of his way.

Toni was very proud of his small garden next to the house where he kept a sheep. In the late fall, the sheep was brought to the butcher, where it was cut in pieces so Aunt Leni could cook it and bottle it in glass for the winter. The sheep meat was mostly cooked in soups. This was not tender lamb cooked fresh. This was a tough old sheep that tasted to me like some kind of stringy hard-to-chew rancid fat. I hated even the smell of it. We didn't eat meat very often, perhaps only once a week, and the first time the sheep was served was on a week night when my aunt Leni was away for a day. A friend of aunt Leni's from next door had come over to serve dinner for me and Toni. Toni had already eaten by the time I came home from school, so while they sat at the table talking I was served the horrible soup. I knew I had to eat my food, and so I started eating. In a few seconds the couple of mouthfuls I had swallowed came right out again. I vomited into the soup bowl. My step-grandfather was cold like ice. He didn't care how much I didn't like it, he demanded that I finish my soup. He held me locked in my chair with only the look in his eyes. I'm sure I ate half of that bowl, sobbing all the time, before our neighbor, expressing her compassion, convinced Toni to let me stop.

I avoided Toni after that, but I didn't show my fear of him. I was still always very social, and so I often visited our nearby neighbors. There was one kind woman who liked to talk to me. She had a son who was fifteen years old. I liked him as well. One day when I went to visit his mother, he answered the door. He asked me to come with him behind the house. There was a high wall near the back of the garden. I walked towards the wall and saw his family's large German Shepherd. The neighbor's son stood in front of me, blocking my way, while the dog stood next to him. He opened his pants, took out his penis, and started to masturbate. I started crying horribly. My nervousness made the dog nervous, and he started to bark and growl at me, and then jump up at me. The son didn't let me go until he had finished, and so I stood there pinned between him with his menacing lust and the dog barking in rage. When I could, I ran from the yard. My aunt saw me and saw immediately that something was terribly wrong. I told her what had happened. She went immediately to the neighbor's house to tell her friend. The two women confronted the son, but he completely denied that any of it was true. There was little my aunt could do, but at least I felt like she believed my story. She could see by my condition that

I could not be lying.

I lived for nearly two years with my aunt Leni and my step-grandfather Toni before returning to my mother's house. I thought I would be happy once I returned home, but for most of my life as a young girl I was always in one way or another attacked by men.

Soon after I returned to my mother's house I became twelve years old, and once again I became paralyzed with fear and guilt. I was alone in the apartment with a male relative who was only some years older than me. He took me by my hand, and led me into the bedroom. He pulled me down onto the bed, and again I was falling, frozen with fear. He took my small hand onto his erect penis and showed me how to rub it up and down. I did as I was told, and after a while I felt this warm sticky liquid on my hand. I didn't know what was happening. I didn't know what the liquid was, only that it seemed disgusting, mixed with the ache in my hand from rubbing, and the terror that gripped every frantic thought. I started to cry, but he stopped me with the warning. The same warning I had before, now deeply hidden in my subconscious. He looked at me with menacing eyes and told me not to tell anyone.

Some days later I told my best friend Ilka, one of the daughters of Hilde, who escaped with us from the East. It is strange to say that I told her about it in the way that young girls eagerly talk about all the events of their lives - a little more interested in the act of sharing secrets rather than caring about their meaning. I of course told her not to tell anyone. Some nights later Hilde visited us, and my mother woke me from bed to bring me into the living room. I looked at Hilde and my mother, and I suddenly became very cold. My mother asked me what the older relative had done to me. "Tell me what he did!" she demanded. I heard the horrible accusation in her voice, as if she had asked me what I had done to him, this older relative who she knew and trusted so well. I had agreed with the older relative not to say anything, and here was my mother demanding to hear my story. I was immediately in panic. I lied. I told them that I had made up the whole story, that what I told my friend was not true. I felt lost and alone at that moment, abandoned in my shame and fear. My mother and I never talked about that incident again. Another abuse hidden in the past.

Parents try to protect their children from danger, but also from growing up too fast. Information that should be shared often never comes into the light, and children suffer from that ignorance. Parents pass their fears and embarrassments on from generation to generation. This habit should change.

When I was thirteen years old, I was sitting on the toilet when I noticed a little bit of red from blood in my urine. I can't even say that I knew what was happening to me. I had no education or information from anyone about how my body worked, only fear, guilt and shame if I were to even think about it. I came out of the bathroom and saw a friend of my mother, Frau Oberbeck, a kind woman I liked who lived in our house. I asked her if I could talk to her privately. We walked down to the cellar, into a small dark room where we kept potatoes and coal for the winter. I told her that I was bleeding, and I was too ashamed to tell my mother. I was usually a joyful child in play, enjoying most every moment, but within any moment I could be reminded of some horrible episode in the past, or one of the terrible secrets. In all these moments related to sex, I was not consciously aware of the connections to my abuse. I only felt the shame. Kind Frau Oberbeck laughed when I told her my news, but it was that encouraging laugh that friends share when conspiring in a cellar. She told me not to worry at all, and she smiled reassuringly when she said I would have my menstruation from now on every month. She took me upstairs to tell my mother. My mother was surprised I didn't simply come to her at first. Both she and Frau Oberbeck laughed when my mother asked, "Why didn't you just tell me that?" I was too embarrassed to offer an answer, so I said nothing. After that, my mother and I never talked about it again. My nice mother and her nice friend were laughing at my embarrassment, but I think within their laughter was their own embarrassment. Children so often pass on misinformation from the little pieces they fit together about life. I had a lot more questions than answers about life, but I so seldom got an answer, that I seldom asked. I felt some comfort in seeing that my mother and her friend thought the matter was not so serious or dangerous, but no one explained to me what menstruation really meant. No one talked about sex, they only laughed as they talked around it. With metaphors and innuendo, I grew up seeing sex as both unavoidable and mysterious, and from my experience, painful. For many children, with scars and threats, sex becomes a dark unavoidable mystery.

About a year later, I was standing at the bus stop, and a car stopped in front of me. Our neighbor, Herr B., offered to give me a ride home. I was happy to get a ride home. I was happy any time I could ride in a car. After passing a few streets I realized we were not going home. He drove the car to a quiet street and came to a stop. Without even looking at me, he opened his pants, took out his penis, and then swiftly grabbed the back of my neck and pulled my head down. He forced my mouth onto his penis, and wouldn't let me out of his grip. My mind froze. I only wanted to pull my head away. After a while his sperm filled my mouth, and I can not accurately describe the horror of that moment. I was nearly suffocating, not wanting to swallow, unable to breathe in, and feeling helpless under his brutal control. When I could, I ran from the car, but I now remember how quickly I put what had just happened out of my mind. I walked home, not thinking. I had experienced a violent sexual act, and with no experience of sex in any other context, for me, sex was violent, and frightening, and I never knew when it may come. I felt only shock, and then guilt and shame for simply being a participant. I was too young to understand the dynamic. I couldn't understand why men were so often attacking me. I couldn't make sense of this frightening reality. So I didn't try. I let these shameful scenes fade from memory, not knowing that they never left my subconscious mind.

Before I graduated from *Volksschule*, Middle School, when I was fourteen, the government provided a morning program for the whole class. We were to watch an hour long movie about the persecution of the Jews. The teacher told us that we would be watching a movie that morning, and I was at first excited just to see a movie. As we watched the black and white films of horror I could not believe what my eyes saw. My brain was so shocked at what I saw that I could barely process the information. At home my family had only talked about who they had lost in the war. My mother lost nearly her whole family, but nothing else about the war was ever discussed. Now I was watching the truth about people herded into trains, concentration camps, mass graves with countless emaciated bodies. I couldn't watch the whole film. My stomach pulled in on itself and I could only vomit. The pressure of war had been all around me as a young child, but I had never seen the whole truth. I could not believe that people could be so brutal. I came home to my mother that day with only questions for her. What did she know of all this? Did she know that all this had been happening around us? She told me that she thought the Jews were living in work camps, along with others who were not Aryan, and along with the handicapped, and Gypsies, and intellectuals who spoke out against the Nazis. The truth about what happened in the camps was hidden from most people by fear and secrecy. However, many people simply didn't care. They believed in that Aryan nightmare. In either case, the government held the secrets, and most of the people feared whatever the government told them to fear. That the people also feared the government, only made the whole tragedy that much more of a dark spiral. With years of terror and deception, and the fear that any neighbor could be the enemy, or a spy for the Gestapo, most people could not bear to look into the center of that dark spiral.

The day I saw that film in school my perception of reality turned inside out. Some years later I spoke to my mother's niece, who was half Gypsy. I saw the number burned into her arm, evidence of her five years suffering in Auschwitz. I wanted to ask her about it, but the experience was far too painful for her to picture again in her thoughts.

As a teenager I was overwhelmed to see the full scope of the war I had lived through. I remember when I was nine years old, and thinking that the war was for me finally over. I had thought then that I could let go. Every night at seven the Red Cross broadcasted a radio program. In 1951, Chancellor Adenauer signed a treaty with the Russians to release all prisoners of war who had been captured in Russia. The Red Cross would read the names of newly released prisoners, and every night for weeks and weeks, I would hope to hear my father's name. Finally in the end, I came to realize that he would never come home, that my father was dead.

When I was fifteen I met Rolf Meesters, who became my first boyfriend. Rolf was nineteen years old, and had just completed three years of training to become a seaman. He was often a week away at a time taking cargo ships up and down the Rhein River. Rolf came from an old Weselaner family that had for generations been members of the *Handwerker Zunft*, the Craftsman's Guild which originated in the Middle Ages. He looked nice, a little bit conservative, but with an agreeable manner. My mother saw him attending church after she learned that we were friends, and I think altogether Rolf left a good impression on her. I liked that Rolf liked rock 'n' roll and Hollywood movies. He liked that I looked good, and came from a respectable church-going home. We loved to see movies together, but we didn't go very often. My mother was very strict about what the church considered sinful. Movies were forbidden. A few times when I didn't go with Rolf, I would sneak off to the movie theater with my brother Günther. We were also not allowed to dance or drink alcohol, unless of course we were celebrating a family holiday, Christmas, or a birthday. The church was lenient in some cases.

In 1965 I saw Alfred Hitchcock's film *Marnie* in the movie theater. I didn't directly connect myself to the psychological drama of the woman in the movie. I wasn't Tippi Hedren's character, but for a long time I thought about that film, not consciously realizing what I needed to understand. I didn't know at the time that I too was hiding something in my past. In 1997 I saw the film *Bliss*, staring Sheryl Lee, Terence Stamp, and Craig Sheffer. With painful truth and humor, this film exquisitely explained the web of patterns that can trap the abused women.

Once when Rolf and I were alone in the house, we were laying on my mother's bed. I wasn't thinking that we were laying together in bed. I was naive enough to just think it was nice to lay next to my friend Rolf. Rolf's thoughts were not so innocent. He put his hand under my clothes and then, with no finesse, no foreplay, he began to play with my vagina. Six years before, the threatening man said to me, "Don't say anything!" and now my pattern clicked on like a light switch. Rolf was perhaps more inexperienced than threatening, but it didn't matter. I froze. I pretended that I was sleeping. I felt nothing physically, no arousal. I only felt fear, shame, and guilt.

One summer day we were walking in nature. We stopped in a soft meadow, and Rolf started to kiss me and touch my breasts. I was again paralyzed, and didn't know what to do or say. On that day I lost my virginity without even fully knowing what the word virginity meant. Rolf was completely in his hormonal instinct. This was new territory for him, and he was far too excited and unskilled to get it completely right. When he brought his penis at first into my vagina, his aim was not even very good. I felt a lot of pain, and then shame. I had no experience with sex that did not involve fear and confusion. I could only cry. I could not even explain why I cried. After Rolf had an orgasm he became impatient and angry with me. He told me I was not a little child. He told me to stop crying. All the men told me to stop crying. For years I would experience no pleasure in sex. I would only learn to hide my feelings. I didn't blame the men. I didn't understand enough about my situation to blame anyone. As I say, I really didn't think too much about it all. When I felt I was in danger, I felt afraid. When the danger passed, I let it pass, covered over by my unending interest in each new moment. I have always had a passion for life. Born into chaos, I learned from birth to value spontaneity. In war, sometimes there is no time to think. However, there is always time to trust the heart. Even in chaos, the heart instantly knows the way. In danger my heart protects me. The rest of the time my heart leads me on wondrous adventures. I didn't blame the men. I usually liked them. I admired their strength. I learned from their intellects. I was often comforted in their arms. I was an attractive young woman with an appealing smile and a desire for adventure. I had a lot of opportunities to be with men, and I seldom said "no" to them. My training from abuse instructed me to always comply, and never complain. In time I became a co-conspirator. I began to always pretend to have an orgasm. Before I would experience my own sexual pleasure, before I would have an orgasm with a man, I would have to wait until my fourth husband Bastian, and my lover Rasa. Finally I found relationships with balance. Before them, I was always carrying my confusion with me. I was always missing my father, and looking for someone I thought was mature. In my search I went from man to man, never really happy or content.

I liked the idea of sex - the exciting sensations, the intimacy, the communion with tender loving male energy. I gradually came to understand what sex could be, but as often as I tried to find the genuine experience, neither the men nor myself were able to properly approach the art of sexuality. Now, in the twenty-first century, more and more men have become sensitive to the balance required for enlightened relationships. My first sexual experiences were all part of the dark ages of human sexuality. In most cases, the men had no sensitivity at all to what women experience. I sometimes think that I could have earlier overcome my conflicts with sex if only I could have found a man who could understand me. Where was that man who could be both strong and tender, and who had the strength of character to control his orgasm? Sex was supposed to be a duet, but the men were always rushing ahead to the crescendo. For me, pretending to have orgasms was a step up from the terror and shame I previously felt in sex. At least I was not crying. On the outside. As I gradually learned from my experiences, I saw more and more of what I was missing. I didn't understand the full power of sexual energy, but I could feel the emptiness. I longed for the totality of the sexual experience.

Sometimes I have looked back on my life and felt that I was always alone, but I was never alone. Within me was everything my mother and father created with their love, and all that they could give me as a child. I barely knew my father, but my mother was always there in my life. Not always immediately there, or even nearby on the planet, but through all my life I regularly visited my mother in Wesel. We sat together in her kitchen again and again, drinking her delicious coffee. She would tell me about the family. I would tell her about my strange and wonderful life. She would not always agree that my life was wonderful, but she usually agreed it was strange. Even so, her heart was always open to me.

My mother made friends easily. She was a good listener, meaning she didn't talk a lot. She did listen carefully, though, and when she gave advice, her friends and family listened. Not all of her family. Her advice was usually too conservative for me. My mother followed the strict moral teachings of the church, but she was not personally judgmental. Not in any severe way. She might respond to me by saying, with some doubt in her voice, "Well, we will see what happens," or "Don't complain if that doesn't work out, child." Then she would be sure my coffee cup was hot with fresh coffee from the pot. She excelled at preparing coffee and keeping her kitchen warm with hospitality. She would often have friends visit for coffee and conversation. I think of myself, and how I am with housework, when I now remember her care and sensitivity to every detail in the kitchen. Making coffee for her was a kind of ritual. She would grind fresh beans with a steel hand grinder she got from her mother. She would pour hot water into the pot to warm it up before making the coffee, and then pour it out just before pouring boiling water into the filter holding the fresh ground beans. Always the right grind, and always the right amount of coffee. Always delicious. And all the time that my mother made her coffee, she would be humming little tunes or church hymns. I grew up with the impression in my subconscious - that singing was somehow a vital part of house-work. I don't know how much that affected the last years living in my mother's house, that little secret about housework, but it was certainly in me somewhere at that time as I began my professional training.

Chapter 5

Professional Housekeeper

Wheresoever you go, go with all your heart.

- Confucius

When I was fourteen I reached a stage where working class children might have an opportunity to move into a higher working status. I had finished my middle school, but my parents could not afford to send me to the *Gymnasium*, the high school, and then to college. Instead, I went to a professional school for cleaning and cooking. I was to learn every theory and practice in the care of a home and a family. Mondays I would attend eight hours of classes at the vocational school. Tuesday through Saturday I would work as an apprentice in a middle class family's home.

I went to work for the Rosendahls. Herr Rosendahl was a butcher. He had his shop in the front part of the house. It was a very nice building with nice grounds and a garden, but of course his shop was in the house. My sensitive nose could smell the difference between a dozen different wild flowers, and she loved to do that, but now my nose was in a house filled with the smell of blood and freshly killed flesh. I never liked the smell, but I did like the Rosendahls. Herr Rosendahl was friendly to me, and Frau Rosendahl was a kind woman who showed me every detail of how she kept the house and shop so spotlessly clean. She could have been a tough teacher over three years time. There were a lot of details to learn.

But Frau Rosendahl was always kind and helpful. She cared with great skill for her two children, Klaus and Gisela, her husband, and the needs of the home and the shop. I think they could see in the beginning that I didn't really like the shop, and so they only had me in there on the weekends when Frau Rosendahl and I would scrub the shop floor. We used soap with lots of hot water and a special kind of hard brush. We used a lot of very hot water, bucket after bucket, to clean the butcher's floor. I didn't mind the hard work, perhaps because of Frau Rosendahl's kindness, but also because I appreciated the results. At the end of the day, the house and family were cleaner and healthier. When I went into the bathroom to take a bath, I appreciated the compelling logic of housework. *How can I clean myself in a dirty bathroom?*

I was an attentive student. But these were lessons that were easy to put into practice in the real world. They were not the lessons I needed to clean up my inner world. During this time I was not very happy with my life, but I was too shy, and ashamed of my situation, to appear unhappy. I worked hard to become as expert in her skills as Frau Rosendahl, and I know she appreciated my effort. I would sit with the family, Frau and Herr Rosendahl and their two children. We would eat delicious meals with of course always generous amounts of meat, a real luxury in those times. I would enjoy the food greatly, but I never really enjoyed the meals. I was too often overly conscious of my family's own poor circumstances. I always wanted to simply eat my fill of food like every one at the table, but I usually felt some shame. I never wanted anyone to think I was too eager. Perhaps they would think I was too hungry because there wasn't enough to eat in my mother's house. My mother had enough food for each meal, but certainly not the luxury of meat every day like I knew from the Rosendahl's table.

One day after I had worked there for about a year, I was very busy with my chores, and I told the Rosendahl's son Klaus to do something. I don't remember what exactly, but I was responsible for the children at times, and Klaus was supposed to listen to me. Suddenly he turned to me and said, "You can't tell me anything. Look where you come from!" He was only eight years old, but he knew exactly what he was saying. He knew exactly how to put himself above me. I said nothing. I just took my handbag and left the house. My mother was very surprised to see me return home on a Saturday morning. The butcher's shop is always very busy at that time, and

I was responsible for answering the phones. My mother told me I couldn't just walk away. I explained what happened, but she firmly believed that we should keep our feelings inside, and always keep a smile on our faces. I had no desire to smile. Soon there was a knock on the door. It was Herr Rosendahl. My mother told him that I didn't wish to see him. He insisted that he talk to me because he really didn't know what had happened. I agreed to explain the morning's events to him. Herr Rosendahl did not like to hear this story about his son. He apologized to me. He asked that I not feel so bad, and that he would clear up the matter with his son. I had always like the Rosendahls, so I was easily convinced by his sincerity. On the way back to the Rosendahls' house I began to feel bad for what young Klaus was going to hear from his father when we returned.

This defiant moment was unusual for me. I had long decided for myself to follow a version of my mother's advice. I would smile on the outside as I usually retreated into my inner world, dominated by shame, even though perhaps I was fortunate to have my own world, my own silent creation. Even though I could easily escape into the silence of simply not thinking about it all, part of me was always alert and present. So I learned a lot in those years, but was very happy at the end of nearly every day to leave the Rosendahls. I didn't really want to be there when I was there. I really didn't want to be at home either. For two hours or so in between the two, I usually went to the local ice cream parlor. I would eat ice cream and listen to rock 'n' roll - Elvis, Bill Haley, Fats Domino, Chuck Berry, Little Richard, Jerry Lee Lewis. When I began my apprenticeship in the house of Frau Rosendahl, I left my old school life and school friends behind. In these years with the Rosendahls, I really didn't have any friends. And for many years after, I had no friends, only husbands and lovers. I went nearly every day to the ice cream parlor and sat alone, eating my ice cream with the rock 'n' roll stars. At the same time, I was becoming an expert in that euphemism called *domestic science*. I graduated from school with high grades in my classes, and a good recommendation from the Rosendahls. My mother was fully supportive. She loved the idea of her mischievous daughter learning the solid skills every proper young woman should know. I did become an expert in many areas related to cleanliness and good health, but these are skills society undervalues. Most people would say I was simply trained to be a housekeeper.

Chapter 6

Husbands and Lovers

I have always believed, and I still believe,
that whatever good or bad fortune may come our way
we can always give it meaning
and transform it into something of value.

- Hermann Hesse

Rolf had been my boyfriend for two years when he received his orders to report to the military. Sitting in a cafe, Rolf in his new uniform, he looked to me and simply said, "Let's get married." I said immediately, "Yes, let's get married." Rolf was thrilled that his girlfriend would remain faithful to him as his wife while he was away and serving in the Air Force. I had other motivations. I was seventeen and desperate to leave my mother's house. My abusive older relative continued to be always present, leering at me, often simply walking in when I was washing myself in the bathroom. In the simple fantasy of a seventeen year old, I imagined myself married with my husband away much of the time. I would have my freedom. I was excited to be in love with Rolf, but I can't say that I had any idea of what it really meant to be in love. I liked Rolf. I was not afraid of him. That was a lot.

My mother was not so eager to open that door, and she held the key. I would not legally be able to marry without my mother's consent until I was twenty-one. I'm sure that some of my mother's resistance came from me not being able to explain my reasons. I looked to her like an obsessed teenager. I could only say that I would marry Rolf. We could have our own apartment. I could work while Rolf was away. I was too embarrassed to explain why I was in such a hurry. She thought I was running into a relationship because I was a young girl with her first interests in sex and romance. She was right about the running. I was not thinking clearly as I was running into marriage, but I wasn't running towards sex and romance. I was running away. My mother shrewdly accused me of being pregnant. She told me she believed me when I looked her in the eyes and said I was not pregnant. Still, I could feel that she was suspicious, and I'm sure that she was not completely convinced until some many months later when she had to eventually see the lack of evidence. I hadn't even thought she might think that I was pregnant. My innocent honest "no" to her question only made her rethink her strategy. She changed the subject and simply said that she would not give her permission. I then turned her idea around, and told her that if she didn't give me permission then I would get pregnant, and then before the church brought ruin on our house, she would have to give her permission. My desperate logic won in the end.

On Saturday September 12, 1959, Rolf and I were married in our local church. The church was full with all of its regular parishioners, our spiritual community, which included Rolf and me and our families. I don't remember the exact words of our minister, Priester Keires. He spoke about our two souls coming together, sharing our lives. It was very nicely spoken, very touching. You could think I was crying because of his soft eloquence. While we stood together before our community, I cried because I knew with all certainty that I was making a mistake. Instead of the freedom I had sought, we would say *Ich falle vom Regen in die Traufe*. I got out of the rain only to land in the gutter. I smiled throughout the whole day, through the ceremony in the church, and through the party afterwards. My wedding night was a catastrophe. I told Rolf I did not want to have sex with him. I could not explain to him the history of experiences in my life that I could not even explain to myself. I could only cry. Images passed through my mind. One image was of Rolf taking my virginity two years earlier. How could I explain this complicated confusing distress?

I realize now the paradox I have always been living with. I have always been attractive, and often seductive. I didn't consciously know that I was always seeking approval to overcome the guilt and shame. I would dress elegantly for every occasion, knowing the effect it had. When eventually I overcame the guilt and shame, I would still dress elegantly for every occasion. Now, however, I was dressing simply to appreciate the beauty.

In the course of my life I have had four husbands and many many lovers. With only a few exceptions, with each of my lovers, I only had sex one time. Arousal and excitement carried me into bed, but as soon as a penis came into my vagina, the unconscious trigger activated. Events hidden in my past mixed with my conscious memories of a penis violently attacking me. These were my first conscious memories of a penis. With each new man, I would let him come in me, but then, automatically, I would become paralyzed. And I would cry. The men were usually surprised or even shocked, not knowing what was wrong. I was often asked why I was crying, but I never gave an answer. I didn't have an answer. In time I felt that my crying, this simple act of pain, was itself embarrassing. One time after laying motionless in bed while *having sex* with Rolf, he looked down at me and said, "You are as cold as a fish." I hated those words. I hated that image. I wanted the men to see me as happy as well as attractive. And so I learned to act my part in sex. I acted out the orgasms I never experienced.

My marriage with Rolf Meesters lasted four years. Even though I was a married woman, I was still under twenty-one. By German law at that time, I could not file for a divorce until I was at least twenty-one. Even though I knew from the beginning how unhappy I was, I had no choice but to wait before I could move on with my life.

When I was eighteen I became pregnant. On the twelfth of February, 1961, my first child was born. With my brother Walter, my father Walter, and my stepfather Walter, I didn't want to name my son after his father, but I liked the idea of finding something similar. Instead of Rolf, with an "o" we chose another common German name Ralf, with an "a."

It still amazes me today to think this, but in my family there was never any communication about sex, that even after I was married I really had no idea of the actual process of childbirth. With every pregnancy, even though the mother would routinely have a gynecologist working with a hospital, there was always in Germany a midwife helping with the birth.

When I was eight months pregnant I was sitting in our local hair salon when I suddenly started to bleed profusely. The hair dresser, who knew me well, immediately called my midwife, and then took me literally just around the corner to the hospital. When I came into the hospital my gynecologist at that moment was just leaving for the weekend. He saw that I was bleeding, and said that I should immediately be brought into the operating room for a Caesarian birth. While we were discussing this my midwife arrived. She asked the doctor if we might wait and see if the pregnancy could more naturally come to term. I believe the doctor agreed, in part, because he really wanted to go home for the weekend. I was admitted to the hospital, and my midwife attended to me. It was then that I naively asked her, "How does this work? Where does the baby come out?" She laughed and said, "Where the penis goes in, that's where the baby comes out!" I think, like a lot of inexperienced young women, I couldn't imagine that a whole baby could come out of such a small place.

I was in the delivery room for the next thirty-six hours. I was in a lot of pain and nauseous most of the time. At the faintest whiff of any strange smell, I would immediately vomit. This was an old hospital. The delivery room had tall ceilings and the walls were all white tiles. It was a very cold environment. Usually the expectant mother would walk a bit, as the movement would help to bring the birth along, but because I was bleeding so much I could not get out of bed. The midwife came and went during that time, but mostly I was by myself and in great pain and fear, lying alone in that cold room. At that time there was little thought of pain relief given to women during a painful birth. It was normal to think that birth was painful.

When my baby finally came out, a very tiny child only a little over two pounds, the doctor told me that I gave birth to a healthy baby boy, downy blond locks here and there surrounding a tiny round face with serious brown eyes. Even though healthy, Ralf was so small and weak that he was isolated in the hospital for the next three months, receiving milk from me but fed through a tube in his nose. I saw him every day through the glass window, but I felt a great loss the first three months of Ralf's life where he didn't have the touch of his mother's body. After only three weeks my milk stopped and I had to travel two times a week to a special clinic in Essen, about an hour away, to buy the mother's milk he needed. When he had gained enough weight, about five pounds, he was finally able to come home to us.

I never really wanted to be a mother. My self confidence was so low from so many bad experiences growing up that I had a very hard time seeing myself with the responsibility of motherhood. On the other side, I loved children. I was often throughout my child-hood a cheerful and reliable babysitter. Suddenly, having a child of my own brought many parts of my being into both a sharp focus and a deep conflict.

When Ralf was one and a half years old I realized I was preg-nant again. I knew I didn't want to bring another baby into this marriage. In my panic I could only think to have an abortion, at this time completely forbidden by law. Any doctor was required to report evidence of an abortion to the police and the penalties were severe. The penalties were severe because the authorities were alarmed at how many women were getting abortions. I didn't talk to my husband or my mother about my decision. It's not that I didn't want to talk to my husband or my mother. I couldn't talk to anyone about such a decision unless it was the person helping me to find a midwife willing to break the law. In any case, I felt this had to be my decision. My mother would have quoted the Pope to convince me to have the baby. Rolf was on his ship on the river Rhein, and I felt I had to act immediately.

A male friend knew, from within his family, of a midwife who performed abortions. He was kind enough to come with me, and then accompany me home in his car. The midwife lived about five kilometers away from Wesel in a small village. We were both a little nervous and cautious not to attract attention as we walked into the midwife's house. I only remember these details now in recollection. At the time I didn't see or think much about anything. I could only think I needed help.

The midwife was a small round older woman. She had long been a midwife and was now retired. She took me into an adjacent room. She explained to me what she would do, and what I should do in the coming hours. I laid down on a table as she prepared her materials. She filled a large catheter with a strong solution of water and soap. She inserted the catheter into my vagina and injected the solution into my uterus. This was not a simple procedure. Women had died as a consequence of a midwife's inexperience. As I got into my friend's car for the ride home, I didn't yet feel any of the extreme pain that would follow in a couple of hours. I was instead thinking that if I went home then my mother-in-law would ask why I was home and apparently ill. I told my friend to take me to work instead. Over the years I worked as a waitress, a factory worker, a salesperson, a housekeeper, and as a laboratory assistant. At that time I was working as a waitress in a cafe. I came into the cafe and for a while I was okay. After some time, I simply couldn't take the pain any longer. I asked my same friend, who was still watching out for me, to drive me home. For another hour I laid in bed, but as the pain grew stronger and stronger I cried out. My mother-in-law heard me and very quickly wanted to take me to the hospital. I couldn't allow that to happen. I couldn't let the doctor see my condition. I tried to calm her down, just to give me more time. Soon after she left me, I again fell into the pain. My mother-in-law finally convinced me to trust her judgement. We went to the hospital. My doctor examined me and I knew that he knew the truth. He said nothing to me. He only followed his heart when he pronounced that I had had a miscarriage.

I think you can understand my conflicted emotions only if you have had a similar experience. I felt the pain of that tiny life lost, along with the relief of not being pregnant. I wasn't thinking, you could say, only reacting. Even as a married woman, my society was so constrained by habit and insecurity, that I understood almost nothing about even the workings of my own body. For years I believed the folk tale that I would never get pregnant if I always just peed after sex. Everything I learned about sex came from adult's jokes, children's whispers, or abuse from men. Strange to think that my old war-time strategy of acting-without-thinking would still be my only rescue.

On my twenty-first birthday, May 14, 1963, I went to a lawyer and filed for divorce. To avoid airing our dirty laundry in public, I told Rolf that he could have all of our belongings. I also told him that I didn't want any money for support. The only possessions I took with me when I left the marriage were my books and what we call *die Aussteuer*, what you might say is something like part of a dowry - not money, but only some possessions. This was a box that I brought with me into the marriage that contained our silver flatware, towels, tablecloths and all the bed linen.

Rolf fell into a deep depression when I left. In desperation, he swallowed a bottleful of sleeping pills. He left a conspicuous note, and took just enough pills to become unconscious, but not enough to quickly take him away. His parent's found him and took him to the hospital to have his stomach pumped. His brother called me and told me that Rolf was in the hospital after trying to commit suicide. I went to visit him, and found him already recovered, sitting comfortably in his room. When he saw me, he got out of bed and knelt on the cold hospital floor before me and begged me to stay with him. I told him no, I would not. A moment of trembling tension filled the room, but neither of us said anything more. I knew in that moment that if I replied to Rolf's emotion, I would be stuck. I would not be able to move on. I turned and left the room, and I could feel that he was following me with his eyes. I walked down the long hospital corridor, never turning to look back. I didn't want to see him standing there, or still hesitantly walking after me. I came to the large swinging doors at the end of the hallway, pushed them open, and then heard them swish together behind me. As I heard the doors close, I immediately felt a joyless but nonetheless empowering freedom. I didn't have a conscious understanding of the dynamics of my decision. I could feel no lower emotions pulling me into a disastrous compromise. I acted with a clarity of mind propelled by the energy of a newly liberated heart.

After deciding to file for divorce, I took two year old Ralf with me to stay at my mother's house, but only for a short time. For the same old frightening reasons, I didn't want to stay in my mother's house. I looked for a job, but realized I couldn't work as a cook or maid in a home and bring a young child with me. I have always been so grateful for my mother and my sister Rita who took care of Ralf when I had so few choices. On an unspoken level, my mother understood my need to leave Ralf with her, and why I couldn't simply stay with Ralf in her house. She simply took him, as I found my way on my own for the first time in my life.

I had painful reminders from my childhood about the differences between the working class and the middle class and the upper classes. My mother's decision from her heart, an emotional response to my desperate needs, was typical in our family. I would leave the small city of Wesel where I grew up in the working class, and where I had served in the home of the butcher, a member of the merchant class. I would now experience another level in the social divisions. I took a job as a maid in the home of a banker in Duesseldorf, sixty kilometers away from Wesel. I moved to the elegant home of Herr and Frau Ebert. The Ebert family was very impressed with my cooking and cleaning skills, but also with my keen interest in my new environment. I lived in their house, cleaning until three in the afternoon, later cooking dinner, and then most nights I would sit in the living room in conversation with Herr and Frau Ebert. We would drink the finest wines brought ceremoniously up from the wine cellar each night after Herr Ebert's careful examination of the choices.

I worked for the Ebert family for a year and a half as their maid and cook. Unless the Eberts had a weekend party, every weekend I would take the train to Wesel to be with Ralf and my family. I felt comfortable in the banker's home, but I kept to myself when I wasn't with the Eberts. I usually never went out at night, and I had no friends in Düsseldorf. My only change of scenery was that weekend train ride.

Some days before Christmas I took the train to Wesel. Ralf was staying with his father for the holiday, but I had the idea to stop by their house and just see Ralf once during the Christmas season. The court had given custody of Ralf to me, with his father Rolf having visitation rights. Neither of us, however, was in a position to support Ralf at that time. Ralf was living mostly with my mother and her family members while I was working for the Eberts in Düsseldorf. When he saw his father, Ralf stayed with his grandmother. Rolf's family were bitterly angry with me because of the divorce. They filed papers with the court to take custody away from me. I knew they didn't approve of me leaving the family, but I didn't realize the level of their anger.

Rolf had an apartment in the building next to his mother's. When I arrived that winter day at Rolf's apartment, what used to be our apartment, I found both Rolf and Ralf were gone. Instead I was met by Rolf's brother Heinz. Usually Heinz had been kind to me, but now he stood like a determined soldier, frowning at me and defending the family against me. He told me that I would not be allowed to see Ralf. He sternly criticized me for all that I had done against his family. I simply crumbled. I cried. I pleaded with him to let me just see my son. He was unmoved. After the holidays my lawyer and I went to court. The judge ruled that Ralf should be immediately returned to his mother. Of course, that meant that Ralf was returned to his grandmother's house, and I would ride the train back and forth from my work in Düsseldorf to my family in Wesel.

One night when I had just returned by train to Düsseldorf, I was waiting for my bus, and looking in the window of a shoe store next to a small cafe. A strikingly handsome older man came up to me and invited me to have a coffee. This was Alfons. He was the owner of a fashionable boutique and living in the nearby city of Krefeld. He was fifty-five at the time and I was twenty-three. We talked over coffee (not only about shoes), and I was quickly fascinated by his intellect, but also his humor and free thinking. I was also soon to be fascinated by the people he knew as a prominent member of the bohemian underclass of the upper class. I had been impressed by the dignified refinement of life in the banker's house, but as I rode off in Alfons' speedy Porsche, I was very quickly accelerated into an unfamiliar, but eccentric and exciting social scene.

I began to spend more and more time with Alfons and his friends. There were parties, and regular gatherings in homes and at bars and cafes - artists and intellectuals all intoxicated with creativity, and other things, and everyone having sex with anyone. Some months after I met Alfons I quit my job with the Eberts and moved into his house. We didn't have sex together, but I did learn to masturbate with him - something my next husband was shocked to learn. I didn't have sex with any of Alfons' friends either, and because I was outgoing and well-dressed, always wearing Alfons' latest collection, and easily making friends, I was also the object of a lot of sexual attention. That became even more intense in the scene the longer I went without sex. I was a mysterious unattainable desire. I talked easily with everyone, and enjoyed the diverse and extraordinary topics discussed with such passion. Even though divorced, I was still Marlis Meesters. In the scene I was called *MM* which people liked to say with merriment as MM was also the name of a popular German champagne. I usually never drank champagne, or other alcohol. I always had orange juice, and good food at parties. I met a lot of interesting people, and, as I say, I didn't have sex with any of them. I was not against having sex. If you could say sex is an intimate dance, then you could say I just didn't care for their style of dancing. For about a year I only pleasured myself, sometimes in the company of Alfons, when we masturbated together.

Alfons was extremely kind and generous. He saw me in his imagination as an exotic princess who could be his friend and fashion model. I too enjoyed his fantasy, but after a while I felt always uncomfortable with him paying for everything. I felt uncomfortable, perhaps unworthy, if I needed to ask him for money. This had nothing to do with Alfons and everything to do with me, and my need for independence. With good wishes, I left the *glamour* of Krefeld, and returned to Wesel.

After I had been back in Wesel for only a week, I was walking down the main street and spontaneously walked into a women's clothing shop. I asked the sales person for the manager, and then walked up the stairs and went into his office and asked him for a job. He looked me over very carefully from foot to head in less than a second and said, "I will hire you, but you will have to wear stockings on your legs." I hated stockings. I was used to wearing them, but I really didn't like fashions that would bind you up like a package. But I did like the idea of working in a clothing store, and so I wore stockings. I wore stockings and sold dresses and hats, scarves and coats, for nearly half a year. Near the end of my time there, for the entertainment and benefit of their many customers, the store sponsored a fashion show in Wesel's large town hall. I was excited to be one of the models in the show, but I was so nervous that I had planned to pretend that no one could see me as I walked down the runway. As it turned out, before I could walk on the stage, there was some sudden mix up in time, and I couldn't model after all. I was actually relieved. As much as I wanted to be a model, I also didn't want to be a model at all. After the show I went by myself to a local cafe-bar where I was friends with the owner. I often went there and talked with her, but I almost always drank coffee. As I sat at the bar, I didn't notice a man sitting with a group of friends at one of the tables. With great confidence and ease, he would soon introduce himself to me, and not long after that he would become my second husband.

Klaus Rosenthal was born into an academic family. His father and mother were both pharmacists. Klaus had the meticulous study habits of a pharmacist, and a serious hard working social ethic. Klaus, and his family and friends, were totally different than Alfons and his friends. I didn't prefer one over the other, but I did enjoy the change. Alfons was athletic. I think he had to be, to keep up with his wild lifestyle. Klaus was tall and slim, but he looked as if he spent his hours indoors leaning over a thick book. Klaus had a hunger for knowledge. I loved his ability to learn a new idea, and then take it apart to see it from the inside. When I met Klaus he had just completed his university studies in Computer Science, what we have now come to call Information Technology. This was a very new field at the time, and Klaus quickly was offered a position at Kienzle GmbH, a computer company with offices in the small city of Villingen, in the Black Forest.

Soon after I met Klaus, I left the clothing store and got a higher paying position working for the giant Dutch corporation Philips. I was assembling extremely tiny electronic components, something women with small hands do in factories all over the world. I worked for Philips for about four months before I moved with Klaus to Villingen. For a third time in my life I was moving to the Black Forest.

My reliance on intuition made me very fast in making decisions. The heart thinks very fast, at the speed of passion. I saw in Klaus a kind of stability, a solid structure appearing in the landscape of my war ravaged experience. He had the intellect and bearing to move confidently through the world, and the ambition and social connections to guarantee financial stability. After we had been in Villingen for about a month, in March of 1964 Klaus and I were married. Shortly after that I was pregnant with my second child, Claudia Susanna.

Around the same time I discovered I was pregnant, I discovered a realization growing in me. I realized that through my innocence I had never seen Klaus clearly. He was often sarcastic, and in the beginning, in my inexperience, I took his wordplay as evidence of a high intellect. He was very intelligent, but I was far too enamored by his intellect to see him clearly. I began to feel that his sarcasm held a deep rooted, but carefully hidden delight in his rudeness. In his mind I should be a pretty housewife, and modern enough to be lively and intelligent and independent, but at the same time totally obedient to my husband. I too had my illusions. I had a model of life in the upper classes. Klaus' family were the upper classes for me. Klaus carried himself like an educated man. I naively thought I would learn a lot from Klaus. He would educate me about the world he knew so well. When I found myself in the upper classes, I found myself only thinking about my working class background. My experiences of abuse all pushed me into a smaller and smaller image of my self. With Klaus, I simply retreated into my low self-esteem, and seldom questioned his actions. During our entire time together, he never once said, "I love you." I remember one day we walked home together from my work. I was tired. My hair was a mess. As we walked he looked over at me and coolly said, "You look like a whore." I was so hurt in that moment. My pride was injured, but my insecurity kept me from confronting Klaus. In moments of painful embarrassment, I have often spontaneously protected myself by simply laughing. I laugh from my heart, an honest laugh, but of course often an unexpected response. Perhaps as a child I found that people nearly always respond well to laughter. As an adult, I often hid my low sense of self behind laughter and a spirited personality.

When I was married to Rolf I began to have problems with my kidneys. I realize now that my kidney and bladder illnesses had a psychosomatic connection to the relationships in my life. While living with Klaus, and realizing more and more every day how difficult our relationship was becoming, I carried these troubles into the processes of my body. In that two years in Villingen I had two operations on my kidneys.

When married to Rolf Meesters, I would cook and clean. Rolf would bring home the money he made from work, and we would buy what we needed without thinking the money was his or mine. It was our money. With Klaus Rosenthal, I received a small allowance. I did my work as a housewife, but the money he received for his work mostly stayed in his pocket. He seldom allowed me to buy anything I wanted. I always felt like an underpaid worker. From this time I have often felt guilty when I have thought about spending money for myself.

I wanted my new baby to be born in my home town of Wesel because my whole family from my mother's side was from Wesel. As Christmas was approaching, I wished to spend the holiday with my family, and not alone in the Black Forrest with Klaus. Three days before the birth, Klaus and I drove the 600 kilometers from the Black Forest, while all the time I felt the contractions from my labor. I went immediately to the hospital when we arrived. Claudia Susanna was born two days later, December 17, 1965.

I had a difficult delivery with Claudia Susanna. During the whole pregnancy I had trouble with my kidneys. Nearly every day I had to go to a urologist to have my kidneys drained through a tube. I would lay for two hours on a cold table through the freezing Black Forest winter. During all this time I could feel Klaus' disapproval. He was a very domineering man who never consulted with me over the plans for our lives. When we later moved to South Africa, he simply announced to me that he had a new job and we would be leaving Germany. I felt little better than a servant. I realize that from Klaus' perspective, he was forced to react to a wife with a troubled psychology. Perhaps he felt he could best deal with the situation by keeping me at a distance. As we drove north to Wesel that December, I fell into a deep depression while at the same time feeling a sense of urgency. The whole drive I felt as if I had to keep the baby inside me until we arrived. Along with this feeling was my conflict with having children at all. All through the pregnancy I could feel Klaus' cold behavior. I always had the feeling he was never really with me. In his cool sarcasm he verbally abused me in a thousand tiny ways. Eager to return to his work, he left me in Wesel and drove back to his job while his daughter was entering the world. When Claudia Susanna was born I excitedly told the doctor to call Klaus and tell him we had just received a daughter. This was five o'clock in the morning. Klaus later complained to me that he thought it was rude of me to have the doctor wake him up so early.

In a strange way while laying in the hospital I felt as if I didn't want to bring this child into the world, but when the doctor told me that I gave birth to a healthy baby girl I was suddenly extremely happy. Claudia Susanna was six and a half pounds. She was a beautiful child with thick dark hair and large almond shaped eyes.

Chapter 7

South Africa

In time, we shall be in a position to bestow on South Africa the greatest possible gift - a more human face.
— Steven Bantu Biko.

Klaus moved to South Africa around three months before I followed him with the kids. At first we lived in a two bedroom urban apartment near Johannesburg. Some months later we moved into a house with a wonderful garden and palm trees. Klaus was never a loving family man. He treated Claudia Susanna well, enjoying his delightful baby girl, but he usually ignored Ralf, often acting as if Ralf was not even there. Ralf was five years old when we moved to South Africa. He was a shy insecure child and as he listened to the few friends he had talk proudly about their fathers, he began to notice his distance from Klaus. Ralf wanted to call Klaus *Vater*, father, but Klaus got very angry one time and told this little sensitive five year old, "I am not your father! Your father is in Germany." In that instant both Ralf and I were deeply hurt. I never fully confronted Klaus, but I did ask him why he couldn't let Ralf feel he had a father nearby. He explained with a great intellectual rationality that Ralf's father was in fact in Germany, and he did not want to be something he was not.

When I moved to South Africa there was still apartheid. My husband took me to this unfamiliar land, but I quickly saw and felt the reality. All around me were a people who lived like slaves in a brutal social structure. I always had a lot of compassion for all oppressed people, but especially for the black South Africans. I grew more and more unhappy living there because of apartheid. The white people lived in a totally separate world. Whenever I was with a group of white women at a party or any gathering I was astounded at their thoughts and actions. It was common to hear a woman advise, "If ever you drive over a black with your car, be sure to back up and drive over them again to make sure they are dead." That was a joke that traveled through the party circuit. A murderous joke.

I remember when I went to the bank. There were two entrances, one with a sign that said White and another that said Colored. I purposely entered through the Colored entrance. Everyone in the bank stared at me. The manager came to me and told me that I can't enter through the Colored entrance. I politely acted surprised, "Oh, I didn't know that."

One day when Klaus was working for a giant steel manufacturer, the managers of the company invited me and some other wives to take a tour of the facilities. All the white people worked in offices overlooking the factories. When I took the tour I felt as if I were entering not only another world, but another age, perhaps the Middle Ages. All the laborers were black, working only in short pants, sweating profusely in the burning African sun. But these were a dignified people, carrying a great pride from an ancient culture even while they worked like slaves. I was shocked to see this scene, slavery in 1966, witnessing the oppression of blacks who were suffering to make the steel to build a modern white empire. It was often my habit to look at people directly in the eyes and share a smile or kind thought, but when I tried to make that connection with one of the black workers I remembered that in this culture a black man was not permitted to look a white woman in the eyes. As I carried this thought and the vision of that black worker, sweating, thirsty for water, I imagined him having an even greater thirst for some rest, some end, some change from this horrible existence. I carried this thought with me as I was escorted back into the world of whites. We were brought into the cool office building and politely served tea. I couldn't drink it. I only sat there in shock, watching the women sip tea while in my mind a proud African man could not even risk a moment to look at me, human to human.

In our house we had an African maid. Her name was Paula, and she reminded me of the large friendly black women I saw in movies of the American South, the loving black servant who was always so good to the white master's children. Even with this disturbing image in my mind, I found myself becoming closer to Paula than to any of the white women I met in South Africa. One Christmas Eve I asked that Klaus take me to Paula's house in the slums nearby to where we lived in Vanderbijlpark. I brought some gifts for Paula and her family. She was very happy to see me, but I could see that she was also ashamed to have me visit her in a home that was really a shack built in the mud, made from tin walls and a tin roof - so hot, hard and unforgiving.

After living nine months in South Africa, I left with Ralf and Claudia Susanna to return to Germany. Klaus followed some months later. With only three weeks notice, Klaus had told me that we would be moving back to Germany. I would leave with the children and he would come some time afterwards. He didn't tell me why we were leaving, or how long we would be waiting for him. I wanted to protest somehow, but I didn't know what to say. I was happy with the idea of leaving South Africa, but in some way I felt the need to rebel against Klaus' control. I said, "I've never even seen Kruger National Park!" A ridiculous thought, but he immediately saw a way to appease me. He said, why not? Why not tour the famous wild animal park. He bought me a week long bus tour through the park, and a week before I would fly with the children back to Germany, I went by myself on a tour of wildlife of South Africa. I have to thank Klaus for that trip. I was fascinated to see wild lions, giraffes, monkeys and crocodiles, but I was even more excited to meet a young Englishman named Michael. His parents were German Jews who fled to England when Michael was a child. I had a short love affair with Michael in the romantic light of the South African savannah. I had no idea that in a very short time I would see him again in England.

Klaus had told me that he would book a flight for us direct to Brussels, and that he would write my mother to arrange for her to meet us, and drive us back to Wesel. He was a little sad to see his family leaving him alone in Africa, but for whatever reasons, he was also happy that he was free to be alone. He had to deal with something before he left where having his family's presence would be inconvenient, but he didn't feel it was necessary for his wife to know the details. As I walked to the plane, Klaus handed me a letter and told me to read it after the plane had taken off.

As the plane was leaving the terminal, I opened the letter. Klaus wrote that he thought I would complain if he told me about the change he had made in our travel plans. He had found a flight that landed first, overnight, in Barcelona, before heading on to Brussels. He explained that he had already written to my mother about the change in plans. He simply didn't want to have to discuss the matter with me. As it turned out, we three cheerfully decided to enjoy the unexpected. The children quickly made friends with all the flight attendants, and we had an interesting evening exploring a small part of Spain, and then enjoying the night in a nice hotel. The next day our flight to Brussels could not fly through a rough winter storm, and so we were forced to land and spend the night in Gatwick, England. I called Michael. I thought, naively, that since I was in England, I should just see Michael. He thought that was a wonderful idea, but he didn't tell me he would have to drive six hours to get there. At four in the morning he arrived, and we stayed up together until my flight left the next day.

Chapter 8

Now again in Wesel

*There are two mistakes one can make along the
road to truth - not going all the way, and not starting.*

- Buddha

*U*ntil we had our own apartment, I lived for a while again in
my mother's house. I think that from the moment I had that
tender touch with Michael, I knew my marriage with Klaus was
over. Klaus and I and the children lived for a short time in Wesel
when Klaus announced that he was moving the family to Basel,
Switzerland. He said that he would leave first, and as soon as he had
an apartment, he would send for me and Claudia Susanna. Young
Ralf would follow a different path.

During this period I spent weeks or months at a time in the hospital, one kidney infection after another - pain and exhaustion with
days of walking back and forth to the toilet, often wishing to stop
walking and only sit on the toilet, not even able to pee very much
but weary from my bladder trying. Despite the discomfort, I felt
joyful about my strength to see myself independent from Klaus, and
yet, I was still married to him. I realized some years later through
a particularly insightful moment of clarity in meditation that my
kidney problems continued to exist as long as I ignored certain
frightening imprints from my past - imprints on my consciousness,
so terrible they are hidden by the clever and overly protective ego.
I suffered the pains in my body and heart, but I savored the feeling
of freedom. Just the knowledge that I felt free made me feel more
free. The combination of healthy optimism and good hospital care
gave me strength in what is for most couples normally a painful and
chaotic process of separation and divorce.

Klaus was gone until late every day at his job in Köln. My mother was watching the children. I was able to bear the drama of my life, but I didn't like that my mother, as a grandmother, had so much responsibility for Ralf and Claudia Susanna. Ralf was often visiting with his father and his father's new wife. Rolf had married a kind-hearted woman named Lisel. Compared to the travel and turbulence in my life, with Rolf and Lisel, Ralf had found a more typically normal and secure environment. He enjoyed the experience. Ralf was seven and Claudia Susanna was three when I made the decision that Ralf should live with his father, and Claudia Susanna would live with me, and her father. There is a feeling one feels when doing the right thing. I don't know if there is a way in words to describe it, but even in the sadness of seeing Ralf go, I had the feeling this was the right thing to do.

While in and out of the hospital, I had a love affair with my doctor. Because of Klaus' excellent health insurance, I was fortunate to often have a hospital room to myself, and my choice of physician. This urologist, well-known and respected in his field, soon became a close, compassionate, and even a passionate friend. After I recovered, and was out of the hospital and well enough, we would often drive to the countryside, find a quiet meadow, lay out a blanket, talk for hours, and then playfully make love in the soft meadow.

Over months of treatment, he figured out that my ureter, the pathway that brings urine from the kidneys to the bladder, was too small and thin. He proposed an operation, and with skillful hands, I was much improved. Under an open sky, the doctor figured out that his touch in our lovemaking was not as successful. He was the first man who noticed that I didn't have an orgasm. He suggested that I pleasure myself, if I liked. I did like that. I liked the whole idea of that understanding from a man, and the opportunity at last to have control over my sexual experience. The operation was successful. I was healing well, and seeing the benefit of both improved anatomy and an improved relationship with a man. Unfortunately the man was not my husband.

Once during this time I had sex with Klaus, and after Klaus had his orgasm, I was brave enough to play with myself, hoping that I too could feel that great release. I had never dared to masturbate in front of Klaus. He was far too conservative to allow what he considered immoral behavior, from his wife. The voice of my mother from years ago came into my thoughts. She asked me why I wanted a divorce from my husband Rolf. I told her that I didn't like to have sex with him because I never had an orgasm. She looked surprised, and said, "That is not a reason to get a divorce. I never had an orgasm with your father or your step-father. Orgasms? Women don't have orgasms!" I immediately started to play with myself. Klaus looked at me as if I was suddenly acting out some terrible hidden nightmare from his past. From the tortured expression on his face, I would guess it had something to do with spoiled food.

Not long after that, Klaus would be in Basel waiting for me to join him. I went one time to Basel. That one experience told me that I should not move there with Klaus. We were invited to a dinner party at a typically upper middle class home. Again I was confronted with my insecurity over my working class history. I was speaking an upper-class form of German perfectly, like everyone else. I was knowledgeable enough to add an occasional intelligent comment, but as all of them at one point were talking about what universities they had attended, suddenly I was asked that simple question. I started to answer the question, but as soon as I said, "I didn't attend a university" I felt as if I were alone in the room. The faces of everyone in the room suddenly became a mirror for me. I was the only one who had not attended a university. I could have instantly thought of a dozen other times in my life in which I felt inadequate, this was not an unfamiliar feeling, but I was too lost to even think at that moment. As soon as I could find the words, I told Klaus that I didn't feel so good and I'd like to go home.

What I wasn't thinking about was the vast difference between this dinner table and my own family's dinner table. It didn't matter that one table had better linen or china. The wealth the upper classes displayed was programmed into the rigid social structure. I was programmed to believe that the wealthy people were worth more than the poor. For me that worth was not measured in linen or china, but in the freedom that I thought the wealthy possessed.

I returned to Wesel. I talked to a new friend who I thought would certainly have an appropriate perspective to offer. I knew of Christian when I was a young child in Wesel, but his parents would never have let us play together. Christian's family came from the rich elite of Wesel. However, he was that kind of upper class kid who didn't care about the rules of class. Even though he was learning to be a banker, he didn't stick with that conservative job for very long. He was very intelligent, but like me, he preferred to express his heart more than his mind. However, his mind was quick and funny. He could easily find the humor in a moment, but he was never laughing at others, only enjoying the lighter side of life. I was slowly falling in love with Christian, while all the time preparing to leave for another life in Switzerland.

When I later met his parents, Christian and I had become more than friends. Christian had already told his parents that I was twenty-six, married with two children, and they knew that I came from a working class family. For a moment, as we stood at their doorway, they were speechless. I believe they were too proper, and embarrassed, to honestly express their feelings, but I'm certain Christian's mother and father had discussed the situation, and their strategy, before I arrived. As we sat in the living room sipping coffee, they both began to list all of their son's supposedly bad qualities - perhaps hoping that I would at some point recoil in horror and spring from the house. I considered Christian to be a wonderfully kind-hearted, intelligent and humorous gentleman. After a short while of listening to his parents searching for more and more exaggerated or imaginary faults, I interrupted their litany with a simply stated observation, "I never had an experience where both parents talked

so negatively about their son, especially when he is your only son!"
Both parents were again speechless, but they recovered quickly. I
believe my honesty interrupted their drama in much the same way
turning on the house lights in a theater erases the distance between
the actors and the audience. Suddenly a real twenty-six year old
married working class woman with two children was sitting in front
of them, and my honest remark shocked them into looking at me as
more than a stereotype. Once that wall was broken, they showed a
generous part of themselves that reminded me of where Christian
may have learned to have such a good nature.

In the summer of 1968, Klaus decided we should go together to
Italy for a holiday. We met in Basel and went by train through the
Alps to Italy. I made the decision to take Klaus' temperature during
this trip. I wanted to see if he would be warm, happy to see me, or
simply kind in his manner. Or would he be cool, mocking me with
his distance and silence and disapproving glances. I was really unsure of whether I could live with Klaus at all. Was this really the end
of our marriage? We stayed for two weeks in Italy. After the first
week, I told Klaus that I would divorce him. In his way of dismiss-
ing the parts of life he felt were beneath him, he agreed to a divorce
without really saying anything. I returned from Italy to Wesel, and
once again I shocked my mother.

Claudia Susanna's security came up first in the list of my mother's arguments. Klaus provided money and a stable home in my
mother's view. I could not guarantee that same monetary security,
but my decision was not about money. I could only think of the
security that grows from a loving environment. I didn't want Klaus'
money. I wanted a husband who cared about me.

In comparison to Klaus, Christian was a kind and joyful man.
For one year Claudia Susanna and I lived with him in an apartment near Wesel. Claudia Susanna enjoyed Christian's good spirit.
The two of them could easily laugh together, but at the same time,
I could see in Claudia Susanna the little signs that suggested it was
not so easy for her to replace her father. Within that first year after
my divorce, I learned that Klaus had remarried. At that time in

my life I didn't have the analytical skills to understand how much my low self-esteem affected my decisions. I could feel Claudia Susanna's loneliness. I would wonder about my life and try to measure the value of my abilities and actions. I enjoyed living with Christian. My life was easier and more joyful, but living free and unmarried, I struggled with my mother's definition of a stable home. Even with the new freedom, I was living still in my wartime fear of the future. I was unable to see myself providing Claudia Susanna with the stability she would need in the next years. Claudia Susanna's sadness in missing her father mixed together with my own sense of inadequacy, and the two realities became a bitter drink I felt compelled to swallow. I decided that Claudia Susanna should move to Switzerland and live with her father and her father's new wife, Beatrice. Switzerland itself is practically the definition of national security. Even the cliches supported my decision. Claudia Susanna was only four and a half years old. She didn't fully realize how different life would soon be for her, but like most children, she was very excited with the idea of something new, and especially with the idea of seeing her father again. Klaus and Beatrice drove to Wesel to pick up Claudia Susanna, and then they headed off to Switzerland, as I began yet another new period in my life.

After Claudia Susanna left, I decided that I needed to somehow come away from always depending on men for my financial security. While still living with Christian, I started attending a school where I learned to become a secretary. I studied typing and stenography but also mathematics and grammar, and after only half a year I completed all the requirements and passed my final exam. However, before I even began a new career, yet another man would come into my life, and through his influence my life turned in ways that I never could have expected.

In the summer of 1969 I went with Christian to a popular festival held yearly in Wesel. When we entered the large hall, crowded with hundreds and hundreds of people, I noticed immediately a very tall man. I pointed out the man to Christian and asked him, "Who is that tall man?" I learned that this was Joachim Hassenburs, a photojournalist for the *Rheinische Post*, one of the largest newspapers in Germany. Christian told me that Joachim was not only a well known news photographer, but also an accomplished artist. He had gained a reputation for uniquely capturing through his black and white photography the natural beauty of the region's landscapes. Christian introduced me to Joachim and immediately we felt a special bond. Quite spontaneously and with a great enthusiasm we ended up talking and laughing all through the night. About a half a year later, Joachim became my third husband.

The second time I saw Joachim, we were sitting in his studio and he put John Coltrane's LP *Olé* on the record player. He said, "Let's listen to Coltrane." I knew nothing about jazz. I didn't know who or what *Coltrane* was, but I immediately loved the sound. Joachim later told me our session with Coltrane was for him a sign, a reassurance that I was able to appreciate abstract music. He presented abstract paintings to me with the same curiosity about my ability to understand what I was seeing. Through Joachim's passion for jazz and abstract art, I was invited to travel from one reality to another, to transcend the familiar concepts my brain associated with sights and sounds. Perhaps my ability to quickly observe, and then immediately act without thinking, let me understand improvisation so easily. And with my early life so entangled in the chaos of war, I could imagine myself as a single brushstroke in a chaotic abstract painting. But before I met Joachim, I was an improvisational actor, reacting, often desperately, to my environment. Artists, I came to realize, could improvise not out of desperation, but with the joy of creativity. I am eternally grateful to Joachim for helping me to see beyond normal expectations, and learn how to express myself with freedom.

Joachim had two daughters from a previous marriage, Ulrike,

fourteen, and Klaudia, thirteen. When I moved into Joachim's apartment I suddenly had two stepdaughters. Joachim's divorce settlement had not yet determined where the children should live, but they enjoyed living with their father for as long as they did. Both children adjusted remarkably well to the changes in the adults' lives. They both loved their father greatly, and Joachim returned that love with kindness and an easy manner. Arguments from these teenage girls were usually given to their mother. I had an open and loving relationship to them both, even if I was taking their father's attention away from them. Ulrike was intellectual and philosophically minded. We easily enjoyed hours of discussing her life in Wesel and her future in the world. Klaudia, a year younger, and more inspired by her emotions, still struggled a little with the emotional space left by the separation of her parents. Ulrike and Klaudia moved in with their mother Christel, but I would see them often as they came nearly every day to visit us. That respect they had for their father's good nature and his artistic ways resonated well with their generation's struggle to define a new world.

This was 1969 and young people all over the West were listening to a new kind of music, and creating a revolutionary counter-culture. We called this the Hippyzeit - the time of the hippies. Ulrike and Klaudia both thought of themselves as young hippies. When I met them for the first time I hadn't thought at all about hippies or what the hippie culture meant. Through Joachim's work as a journalist, he photographed a wide variety of newsmakers. At around the same time I met Joachim, a rock 'n' roll group from America, Sweet Smoke, had moved to Europe, and by chance they had moved to a small town very close to Wesel, just a short walk from the Dutch border. Within a couple of years they would become one of the most popular rock bands in the European music scene, but when Joachim met them they had just arrived, and Joachim became an important early supporter of the group. With his connections in the area, he helped them to set up their first concert. Of course Ulrike and Klaudia were thrilled with their father's support for Sweet Smoke. That meeting of cultures ended up having a profound impact on all of us. Joachim was taking photos of the group for the press, while Ulrike and Klaudia were following the band around from clubs to concert halls as two of their most devoted fans. I was at first feeling a little out of place. I had just spent nearly two years living with Christian, enjoying fine restaurants, the tennis club, and intellectual conversations. Now I was enjoying the music and the scene in smelly clubs and concert halls. Compared to the heart and energy of a Sweet Smoke concert, conversations at the tennis club now seemed hollow - high minded, but unconnected to the heart.

After many of these concerts, the evening continued into early morning at our new apartment on Breiter Weg where Sweet Smoke would come to relax. This was where Joachim, and then later I, would be first introduced to the substance after which the rock group had named themselves. Our new address Breiter Weg would become within a short time *the place to know*. Our street name suited us well. Breiter Weg is translated into English as Wider Way.

For several months after we got married, Joachim and I lived in a one bedroom apartment on Brahmsstrasse in Flüren, a part of Wesel, but then moved to a very large apartment on Breiter Weg in downtown Wesel that served as well as a studio for Joachim's art work. Later that studio became the home for my first paintings. With Joachim my consciousness turned around one hundred and eighty degrees. Joachim not only photographed local and national celebrities and captured wonderful black and white images of the West German countryside, he was also an intellectual who took great pride in his knowledge and philosophy. Many years later I would see the difficulties in so much pride and philosophy, but in the beginning I really enjoyed Joachim's humor and love of nature, art, and interesting people. I was introduced to people and ideas that made me question all that had come before in my life. I had grown up in the deepest chasm of chaos wrought by the most disastrous political and social struggle of the 20th century, but I was throughout the horrors of war and destruction only a child picking flowers on a battlefield. I had never been interested in politics or social structures, except in that I had a sense that my class would so often prevent me from having a voice in such conversations. With Joachim, I was introduced to society as the partner of a successful journalist and artist. We would talk easily and about any subject with the leaders of the society's mainstream as well as with society's most controversial and outspoken critics.

My mother was somewhat unusual for the working class in that she carried herself with pride for the elegance and learning she brought to our humble condition. She was very clean, orderly and strict with her conception of what was proper. She never hid from the fact of her working class status; she simply elevated her position in the few ways open to a woman of high standards in a class of low opportunities. My stepfather always had a fairly good paying job. My mother expected me to dress and act as if we owned our own lives, even if for most of my early life we were lucky to share someone else's crowded apartment.

For most of my life I was oblivious to the hardship my family lived through. I was so young and innocent that I seldom noticed the ugliest sides of my family's experiences. Of course in a child-like way I always had compassion for the harsh emotions I felt from all the adults around me, even if I didn't fully understand the cause. As I grew older, noticing how my family fit into a larger society, I lost some of my childhood joy. When I was twelve years old I had a friend from a very wealthy family. I always dressed myself as best as possible with the nicest clothes I could find, and so my friend's mother was impressed with my manner. Soon she asked me about my family. When I told her that my step-father was a laborer building houses she was still polite, but the next day I found out that my friend was no longer permitted to play with me. I learned for the first time my expected role as a pawn in a chess game that was suddenly appearing all around me.

When I was fourteen years old I would take the tram to school every morning. The tram station was just below a boy's Gymnasium (upper school). Nearly every morning for a while when I was waiting for the tram to take me to the bus that then took me to school, there was a boy watching me from one of the school's windows.

After some days he got the courage to talk to me. One of the first things he asked me was what school I attended. As soon as I told him that I went to a regular coed high school, and not the local girls upper school, suddenly all the enthusiasm fell out of him. We had already planned to meet the next day in a little cafe, but I waited there for an hour before realizing that I would never see him again. That window above the tram station was always empty after that day.

Chapter 9

Breiter Weg

If you want to change the way people respond to you,
change the way you respond to people.

- Timothy Leary

$\mathcal{I}$ have only in recent years come to weigh properly all of these childhood traumas I took in, whether I remembered them or not, or understood them or not. I have examined all of these events over these last many years through the guide of both therapists and shamans.

For at least five thousand years shamans in the Amazon have used psychoactive plants to journey out of their normal ego worlds and into a space where they could connect to a different world, but one very closely connected to our own. The alternate world is often inhabited by animals, totem animals that represent different aspects of the struggles in our lives. The shaman is the experienced guide who helps you make your way through this world, and understand its meaning. Therapists in the West from many different schools of thought offer a similar possibility.

Joachim was imprinted as a young teenager after the war with the jazz a lot of American soldiers brought to Germany. After meeting Sweet Smoke and the music scene that surrounded the group, he sat deep into a chair in the living room, smoked hashish from a pipe, and listened to a new music with altered processors in his brain receiving the information coming from his ears. The information appeared to be music, but suddenly viewed from an entirely different dimension. Both Joachim and I learned a lot from these altered states of consciousness, each of us confronting our own individual ego issues with novelty, chaos, conformity, and improvisation.

When I was two years old, and my mother was ordered by the Nazis to bring her family and work on a farm in the East, Joachim was twelve years old and standing tall in the front of a parade line of ideal German youth, honored to be chosen to shake Hitler's hand.

Like all German boys and girls at that time, when Joachim was seven he left home to live in a Hitler Youth Camp. He once told me that he cried when he was sent to the youth camp. Joachim was tall and strong, but he was easily swayed by his emotions. Once in the camp he gladly joined in, especially in any physical activity. He was trained, each year with greater challenges, and because of his size, strength and intelligence, he was chosen to follow the special training that led to a place in the elite *Werwölfe* (the Werewolves). The Werwölfe were to be a highly trained guerrilla force that would attack occupying forces if ever the Third Reich would fall. When the Reich did fall, Joachim had just turned thirteen years old and was stationed in a training camp in Yugoslavia. His small unit of fourteen boys were left to find their way home on their own. Joachim was one of only two boys who survived the journey. He walked from Yugoslavia, across the alps, and back to his home town in Duisburg. It was a distance of about a thousand kilometers.

Joachim had been indoctrinated to believe that he was a leader of the elite. The war was long over, but Joachim's familiarity with that form of fundamentalist persuasion was still with him. Joachim understood all the popular new and old philosophies that came from both east and west in the 1960s, and he expounded on these ideas with the certitude of a newly converted preacher. He once compared his children's generation, the new generation of the 60's, to his own, where as a child he remembered the depravation of the war time. Thinking of the rise of materialism, he said of the 60's, "Ihr seid die Kühlschrank Generation." *You are the refrigerator generation.* "You don't even think of where your food comes from," he would say. "You just open the refrigerator, and there it is." He had a lot of humor in his sermons, and people liked to hear the new ideas delivered from a towering German archetype, but still they were sermons, and in time people began to get nervous sitting so long in Joachim's church. The church, however, was also our living room. I too thought of the living room, the place where we honored our guests, as a kind of temple, but like all of my perceptions and ideas at that time, this was not my parent's church.

Through my stepdaughter Ulrike and her boyfriend Heinrich, I heard from the generation that came just after mine, just after the war ended. Without the direct memory of the Nazi past, they had less to process than us, and more to offer of what was new in the world. Some of what was new to them and us was quite ancient, such as the mysteries of the East.

I was reading what for me was a new literature. In our living room, sitting alone for hours while Joachim was off photographing the world, I was reading the *Tao Te Ching*, *The Tibetan Book of the Dead*, *The Psychedelic Experience*, James Joyce, Carl Jung, Hermann Hesse. I spoke often about these books with Ulrike and Heinrich, Heinrich's brother Wolfgang, and their good friends Volker, Raimund and Wolf Dieter. This small seminar of friends quickly grew with more and more friends, the new Weselaner generation, and all of us deep into our discussions - fascinated about new understandings of old ideas in a new world.

I think ever since I was able to talk, I never really liked to talk about my past. When something bad happened, my first thought was to move on. I even thought that to analyze what had just happened, or even think about it later was, you can say, a waste of time. I have always been very well organized. In my training in professional cleaning and cooking I learned to clean up a mess, then move on to the next task, perhaps making tea. In our living room, visited more and more often by a wide assortment of people, I put aside any thoughts about the past, and talked only about the present and the exciting ideas and practices that would take us to the future. I was also usually making a very tasty pot of jasmine tea.

Of course in this time I smoked hashish, as did most everyone we knew. It wasn't just the young people, who like the youth all over the West were smoking marijuana, most people we knew - doctors, teachers, artists, lawyers, even a judge who was an old friend, all the many people Joachim befriended through his work, plus all the people who came attached to the circus that was the American rock group Sweet Smoke - they all smoked.

Our living room became a place where people could talk about any subject, and with such a wide variety of people who felt comfortable around our table, we gained a quick reputation for generating a lot of enthusiasm about a lot of exciting ideas. There were also many troubling ideas, especially among the young people. I was some twelve years older than most of Ulrike and Heinrich's friends, not old enough to be their parent, but much older in life experience than any older sister. I was both youthful and yet far wiser than I really should have been at my age. The people who visited us, who could read body language, either consciously or not, would have seen me as an independent, but an empathetic listener. Through listening, I began to find my own voice. In time, I gave a lot of advice, advice from my heart's experience. I have since then been honest in expressing my beliefs. In the comfort of our living room I talked a lot. But I also listened a lot.

The listening was very important. Second to that was my optimism and encouragement. The young people complained about their many issues with family, friends, school. I always told them they must not expand their perceptions, and then only see the negative in their world. They must not simply hide behind it all in hedonism. In a thousand different ways I told them first they must be aware. Then, in their own way, they have to practice peace and love. And then, not necessarily last, but the third thing I advised was the importance of being clean, meaning purification - the virtue of being pure in thought, feeling, action and body. I didn't say all of this to everyone all the time, of course, but the essence was there, and a kind heart behind my words. Sometimes I was pretty tough with people, people who hid behind ego games. I found in the experience of confronting my own ego, that when you show someone their ego game - then comes resentment. Through the resentment comes anger. Through the anger comes frustration. Through seeing all of this, we can change.

Once on Breiter Weg I had a realization about one aspect of the nature of change. In reading *The Tibetan Book of the Dead*, I began to wonder about the normal human lifespan the Buddhists describe as one of many incarnations. From incarnation to incarnation we accumulate the wisdom of our many lifetimes, but I was thinking about that whole process of spending so much time in each lifetime just growing up and becoming mature enough to use the accumulated wisdom. Why not just live longer in one lifetime, and not just accumulate some wisdom, but have some time to act on that wisdom, and make greater changes in my self and the world? Coming from a Buddhist point of view, I thought, why not use the accumulated wisdom to slow the aging process, and allow for more time to work with what you acquire. I had the thought to jump over a lifetime, and simply live in this life for 149 years. I told Joachim, "I will become 149 years old. I'll just jump over one incarnation. It's really boring, again and again, mommy, poppi, school, teacher, marrying, old age, death." We both laughed at what was perhaps a naive understanding of both Buddhism and the science of anti-aging, but since that time in the 1970's I have always felt my intuition about life extension has been a valuable theme in my life. Over the years I have been amazed to see how the relatively small science of anti-aging has become the established field of regenerative medicine. In 2007, University of Cambridge trained biomedical gerontologist, Dr. Aubrey de Grey, published *Ending Aging: The Rejuvenation Breakthroughs that Could Reverse Human Aging in Our Lifetime*. He has predicted lifespans in the not too distant future of a thousand years or more.

The themes that carried through all my thinking and advice to myself and others, all had to do with opening one's consciousness. I realized through my reading and experience that opening one's consciousness was a major theme in most religions and philosophies, as well as the key to breaking old conditioning and finding your way through the chaos. I was in my own learning process even as I advised the kids. I still had a lot of chaos to travel through. I still had a lot of awareness to gain. I still had to learn how to live with all I was learning.

In reading *The Psychedelic Experience: A Manual Based on The Tibetan Book of the Dead*, by Harvard professors of psychology, Dr. Timothy Leary and Dr. Richard Albert, and Ralph Metzner, I began to see psychology from a fascinating perspective. *The Tibetan Book of the Dead* prepares the living for the experience of death, and the Buddhists emphasize the mind's attachment to the material world, and how non-attachment can lead to enlightenment. Tim, as a psychologist, explored that same theme, emphasizing the ego-death one may temporarily experience during a psychedelic journey, and how that transcendence mirrors the experiences of many spiritual writers over the ages who describe an ecstatic losing of one's self within an enlightened state.

Some years later I avidly read Tim's new system of mapping consciousness from a perspective that went beyond traditional psychology. He called this model the *Eight Circuits of the Brain*. These are the major points in a person's development where mind, body and spirit are imprinted with fundamental lessons about one's interactions with reality. The first four imprints are part of a familiar model in modern psychology. The second four imprints are a map for navigating our way to the future. Tim became one of my greatest teachers, as his writings so clearly described the origins of much of the conflict I observed in myself and others. In using the understanding of how everyone is identified or stuck in the different imprints and conditioning, I became more aware of the games the ego plays.

I saw my own ego, my own resentment, my fears, my frustration, and my reactions to other people and the world. I realized that it was not me who acted. It was a program running in my brain. When I realized that I could act without following my old programming, I came closer to my Self. It was seeing my Self for the first time. That doesn't mean I acted without ego, but I could see my Self and other people more clearly. I was consciously beginning a never-ending learning process.

When I met Sweet Smoke, I was listening mostly to jazz musicians like John Coltraine, Archie Schepp, Charlie Parker, and Albert Mangelsdorff. And classical artists like Bach, Beethoven and Handel. Through Ulrike and Klaudia I listened to Pink Floyd, Frank Zappa, The Beatles.

I first visited Sweet Smoke at their farm house in the tiny town of Hüthum, just thirty kilometers from Wesel. Before I entered the house the first time I briefly said hello to a couple of young men playing frisbee in the yard. One of them was Rasa, sitar and guitar player, who would later become my closest friend in my life.

When I went into the house, I didn't know what to think. With long hair, long beards, for me they were the real hippies from America. Very quickly I realized that they had a deeply spiritual side. They all practiced meditation, and followed the teachings of several different Hindu gurus. Their music was new to me, and very loud in the concert halls, but I became quickly used to the volume. I loved their unusual jazz/rock.

Nearly every time Sweet Smoke returned home from a concert or tour, at any time of night, they would stop by our house for a quiet couple of hours in our living room. We were all sitting on low couches around a long wooden table, sharing the sweet smoke of hashish. I always had a pot of hot jasmine tea sitting on the metal plate of the oil oven that heated the room. There were always candles. I hardly used electricity. The candles created a very comfortable atmosphere. The candle light for me helped to create a peaceful setting. What I do to this day with candles started on Breiter Weg. Every time I light a candle I say *Aum*, the sacred Sanskrit word for the sound of creation. Every time I blow out a candle I say *Aum*.

When Sweet Smoke came from a concert, often on the road for long hours, they were physically exhausted, but not ready for sleep.

They loved the calm vibration of our living room. They loved filling it with the spirited energy from their latest performance on stage, their voices still filled with inspiration. They loved to talk, about their concert, about their experience living in Germany, playing in concert halls in different parts of Europe, and always their intelligence and humor kept us laughing as we discussed rock 'n' roll and the nature of the universe.

Michael Paris and Joachim shared a nearly breathless concern for every detail of the genius of Thelonious Monk. Michael was in every way a musician. He would count the numbers beginning each piece performed on stage. He would often enter a kind of trance as he improvised his jazz/rock chants, sometimes with his saxophone, sometimes with his voice. On stage he was so full of energy, he appeared to be plugged in. His excitement for ideas kept him as the band's leader in our living room discussions as well. In the first year we knew them, my English was not very good, and so I was mostly listening to Joachim talk in English with the band. I would often sit quietly, my eyes sometimes closed, but at the same time regularly arising to keep the tea pot full and fresh, and change the music on the stereo. As time went by, my English improved and the members of Sweet Smoke were speaking in both German and English. The more I understood their words and the way they thought, the more I understood why their music was so good. We loved their music because of their freedom. Not only that. We loved their curiosity, their effort to feel deeply, to explore freely. One time we were passionate in a philosophical discussion. Rasa was intently following the mostly German that was spoken, but he had trouble with one unfamiliar sounding word. His German was not so good then, but he said with perfect pronunciation, "Was ist *Yea-zoos?*" What he heard would perhaps be spelled *yea-zoos.* In German, this is the pronunciation of "Jesus." The conversation stopped. Everyone looked at Rasa. The Americans were immediately smiling, realizing why Rasa would be confused. I turned to him and simply said, "Kennst du nicht Jesus?" "You don't know Jesus?"

We talked a lot about who we knew and what we knew, but

also we talked about what we didn't know - the things we wanted to know. We talked a lot about peace and struggle. Every young American man we knew at that time talked about peace and the war in Vietnam. The members of Sweet Smoke were Americans on an overseas mission of a different kind. Most of them would say that they were on a journey to find themselves. They would use meditation and the music as their tools. They would sing Sanskrit chants with their meditation, and teach those same chants to thousands of fans at a concert, with electronic accompaniment. Sweet Smoke was not from Europe, but they were European rock 'n' roll stars - unknown in their hometown of New York, but famous in Berlin and Paris. As I watched them talk about their experiences, I could see them digesting this foreign diet of fun and fame. I loved to watch them on and off stage pouring their hearts into creative energy. I don't want to seem too romantic. Their lives on the road were not free from stress, but whether up or down, the journey was exciting. It was exciting to watch them perform. It was exciting to watch them later sitting in the living room and talking about what it all meant. I loved to watch them trying to figure out that journey - that journey to one's Self.

When I met Joachim my name was Marlis. Shortly after we met he told me he really didn't like the name Marlis. He said he felt it was a lower class name. He said "let's change it to Ma, that's a nice short name for Marlis." I was immediately sad inside, but I didn't resist. I just took his idea and agreed. Part of me agreed. I fell again into that feeling of low self esteem. From that day on for many many years, everyone who met me knew me as Ma. For the young people this was a benefit. They could see me as someone close to their age but also as a strong mother figure. As an artist, Ma became short for *Malerin* the German word for painter. I signed all my paintings from then on as Ma. I also always drew an Aum as part of my signature. Sometimes I only drew an Aum.

I became quickly used to the name Ma, and it was interesting how people used it. Some people said Ma with a mother thought behind. Some people would ask, "Ma?" and I often had to explain, "Ja, just Ma, M, a. That's all." *Nomen est omen.*

In a very short time I went from Marlis to Ma, I became Joachim's wife, and with so much widening of my consciousness on Breiter Weg, I was seeing more and more how I was Ma and how I was that Aum I put on every painting. I was realizing what was raising my consciousness, and what was holding me down. Joachim identified himself with his mind, with what he knew and who he knew, but the most joy I had with him was our time together being in nature. We drove countless times to the North Sea in Holland. We sat on the beach, Joachim with his camera in hand, and watched as the water sculpted ripples and wave patterns in sand. He would wait and wait until he saw just the right pattern for the camera. One of Joachim's favorite photographic subjects in nature we found in any still water. He would see a reed or grass growing out of the water, and in the stillness of a calm pond, the grass would be perfectly mirrored in its reflection on the surface of the water. We would sometimes sit for hours waiting for the perfect moment to photograph a small scene in nature. Joachim loved that I was able to sit so long and so quietly with him, appreciating these thin abstract lines in water and air, written by nature as a kind of calligraphy. Those were our best moments together, sitting in quiet observation of nature. This appreciation of these seemingly chaotic scenes in nature inspired me to recreate my experience on a canvas as my first paintings of abstract landscapes. Our hours sitting in our living room sometimes offered a similar moment of observation and meditation, but often we were struggling with all the games that egos love.

After four years of being the wife of Joachim, I wanted to be an independent free woman, yet again. I actually didn't want to leave Joachim. I had a lot of compassion for him. I liked Joachim. I didn't like some parts of Joachim, but I liked his spirit. I learned a lot in the time I was with him, especially how not to be. I also learned something about my internal clock. I was married to Rolf for four years before we were divorced. I was married to Klaus for only four years. Now, again, after four years I got a divorce from Joachim. I could see this as a pattern, but it was not the same lesson again and again. I was growing, and learning about many patterns in my life. Some were easier to change than others.

Joachim and I agreed to divorce but we agreed to still live together. I was still living under a roof with a man, but I was thinking I could also be an independent free woman. It took another six years for me to grow more fully out of that pattern.

During this time, I drove in my *Ford* station wagon by myself on a long journey. This was the first time I was alone in my car with no plan other than to travel. I folded down the back seat and put in a mattress, and brought along a butane camping stove for cooking all my meals. I started out from Wesel with only the idea of going to the nearest southern beach. I left Wesel in a spontaneous moment of wanderlust, with no real experience in how to wander by myself. I knew the autobahn would take me to Switzerland, and so I just headed south. When I found myself in Strasbourg, France, I realized that I had no idea what road to take. I was looking for the autobahn south, but of course I was in France, and there was no autobahn. With my four words of French, I went into a gas station and bought, for the first time in my life, a map.

I traveled for about five weeks. My first beach was in Valencia, on the Mediterranean coast of Spain. This was my first of many journeys by car, sometimes by myself, sometimes with friends and relatives. I have traveled in nineteen countries in my life, observing and absorbing the character of different cultures, often finding some inner balance in being outside of my own culture.

For the next six years we lived together in Germany and Ireland. A lot of patterns were changed, but some were not so easy to leave behind. I created a distance between Joachim's domineering behavior and my new understanding of myself, but that new understanding was fragile and still in the first stage of discovery.

As I was moving forward, Joachim reacted to my changes, and his own struggles with growth, by resonating more deeply with the patterns of his dark past. When Joachim was forty-three, he decided to stop working. Five years of exploration, using drugs, meditation, and many hours of conversation and reflection stirred up the caldron that was Joachim's life. All the harsh patterns drilled into him by the Nazis began to surface again in the form of Joachim's defense against the pain of self realization. Joachim had been the ideal example of Hitler's model of German perfection - the tall, handsome powerful well trained warrior - but now he was a grown man living in the new hippie world of peace and love. Finding the better side of his nature, the better side of what a man could be, was for the former Hitler youth a long and painful challenge. Joachim talked a lot about that challenge, but it turned out to be far easier to simply talk about the old patterns, than to actually change them. Joachim, with a powerfully trained ego, cleverly found ways to talk about the future while still using the weapons of the mind the Reich taught him to wield.

We had many friends who thought his war time experiences were powerful lessons, and his enthusiasm and good nature in promoting new ideas were infectious and inspiring, but in time, people began to feel uncomfortable as students learning Joachim's history and social science. As Joachim became more afraid of confronting his past, and more sure in his optimism about all these wonderful new ideas we all were discovering, he used his fear and hidden anger at what the Nazis had done to him as the fuel for the fire of his new dogma. Imagine the power of Nazi propaganda now promoting the most radical of new ideas of the counterculture. Of course people wanted to hear the new ideas, but imagine this dark emotion conspiring with great passion in a quiet comfortable living room. No matter how sweet and fragrant the taste of my jasmine tea and no matter how open and receptive was my empathetic heart, our visitors were often torn between two extremes. Most people didn't see that extreme side of Joachim immediately. But as Joachim became more unyielding in his positions, more emphatic and even outrageous, some friends began to accept him as a modern demanding guru, while others just became irritated.

I was learning to be free of some old patterns, but I was only partially aware of the dark power of Joachim's dreams and illusions. In what looked like an expression of the freedom of his imagination, Joachim was in fact building a very rigid ideal world. In Joachim's new world, his passion recruited many around him, but I would soon feel an irresistible need to escape.

Our German friends watched as Joachim slowly traveled through his struggles. All our friends from abroad, those who did not speak German, only heard Joachim speak in English. His English comprehension was good, but his vocabulary was relatively small, and so his interesting ideas came across with a humble brevity, and lost most of their dogmatic edge. His warm smile and good humor left a lasting impression. I too watched as so many people came through our living room. I was learning something new everyday, but everyday I also struggled. I accepted so much, at least I appeared on the outside to accept so much. I, at least, accepted Joachim's influence enough to allow him to change my name. Throughout the 1970s, Joachim continued to be Joachim, but I began to see that I didn't have to define myself by the complicated paradoxes of his personal struggle. Joachim's blind enthusiasm carried him further and further into his rose-colored nightmare. In the early 1980s Joachim moved to Berlin and became a kind of cult leader for a small commune of followers in what he envisioned was the new state of human independence.

We had our dark moments in our time on the Wider Way, but over six years on Breiter Weg, I grew as much as I struggled. My paintings during this time expressed the energy of all we experienced and learned. Strokes of thick pastel oil colors painted on soft Kashmiri silk. The silk was not stretched on a frame, but laying free on the work table. It is not easy to apply oil paints to a surface so soft and yielding. I learned a lot about the obstacles on our journey during this time. We were taking many different paths in attempts to change our consciousness. Eastern philosophy had a profound effect on us. Meditation, study of ancient texts, and the practice of holy rituals all grounded us to an ancient tradition. We tried to be careful to understand these deep philosophies and use them wisely, not just replace our old religious beliefs with new propaganda. Using psychoactive substances also offered two possibilities. They were powerful enough to break up old patterns, but were also easily abused by many people who saw in them simply the opportunity to escape responsibility. In the famous 60's there were two schools for approaching the use of psychoactive substances. In one school people were mostly interested in hedonistic fun. In the other school, students wanted to use these powerful substances as tools for learning. For us, we combined both schools, having fun while also seriously seeing the tools as sacred objects, used always with prayer and ritual. We traveled as explorers, mapping out the territory of our histories, our dreams, and our ego battles - examining the struggles in our minds and hearts, and finding strategies for the uplifting of our souls.

While Joachim was fighting the typical male battles over the territory of ideas, I was struggling with my old war, best described as the conflict in my relationships. While my divorce from Joachim gave me a certain amount of freedom, as always, that one eye-opening perspective led to a wider view of everything else. I felt deep in my heart how much I missed my children. I came to the conclusion that even though my intention was good in wanting security and physical stability for my children, giving them to their fathers was not an action I could easily judge. I realize how much my children must have suffered when suddenly their mother was gone, but in all the traditional measures, they had good lives, Ralf and Claudia Susanna living in what most everyone would call good and caring households in Wesel and Basel. Ralf had always been a earnest but uncomplicated child. I never had the feeling that I had to worry about him or his future. Claudia Susanna was always a happy child, but very sensitive to her surroundings. She was a curious child, always interested in all things that were new. She loved the new idea of going to live in Switzerland with her father, but in time she came to love the next logical new idea, coming back home to live with me again.

Over the ten years she lived with her father and step-mother, I visited her often. I went to Basel nearly every year, and she would always visit me in Wesel during her school holidays. We always had a deep connection to each other, as she did with her father, but our two lifestyles could not have been more different. Claudia Susanna enjoyed the luxuries of the proper German-Swiss family Klaus and Beatrice provided, but she missed the touch of my simple uncomplicated love as a mother. Following the classic family model, Klaus left most of the family matters to his wife. It's not that he did not care about Claudia Susanna. He loved Claudia Susanna. Like most family men, he saw his main responsibility as family provider, pouring most of his time and energy into his profession.

From the moment I gave Claudia Susanna to her father I felt guilty. All of the logical reasons and good intentions I had, made that first act of sending her to Switzerland seem appropriate. My mind was at ease, my heart's concern for her well-being was answered, but both my mind and my heart had a lot to learn in the coming years. My conscience would always be reminding me of the lessons I needed.

Eventually, after many years, I released the feeling of guilt from giving both my children away to their fathers. This issue, with some other major traumas, I've worked on my whole life since. Transformation has come through many different therapies, deep introspection, devotional practices, and some other great challenges to the ego.

I usually never liked to discuss my problems with others. I had my own way of working on my self by myself. And I didn't want to talk to other people about me when I was giving so much time to helping them work out their problems. No need for them to process my issues along with their own. I also knew that if I told them about my problems, then they would talk to others. Soon a whole negative field would develop. I was careful about sharing anyone's story with another. I didn't want to create a field of gossip. I knew the people around me saw me as Ma, a woman who gained a reputation for speaking the truth brutally, but also listening with an open and loving heart. This is an unusual combination in a person, and people responded strongly. Actually, people came to me like I was a magnet. For the longest time the ego enjoyed the recognition. I liked the thin confidence I gained from people listening to me, and I found that I had a lot to say.

One young good friend of ours began to come nearly every day during his lunch break from work and sit with me in our living room. There were a number of young people in Wesel who used heroin, and after conversations with several of them, over time, they stopped their addictions. They would tell their friends that I had helped them out of their addictions, and so the reputation of Breiter Weg grew further. I suppose I did help them, but I felt I was simply creating a warm environment, and saying what seemed obvious to me. This young friend never talked about his addiction, but after several visits, I figured it out, and asked him if he was doing heroin. He said, "Yes, I have a lot of trouble with my father." The next time he visited, as usual we talked about philosophy and society. Suddenly I said to him, "Okay, so you do heroin because of your parents. You think that because you do heroin that the whole parents issue goes away? No, it becomes worse because you never change anything, you are simply escaping, but only half. Every time you fix, you always come down again, and then need to escape again. In time, your whole body becomes more and more ill, and your relationships with people are still there, only they too become worse and worse. You can't change your parents, but you can change yourself, if you want to." I paused for a short moment. "So, if you want to change, then change. If you want to keep shooting heroin, then why suffer for so long, and make others around you suffer. Why not just sit down and keep shooting and shooting, and soon you are not just half way escaping, but you are completely gone! Dead." As an absurd afterthought I added, "What do you do then?" I knew he was sensitive and thoughtful, and clever enough to want to listen to my harsh logic. My words were harsh, but while sitting with me in our living room, he was, in a way, suspended in a very accepting and loving field. I didn't tell him he was a bad person for doing heroin. I was simply honest with the guy. He loved that loving honesty. The next time I saw him some days later, he already looked different. His eyes were more aware, and he seemed more confident. He told me that he simply stopped. He said he couldn't get my words out of his head.

My strongest personal transformations would come many years in the future, but because I had realized and integrated some major parts of the puzzle of my life experiences, I spoke to others with a deeply felt understanding and compassion. At the same time, I found myself always learning something, especially from the new up coming generation. They spoke often about the value of peace, and their struggles to fit this ideal into their lives. We had a sincere sharing of minds. People trusted the communication in our living room.

I saw that most people's problems were spiritual and social issues. The spiritual question, in one form or another, was "How can I find my Self in a world where I am constantly being told who to be?" I would laugh and say, "Don't listen to those people. Go with your heart."

The social questions in many different forms, were all basically, "How can I have a better relationship with the poeple in my life?" This was a question I often asked myself. I thought about the clarity one can obtain through meditation. I told them to think about the experience of being in meditation. At first our minds are very active, jumping from one theme to the next, without even realizing that we are jumping. Then we realize suddenly what we are actually thinking about, and that is mostly crap. It has nothing to do with our real Selves. We navigate through our relationships in much the same confused state - distracted by the drama - often unsure of how we should act. We can even begin to wonder if we are lost.

We can find a lot of clarity in meditation, and a great help is a mantra, a sacred and healing word or phrase. A mantra can help to bring some order to the chaos of our thoughts much in the same way a melody can soothe a troubled heart.

I say *Aum Mani Padme Hum* many times a day. Aum is a wonderful mantra. I say Aum a hundred times a day. Aum is not only three letters. It is the sound of all creation. It's a joyful sound for our hearts, our minds, our souls and bodies. I say Aum when something positive happens, as a blessing. When something bad happens, I say Aum, accepting the reality of that bad thing. I say Aum before meditation. I say Aum when lighting and when blowing out a candle. Aum is for me a spiritual greeting, a greeting for everything that comes to me. It is honoring my Dharma. With Aum comes joy into my heart. It instantly stops all the crap in my mind. I become more and more free of distraction. Through this process, I can more and more easily see my Self, and then connect to my Self.

One other question everyone brought to our living room - how can we have peace on the planet? When I come to that question now, I feel peace comes from within. We can only have peace on the planet when we are at peace in ourselves. Before my experiences on Breiter Weg, I had a normal German education, with a normal view of the larger issues - God and the world. I had extreme events in my life that left strong impressions, and my perspective reflected those impressions, but I still had very little understanding of a wider reality. I had only the beginning of an understanding of the meaning of expanded consciousness.

With our shamanic experiences on Breiter Weg, expanded consciousness let me clearly see that unlike all the teachings in my church I mostly ignored as a child, I saw a kind of divine spirit in every rock, every plant, every object in my sight, all were connected creations of an infinitely complex and beautiful universe. I could also clearly see how this wonderful concert of the material world is connected to us through our thoughts and emotions. I could see my ego participating in this whole cosmic drama.

One regular visitor to our living room was Chinese physicist and mathematician Tien Zu. He had come to Germany to teach Mathematics and the graceful Chinese art of Tai Chi. He brought with him the dense psychological drama of being the son of a powerful Chinese general. With a child-like innocent face, he sat perfectly straight up in his chair, but moved with the grace of the ancient Chinese arts. Tien Zu was formal and conservative in his manner and habits, but liberal in his thinking, and very curious. He never smoked hashish. He never drank alcohol, but the first time he visited, as was the German social custom, he brought us a bottle of wine. We talked for an hour with him, drinking tea, and joking about the bottle of wine sitting ceremoniously on the table, but neglected. Tien Zu was serious and earnest in discussions, with only an occasional small halting laugh. I could see he was uncomfortable laughing. There was a nervous emotion in that short ha, ha, ha.

Tien Zu visited us often. We talked passionately, exploring his world of physics and mathematics, always impressed with his deep understanding of very specific scientific topics. He often wondered how those topics were connected to the philosophy of Buddhism and the ancient Chinese martial arts. He read widely, and listened to his young students, and he was always interested in any connections between science and the new free spirit he felt in all the new thinking surrounding him. One night he spontaneously asked if we would guide him through a psychedelic journey. He had read that when taking a psychedelic substance one should find a calm and comfortable space and a calm and comforting host. We agreed to be the calm and comforting hosts, and in the coming hours we would see a great transformation in our friend. We began his journey in silence. Tien Zu sat in lotus position on the sofa, his eyes closed. We had some idea of what he may be experiencing, but every person's journey is unique. After many hours of silence, Tien Zu suddenly began to laugh. This was a laugh we had never heard from him before - full throated and full of joy. He still sat in a yogi's lotus pose, but now with relaxed muscles, swaying in the gentle waves of his laughter. He laughed and laughed, and then slowly subsided into a mirthful smile. Over the coming hours he would sit, beaming with his silent smile, and then suddenly for some moments laugh again.

Over a light breakfast in the morning, he described his experiences. In the beginning he said he could somehow feel what he was seeing behind his closed eyes, and what he saw astounded him. All around him was the geometry within all forms. Every image and thought were visible to him as numbers, and all the numbers were formulas in an infinite parade of ordered information. He examined many aspects of his life, and found within the formulas of his studies, his relationships, his work, many patterns appeared that just made him laugh. He laughed at both the simplicity and the absurdity of the patterns of his life, but mostly he laughed in joy at the sheer beauty of his entire existence, and how it was at once connected to a universe of harmonious numbers.

In my journeys into wider consciousness I didn't see numbers, but I saw the same interconnected universe. I saw that all beings were connected to all others, and I saw millions of people on the planet were having similar revelations. I saw in that connectedness a great potential. I saw a world of people connected by a common knowledge of their shared nature, and a great compassion arising out of that sharing. I could imagine a wave of love washing across the planet. When I thought that so many of us were deeply connected in a magnificent web of life, it was easy for me to be optimistic. *The Time of the Hippies* held great optimism for many people. A generation looked deeply into that great web of life, and saw universes of possibilities. I too saw the universes. I had the optimism. I had the enthusiasm. I was ready to create a new world of love and understanding. I had no idea of how much I still had to learn, and unlearn. I had no idea how I was really only at the very beginning of my understanding of expanded consciousness. I had no idea of the distance between the brief glimpses of a paradise we experienced in shamanic journeys, and the deeper understanding found in the long odyssey to discover that paradise.

Chapter 10

Ireland

And the heart that is soonest awake to the flowers
is always the first to be touch'd by the thorns.

- Thomas Moore

In 1979 we got a letter from Rasa by luck, really mystically because the address was wrong. The letter followed us to the southern most end of Ireland where Joachim and I owned a piece of land, actually the side of a hill that was known as *Knoghafrihan*. The name is hundreds of years old, maybe older, but no one could tell us what it meant or where it came from. Rasa wrote only "Hi, I'm living in America." He also sent a little cartoon. He told me many years later that he only thought we might find the cartoon funny. He had no other intention in mind, but when I saw the cartoon I immediately saw my relationship with Joachim. The cartoon was a blind Kangaroo with sunglasses and a cane being led by a little seeing-eye frog on a leash, both of them hopping down the street together.

For six years the Breiter Weg studio transformed into a destination point for people from all over the world. We had friends, and friends of friends visiting from all over Germany. Through Sweet Smoke, their gurus in India and their tours in Holland, Germany and France, word of our living room brought people from Europe, America and Asia. We had Indian yogis staying for days at a time, a Chinese doctor and herbalist, scholars from New Zealand and Australia, and of course many young travelers who at that time found it easy to move overland through the ancient trade routes between Europe and Asia, or even easier to travel on discount and smokey Dutch KLM flights from New York to Amsterdam. After six years we were overloaded. Our house had become something like a combination of an ashram and a cafe. We heard so many stories, ideas, theories, but mostly the tales of everyone's discontent with their busy lives in a hectic world.

In 1977, our friend Wolfgang returned from a couple of weeks in Ireland with an inviting description of green hills and friendly people. Joachim and I were thinking to move to a warm part of Southern Europe, but instead we drove to Ireland, and in the calm lowly populated South, we found a wonderfully quiet and empty property overlooking the sea. On that first trip to Ireland we took my mother along. On all the normal social levels, I had an open and honest relationship with my mother. I would always tell her about the changes in my life, even the ones that might shock someone from her generation. Even though she didn't always approve of my actions, I was always strong enough to do those things I felt I had to do. She would always speak her mind, usually saying, "Marlis, think about the consequences." I didn't want to think about the consequences. I wanted to live my own life, not her idea of life. I wanted to make my own mistakes and learn from them. When she met Joachim for the first time she later said to me, "He has a dark side. I don't know what you see in that man." I told her, "I don't care. I'm in love with Joachim." Even though she had her strong opinions, all my men liked to visit her. She always had a warm hearted welcome, and always offered a cup of coffee. When she saw the property we bought in Ireland, she was surprised that I wanted to live so far out in the countryside, so far away from any social life. This, of course, was exactly what we wanted.

We returned to Germany briefly to close up the Breiter Weg studio. Most everything we had we gave away. Joachim transformed our Ford Transit van into a small camping vehicle. We drove back to Ireland and planted the Ford high up on the side of *Knoghafrihan*.

The property had no running water or electricity. There was a small stream where we could collect water. The neighbors were all farmers, the nearest one only about a five minute walk away from us. Our nearest neighbors, Nora and John, watched us closely when we first moved onto the property. They were curious about who was living in a van on such a remote piece of land. After some days they came and welcomed us. Many afternoons after that they invited us for a very tasty Irish tea with soda bread, that they called cake, spread with Irish butter and delicious homemade Blackberry jam. That hour was for us very enjoyable. We learned a lot about the Irish culture. We made a lot of friends in Ireland, some of them still very close to me these many years later.

Sometimes Norah and John would come to us for tea and bread. Everyday I baked a sourdough bread. Joachim dug a hole in the ground, and I got from Nora an old large iron pot with a lid, what one would normally hang over a fire. The bread was placed in a round bread pan. The pan was placed in the iron pot. In the hole we piled in sticks, twigs, and old dried bushes we found around the territory. The iron pot was placed in the hole, and then the whole pot was covered in more dried wood and twigs. Then we lit it on fire. The heat from the small twigs was so intense that after twenty minutes the bread was done. It was a delicious and healthy bread.

Our diet since the early 1970s was always very simple. At that time we became vegetarians. We were concerned about the amount of chemicals in most of normal food. But I was also impressed by something told to me once in a discussion about the nature of energy. Our friend Tien Zu had once told me that when an animal is killed, all of the fear experienced before that moment of death is stored in the animal's cells, what we then later eat. That immediately made sense to me. From that moment on I decided to stop eating meat. Of course it wasn't so easy.

Two years later, I went with a friend to Amsterdam. We went into a very good restaurant where I ordered a steak. I had been a vegetarian for two years, but our conditioning is very strong. We often go a little backwards before we go completely forward. To give the ego a little leeway, I always said, "two steps forward, one step back." In our Western culture, meat is the main food, so everywhere we went we saw and smelled meat on the table. Vegetarians at this time were uncommon. I asked my friend Raimund if he would take a drive to Amsterdam with me to a fancy restaurant where I could take a small step backwards. When the steak arrived and I began to cut the meat with my knife, I experienced a moment of transcendence. I literally felt as if I was cutting through the flesh on my own arm. I can still feel that sensation today. From that moment on, I didn't taste meat again for almost ten years.

I realized gradually, slowly over time I started to put it together, that whenever I was in low consciousness, whenever I was not connected to the feelings of my heart, when I was in a low emotional state of mind, in these moments of weakness I often had a craving to eat meat. Later on I met people who told me that they believed eating meat helped us to be grounded. Some people have said that their DNA has designed them to be meat eaters, and without meat they have a hard time feeling stable both physically and mentally. All that may be true, but I feel we are grounded, no matter what we eat, by our connection to the planet. We ground ourselves, on all levels, through our intentional connection to Mother Earth. I think that groundedness I craved in moments of weakness was an emotional reaction to my circumstances. The ego wanted the comfort I imagined getting from eating the food society has told me I need. In my weakness my stomach was not asking for meat, my heart was looking for comfort. The ego's association of the smell, taste and full stomach satisfaction of eating meat was just a memory of times, especially during the war when we had so little meat, of times when we were hungry for days and days, and eating meat represented the promise of security. Years later, as a vegetarian, in moments of insecurity, the ego stupidly thought eating meat would give me security, but really I would only be feeding my emotions.

The oldest part of the brain remembers the fears of our ancient primitive ancestors. At one time in our very distant past we always associated eating meat with either killing or being killed - with being the predator or the prey. Today, we of course still have fears associated with our survival, but these fears are now more connected to how we get money to shop for food. Our fear once associated with the success or failure of the hunt, is now associated with our success or failure in the workplace, and in society in general. This connection between fear and diet only confuses us. Fear of having nothing to eat has nothing to do with what our bodies actually need to be healthy. So we eat and eat with an unconscious desperation, as if we are grabbing as much as we can before the tiger can eat us.

We in the developed nations have the resources to eat in a way that maintains our health but also creates a condition where the body, the emotions and the ego can not only relax in security, but also benefit from eating the most nutritious foods. When we eat to satisfy our emotions, we merely survive. When we eat to raise our level of health, we eat to thrive.

In a world where many people are still starving everyday, it is difficult to say we should not eat meat. Too many poor people are still dreaming of sitting before a table filled with every type of food. It may be better to advise that all of us consider for ourselves what our food means to us as individuals, then what it means to others, but then also what it means to the planet itself. Think of our factory slaughter houses where poor animal souls suffer the nightmare of the concentration camp. The amount of grain and water cows, chickens and pigs consume alone could feed and quench the thirst of the starving people of the world. The amount of waste the factory farms create is largely ignored. Just as we ignored our effect on global climate change, we don't even know yet the effects of so much organic and chemical pollution buried in the ground, sprinkled as fertilizer on our crops, and mixed like a toxic drink into our water supply. I can understand a hunter killing a deer or wild pig, and then using the fresh meat to feed a family. This is an old human habit that would still be safe for the planet, if that was the only way we ate meat. I agree with that, but even that model, hunting for survival, I think is an old model we have to change.

When people say eating meat is part of human nature, they are usually pointing back a few million years in time to when scientists think we started eating meat. I am interested in the present moment, where far from a hunting model in balance with the environment, humans now herd millions of sentient creatures to their deaths in slaughterhouses. The sentient creatures experience the smell of death long before reaching the end. Throughout their lives their spirits are broken by confinement and cruelty, and then we eat them. How can we ever create peace when our daily efforts at survival are so similar to the worst practices of warfare?

Hindu philosophy divides all of Nature into three categories which are called Sattvic, Rajasic and Tamasic. The division is often used to describe the nutritional qualities of food, but it also teaches us to view our nutrition from a wider perspective. The three divisions help us to understand the effect of food on our body's health, but also the effect on our minds and spirits.

Tamasic foods, the lowest category, are like poison. Foods like meat, alcohol, processed chemically treated foods and old foods are all considered tamasic. These foods take the most effort to digest. These foods not only add stress and toxicity, they also slow our minds while the body puts its energy into digestion. It is said they promote ignorance, doubt and pessimism. As they use so much energy, they cloud our thinking processes. They lower the rate at which we vibrate on every level. You can imagine the weight of these foods is like trying to make your car carry an elephant. This means they tie us down to our lower emotions, most especially fear.

Rajasic foods are said to increase the speed and excitement of an organism. They give us energy, and while it is said that yogis who spend their days with meditation and yoga never touch Tamasic foods, they also don't eat the Rajasic foods that excite the body and mind. Some examples of Rajasic foods are sharp spices or strong herbs, stimulants like coffee and tea, as well as salt and chocolate. Any food eaten too quickly or in excess is also considered Rajasic. In order to have sufficient energy, most normal people working day after day in the material world need to eat some Rajasic foods.

The purest foods, those which do not stress the body and create the most suitable environment for raising one's consciousness, are called Sattvic. Sattvic foods give energy to the body and mind, but do not need to take a lot of energy from the body in digestion. They include grains, fresh fruit and vegetables, pure juices, legumes, nuts, seeds, honey, milk, butter and herb teas.

Before settling in Ireland, Joachim and I traveled in the camper van through Europe and North Africa for about half a year. We lived mainly on bread, rice, vegetables and fruits. We shopped in farmer's markets and traveled slowly from country to country. We never went to tourist destinations. We simply enjoyed nature where ever we found open spaces, forests or hills. We also traveled along the Atlantic and Mediterranean coastlines, sitting many hours on sand overlooking vast seas.

In Morocco we lived for a while with a Berber family. The eldest son, Mohammed, was married to an unbelievably beautiful little princess of a girl. Her name was Fez. The women in the family worked from the early morning until late at night. They spent hours cutting from the trees and bushes to collect fire wood for the small oven in their mud and stone homes. They worked all day long cooking and cleaning, making all ready for their families. They would hand-grind wheat and bake wonderful flat bread in a special outdoor oven that several families would share. The men of the family worked in the fields and sold goods in the market. Mohammed usually travelled with us to show us the countryside, or to take us to his favorite places to play in the northern cities of Ceuta and Melilla, where we would sleep in the van, and he would stay up all night partying with his friends. At Mohammed's village, we slept in a small room in the family compound. The small window openings in the walls had no glass, and the frigid night air blew around us as if we were sleeping in the open under the winter sky.

When we arrived at our property in Ireland, we simply parked the van in a good location overlooking the countryside. We could see the harbor of the small fishing village of Baltimore in the distance. We began a period of three years with a very modest lifestyle. Twice a week we drove to a friend's house to fill up large bottles of water, and take showers. Sometimes we walked the four miles into Baltimore. Mostly we stayed on the property reading books, talking with friends, or simply sitting quietly in nature. Everyday I would climb up our property to a steep cliff face, one large rock with one of its sides steep like the side of a pyramid. I would climb up and around and onto the flat top of the rock. Sitting there surrounded by moss, clover and flowers, I could see over the ocean and in the direction of America. One time standing below the rock I looked up at my private meditation space and thought, "That rock I will call Cleopatra."

The land around our place was perfect for me. There were flowers everywhere. Flowers over flowers. All my life I have been attracted to flowers and trees. In Berlin, through Claudia Susanna and Klaus, I was introduced to the Bach flower remedies, created by the British Physician Edward Bach. He identified thirty-eight flower essences he believed related to different mental and emotional ailments. Bach used such small amounts of plant material in each bottle that he says only the energy pattern of the flower remains. This is the same idea behind the German physician Samuel Hahnemann's

Homeopathy. From all my experience with flowers, from weaving flowers as a child to using their herbal and energetic healing powers, I believe we are connected to plants in many ways greater than commonly believed.

In time we planted eucalyptus trees and bamboo on our rainy Irish property. I loved the sound of the wind playing through the bamboo, and Ireland had plenty of wind. Sometimes we had visitors. Family and friends from Ireland, Germany, France and Switzerland came and stayed for some weeks at a time, living in a special tent on a platform we had set up as a guest house. During this time I made several trips to Germany to visit my mother and my son Ralf. Frequently through my life I have visited my family in Wesel, no matter how far away I was living. When I would arrive the whole family would come together. I really loved my family, and I know they all loved me and wanted to see me, but none of them understood me really. They thought of me, in some ways, as an exotic bird that happened to be born into the family. Still we were all family, and they always asked me many questions about what was new in my life. Things changed faster in my life than in any of my family. They could barely imagine my adventures as an artist with so much freedom and so many choices. They were perhaps somewhere between enchanted and bewildered with what they heard, but perhaps the stories were less important than the simple happiness they felt to have me home with the family, even if only for a visit. I imagine that for them to make any sense of my life, rather than my perception of the free artist with many choices, maybe I appeared to them as a struggling artist in the chaos of a bohemian lifestyle, avoiding responsibilities, and making too many of the wrong choices. If they really thought that about me, I can't say their perceptions were wrong, only that they lacked the perspective of seeing my life from the inside. I did feel like a free artist, and I did feel like I had many choices, but it is true that sometimes I was only free to make difficult choices.

After living three years in Ireland, even with Joachim and I having exhibitions of his photographs and my paintings in the city of Cork, we were unable as artists to make enough income. All our savings were gone, and so in 1980, we left the property and flew back to Germany. The next year I flew back to Ireland. An Irish art agent arranged for an exhibition of my paintings at the Metropole Hotel in the city center of Cork. The hotel gave me a nice room, and all my meals during my stay. I was impressed that the hotel management so appreciated fine art that they would want an *artist in residence* during an exhibition.

Eventually, many years later, the camper rusting away, I paid a farmer neighbor to tow the car to the junk yard. I had stayed once in the car some years after we left Ireland, but I felt the land was a sacred space, and I didn't want the car rusting away there. Joachim and I both loved our time in Ireland. We left with heavy hearts and regretted never returning to live there again. Even after Joachim died many years later, I still owned that hillside, and Cleopatra's Rock overlooking the Atlantic.

Chapter 11

The Storm before the Calm

Believe nothing, no matter where you read it,
or who said it, no matter if I have said it,
unless it agrees with your own reason
and your own common sense.

- Buddha

In the Niederrhein, in the Rhein region, and its regional capitol Wesel, Joachim's reputation as an artist would enable us to afford a small house on Kirchplatz, a kilometer from the center of town. This was the spring of 1980. Until we found that small but fine house, we stayed for a while with my mother. I understand now how much patience my mother had with me and Joachim. Slowly Joachim's personality became more and more rigid and narrow-minded. His ideas became inflated with his passion, and haunted by the dogmatic Nazi patterns of his youth. With the common insanity of thinking his tunnel vision was everyone's vision, Joachim slowly built a world around him more and more strange and detached from reality. He looked at the hippie lifestyle and what was being called New Age beliefs, and he said, "We are the elite." Grand ideas that had tangible connections to reality were in his mind proof that the counter-culture had eclipsed the mainstream. After a while, most of our friends didn't even listen half of the time to Joachim when they came to visit. They left Joachim's pronouncements hanging in the air like a child's embarrassing interruptions. I too didn't listen, but I always had compassion for Joachim. Although in different ways, we both had been damaged by the Nazi war machine.

A lot of friends had compassion for Joachim, and largely because he never lost his sense of humor. No one really confronted him on his strangest ideas, so he was probably never forced to laugh at himself, but his intelligent eye would quickly see the lighter side in most of life's situations. He also genuinely liked the people he warmly invited into our home. Joachim was tall and his size could be intimidating when he was arguing a point, but sitting quietly outdoors in nature, he could be simply calm. He could radiate that calm easily when quiet, but Joachim loved to talk.

It was while we lived on Kirchplatz that I realized that I could no longer live with him. I didn't want to make him leave, because he really had no where to go, so we continued to live together until 1982. At this time I didn't know about energy between people - how a person can so disrupt another's energy through their actions and ideas.

I of course didn't plan to leave Joachim in the way I did. My abrupt abduction by the authorities in December of 1982 left Joachim alone, and without an anchor.

In some ways, being in prison in Berlin from 1982 through 1985 was a blessing for me. I became grounded during three years as a guest of the German government. I was forced to leave everyone I knew behind as I became immersed in what was certainly a more stable environment than Kirchplatz.

In February of 1981, Walter, a friend from Berlin, asked me about buying our property in Ireland. We traveled together to Ireland for a visit. We stayed with my friend Ulla, who was living in the house owned by her friend Archibald. Archibald, sixty-four when I met him, was a teacher and practitioner of, what was then, a new kind of energy massage created by the daughter of Dr. Wilhelm Reich. Dr. Eva Reich used the ideas in her father's study of Orgonomy and the theory of *body armoring*. Orgone was Reich's idea of how to describe Prana or Chi, the life-force energy. Body armoring means that we take into our muscles all of the imprints and stress of our lives, making our muscles tense and stiff, like medieval armor.

Archibald was a master in removing armor. His powerful hands were as soft as silk. I could see a little of the mythic character of the knight in Archibald, although with his wisdom and discerning humor he was more often like the wizard in the story. He came from a Royal Scottish family who lost their money in the early 1930s, when Archibald was fourteen. Archibald was left with few alternatives, and in 1933 he joined the military. He trained as a pilot and flew against Rommel's soldiers in North Africa. Archibald told me that he really liked Rommel. He was fighting Rommel's army, but in one of the most civilized episodes in any history of war, the German-British battles in North Africa were unique. At five o'clock every day the soldiers would have a cease-fire until the next morning. This was partly because in the desert at night one was so likely to get lost that neither side wanted to fight. In time the soldiers called this battlefront the war without hate. Rommel and Montgomery were using their armies like chess pieces to gain territory. There were fierce battles, but the goal for both generals was victory through strategy, not slaughter. The soldiers on both sides had what even the Germans called tea time starting at five every day, and they began to contact each other, exchanging information, cigarettes, and even prisoners.

Later on in World War II, in Eastern Europe, a German soldier shot down Archibald's plane. Archibald parachuted to the ground, almost making it. His chute landed in a tree and he was violently thrown into a tree branch, injuring his back, leaving a pain that he would carry for the rest of his life.

When we first arrived in Archibald's house, Archibald was not there. Ulla had told him I was coming and he decided to drive into the mountains and meditate before we arrived. In his meditation he had a premonition of something special happening to him. When he returned home he saw me standing in front of his house, looking out over the green over green hills. I turned to him and from that moment we became lovers, and later friends for life. Over the next two years we met often, in Ireland at his farmhouse, in Portugal where he had another house in the Algarve region, and he came several times to Wesel. At this time Joachim had a girlfriend, Laurance, in Paris and was mostly staying with her when I was in Wesel. Still, Archibald met Joachim a couple times. They were both fascinated to talk about their experiences in the war, fighting on opposite sides.

Archibald and I were mostly together in Ireland, and over that period we traveled around the country. I learned a lot about Ireland from this Scottish nobleman. Archibald's connections to high as well as bohemian communities gave me an introduction to people from many parts of Irish society. Archibald's best friend was Jack Roberts, an expert on Druid history, myth and ritual. He wrote a book on sacred spaces, *The Sacred Mythological Centres of Ireland*, and Jack and I traveled to several of those places together. Archibald was also close friends with Jack's wife Julie, who was a Tai Chi teacher, as well as a great masseuse.

In the hours we spent alone at his farmhouse, Archibald taught me the techniques and philosophy of energy massage. I practiced the art of energy massage in Germany in the months before I was arrested. In prison, I gave energy massage sessions to some of the prisoners. Archibald became one of my closest friends. He visited me one time in Berlin some years before I moved to America. He was very happy to meet Bastian.

One evening in Ireland we attended a dinner party where I met Archibald's friends Bernadette and Brian Kearney. They had two wonderful children, Aaron and Fay. Brian was an officer in the county's social welfare department, and Bernadette was a real estate agent. We became very caring friends. I brought Claudia Susanna to Ireland several times, and one time Bernadette suggested that Claudia Susanna stay in their house with them during the visit. Claudia Susanna struggled, like most kids, with finding herself and rebelling against adults and society. She had the added burden of being forced to always compare her father's and mother's very different lifestyles. She was fifteen at this time, and while I was introducing Bernadette's son, young Aaron, to new ideas about spirit and life that he could more easily accept from an older friend rather than a parent, Bernadette and Brian wanted to reciprocate, and offer some Irish lore and insight to my strong-willed daughter.

Years later when I was stranded in Germany, unable to join Bastian in America, I visited Ireland and went with Bernadette to the beach. From the last time I was in Silicon Valley I had with me a bag of silicon chips. These were small shiny pieces of silicon with printed circuits that I got in a rock and gem store in Mountain View, California. With this symbol of the new riches of the West, I had a strong impulse to give something in some way to Ireland. I have always had a very strong love for Ireland. I told Bernadette that perhaps she would think I was silly, but I wanted to perform a little ceremony on the beach, offering the silicon chips to poor Ireland with the heartfelt intention of planting a seed from the new high technology of the information age. Bernadette turned to me and spoke from a memory deeply rooted in her consciousness. She reminded me that years before we were on the dunes overlooking the sea. We saw someone struggling, drowning in the ocean, having gone too far out in the heavy waves. We were too far to reach the beach to help him, and being far from the nearest town, there were often no people walking on this beach. Bernadette told me that she watched me turn towards the ocean, get down on my knees and pray for assistance. We both had our eyes closed for a moment, and then when we looked up, we saw that the man had been washed by a wave to the shore. He was struggling now to pull himself onto the beach. She told me that she felt in that moment that my prayer had been answered. She said that she felt that perhaps the energy of praying had given the drowning man the energy he needed to save himself. She smiled as I threw the silicon chips into a collection of seaweed, trash and foam that had washed onto the shore. I intoned, "From this pile of trash, let there be a whole silicon forest!" We were both laughing as I asked that the information age, with its wonders and wealth, come soon to the shores of Ireland. Ireland became a leader in high technology in the World some years later, but I'm sure it is only Bernadette and myself who think our little ceremony might have had something to do with it.

Before the end of our days on Kirchplatz, Claudia Susanna, nearly sixteen years old, visited us during one of her school holidays. Before she left to return to Zurich, where the family Rosenthal had moved some years before, she asked me if she could come and live with me again. My first reaction was no. I told her it was better she finish her school in Switzerland, but she then told me she couldn't live with her father anymore. She told me that her father was getting a divorce, but that he didn't want to take Claudia Susanna with him. He wanted Claudia Susanna to live with her step-mother, and for the last year or so her relationship with her step-mother Beatrice had become typically difficult as Claudia Susanna found her teenage voice. I agreed that she come back to Wesel.

Later on I really regretted that decision. I was granted full custody of Claudia Susanna, and in the summer of 1980 she moved into the Kirchplatz house. Her family life in Switzerland was not the best of environments, even though for most of her life she really loved living with her father and Beatrice. Now, Claudia Susanna felt uncomfortable in the turmoil of her father's broken marriage, but Kirchplatz didn't seem like the best alternative. In the end, I felt like a mother's love was better comfort for a troubled teen than the indifference she was now receiving. Claudia Susanna saw the situation from a different perspective - one that I should have considered more. She asked me soon after moving into Kirchplatz an important question of which I thought I knew the answer. In easily reading the energy in our home, she asked, "Why are you still living with Joachim?" I told her, "He has nowhere else to go," but I made the mistake of not thinking about what a teenager really needed, security with loving discipline. Claudia Susanna had my love and support, but we were living in an environment strongly influenced by Joachim's imposing beliefs. I never confronted Joachim directly about his beliefs, and Claudia Susanna was suddenly living as his step-daughter, with little control over her situation being the child in a home with two challenging adults. I think about one time when I left her alone with Joachim. I was angry with Joachim, and I needed to leave for a couple of days. I went to visit friends, thinking that Claudia Susanna would be fine in Wesel. I had no sensitivity to the balance I gave our home, and how that balance disappeared when I left, and how Claudia Susanna was left alone to suffer Joachim's increasing instability. This was one of many times I failed to understand Claudia Susanna's needs as I struggled to give her both guidance and freedom.

Claudia Susanna found the school system in Germany much more difficult than in Switzerland, and in other ways she had a hard time adjusting to life in Germany. I didn't know at the time that my love for her gave her support in one part of her being, but I was not the strict disciplinarian that a teenager sometimes needed. I had no idea that nearly everyday when she left for school she instead went to hang out with her friends who were all a few years older than her. She was always a beautiful and popular child. That sweet round face and exotic oval eyes added an irresistible allure to her already bright personality. I don't know how she missed so much school without the school even realizing. Weeks went by before I received a letter from the school's director asking why she was not attending regularly. Claudia Susanna and I then had a long conversation about her life. She talked passionately about her troubles in school, that her friends were all already out of school, that the small city of Wesel was closing in on her. Once I asked Claudia Susanna about her friend's parents. This was my deeply rooted concern over class status mixing in with my concern for Claudia Susanna's welfare. She was correct to dismiss my thoughts. She said, "We don't care who the person's parents are! That's your generation's thing!" We had many good times together during that period, but we often fought about her relationships with her friends. I liked her friends, but many of them were feeling the pressure of old Germany reacting to a new youth culture. Claudia Susanna was in herself usually very centered and nurturing, but some of her friends were far less stable and several close friends were doing heroin regularly. Claudia Susanna kept away from that part of the scene, but I could see that I had to bring her away from Wesel.

In the end of 1980 we traveled together to Berlin. Claudia Susanna made friends easily, and I had good friends there already. We agreed that she could live with a small group of close friends in Berlin. I trusted her judgement. She knew how to set limits for herself, and she was strong enough to live as a young girl in a big city. In 1981 she moved to Berlin, and with a new sense of mission she more easily finished her high school requirements. She worked hard, writing a lot, and completed her lessons at her new home on Seeling Strasse. This was our friend Peter's apartment, where a small group of friends lived harmoniously and economically in the big city.

For our friends in Berlin I was always seen as compassionate but strict in my beliefs. Through my meditations, readings, self-reflections, and meetings with so many teachers, yogis, artists and world travelers, I had gained a reputation as someone from the previous generation who was not so tied to the German horrors of the past that I had to hide my pain within the shadows of denial. After all, I was not an adult participant in the insanity of the Third Reich. Older Germans who lived through the war were happy to forget the past. The younger generation felt pressure from within and without Germany to suppress the largely male aggression that so characterized the Nazi years. Claudia's male friends were happy to embrace the hippie ethics of peace and love. This role suppression allowed German women, who had the strength, to exert a new influence over the hearts and minds of the German youth. When I visited Claudia and her friends in Berlin, all were eager to hear about any new ideas I might have about the nature of consciousness and how to actualize compassion in one's daily life. Young Germans were hungry for this message.

Neither Claudia Susanna nor I had any idea that I would soon be in jail, and Joachim would be greeted as the new father figure of the Seeling Strasse household, and turn that small group of friends into a hedonistic commune spiraling downwards into darkness.

In the spring of 1982 Joachim and I received an invitation from Rasa to attend his wedding in America in the small college town of Northampton, Massachusetts. While we were good friends with the band Sweet Smoke in the early 70s, we never gave a lot of thought to the unusual fact that they were all Jews living and working in a country that only twenty-five years earlier would have been more than happy to cook the whole group in an oven. Sweet Smoke never made a point of being Jewish, and our many hours late at night together always leaned more towards the philosophies of Hinduism and Buddhism, and the dreams we all had of building a better world.

In 1971, when Sweet Smoke split up for a year, most of them traveling to India, Rasa came and stayed with us in the Breiter Weg for some weeks before he headed east. Neither Rasa nor I could speak the other's language very well at that time. Joachim was still working and gone most of every day. Rasa was playing sitar most of the time, and I was sometimes painting, and sometimes just listening. We communicated primarily with our eyes. He was a soft calm guy, gentle and kind. We developed over time a very deep connection between our hearts and souls. Rasa received the spiritual name Rasa Deva soon before I met him. His friends and family in America had always called him Rick, and even the other members of Sweet Smoke called him Rick, but he started to use Rasa Deva as his stage name, and while I was in America I always called him Rasa. He tells me that when his friends heard me use the name, they too started to call him Rasa. After years of introducing him as

Rasa to people I knew, Rasa became Rasa's common name. He later legally changed his name to Richard Rasa. If you were to translate his name full name, Richard and Rasa, you could call him the lion-hearted Lord of divine nectar.

We were thinking about Rasa's invitation when Joachim decided not to go. Joachim liked Rasa quite a lot, and even with the chance to see members of Sweet Smoke again, I realized later that with his past holding on to him, he simply felt uncomfortable attending a Jewish wedding.

I arrived in New York two days before the wedding. I took a bus north the next day, and Rasa picked me up by car in Springfield, Massachusetts. I had never met Rasa's, soon to be wife, Rebecca before. She was a young, innocent, open, and good-looking woman. She was of course on the day I arrived completely in stress. That evening we all went together to the wedding rehearsal where I met Rasa and Rebecca's families and friends. When I met Rasa's mother, Barbara, she greeted me as if I were in the family. Rasa had told his mother over the years how my house in Germany often felt like a home away from home for him while he was living abroad. He was only eighteen years old when he first played with Sweet Smoke in Europe. His mother was very grateful that we offered him a secure and comfortable place so many times while he was away. Rasa always stopped to see us when he traveled back and forth to India. Over the years I've lived in America, nearly every time I am on the East Coast, I drive with Rasa from Massachusetts to Washington D.C. to visit his family. Rasa's mother Barbara, so kind, generous, and joyful - she always welcomes me with an open heart. I was overwhelmed by Barbara's compassion when my mother passed away. This Jewish woman commemorated the life of a German woman by planting, in her honor, a tree in Israel.

After Sweet Smoke broke up for good in 1973, Rasa was on his way to India again. He asked me if he could bring something back for me from India. I said, "Yes, a tamboura." When Rasa returned the next year, I was a little surprised, and actually thrilled that he brought me a tamboura, the Indian drone instrument, the traditional accompaniment for the sitar. I was surprised because the tamboura was large, almost as tall as me, and Rasa had carried it from the other side of the globe. Rasa stayed in Germany for some months. For most of that time he was staying in our house. He taught me how to hold and play the tamboura. We played nearly everyday together, him on sitar and me on tamboura. Rasa played an interesting unique style influenced by classical training he received in Benaras, India mixed with the influences of playing jazz/rock with Sweet Smoke. I remember we were sitting one morning on the terrace. My terrace was a wonderful garden with southern light and a big plum tree providing shade. The plum tree was in full bloom with delicate fragrant white flowers. I had always painted in solitude, but with Rasa sitting in the sunshine I suddenly felt this warm heartfelt vibration between us. I went into my studio and got my painting supplies and I began to paint the plum tree in abstract. When Rasa left for America that time, I didn't know that I wouldn't see him again for another eight years, at his wedding.

Rasa and Rebecca's apartment sat directly across from the Northampton city jail. I stayed in America for six weeks and I sat on their balcony many times. I could easily see bars in the cell windows, and occasionally a prisoner looking out. I didn't know that four months later I would be looking at the same view, only one hundred and eighty degrees in the opposite direction. Every time I sat on that balcony across from the prison, I asked myself what sign is this? I couldn't imagine the simplest of explanations.

America was very exciting for me. A great influence for me, the German artist Joseph Beuys, came to America and said, "I like America, and America likes me!" That was actually the title of an exhibition of his in New York at the *René Block Gallery*. That was the way I too felt in America. I stayed several times with Rasa and Rebecca, but also visited New York, Boston, Washington D. C., and Hoboken, New Jersey. Coming from a little city in old Europe, New York seemed so overwhelming for me; at times I felt as if I were walking through a movie. Other times I felt as if the buildings might come crashing down on me. I was both shocked and fascinated to see places where the buildings were so tall only shadow light made it to the streets below. I've always been very curious about new things, and even in this massive exotic city, I walked fearlessly, taking in everything I could. I walked a lot through Manhatten. One evening I wanted to visit Jay, the drummer from Sweet Smoke who now lived nearby in Hoboken, New Jersey. Hoboken is a Dutch name, and since I came from a part of Germany that at times in its history actually was part of Holland, I thought the name Hoboken would be pronounced something like Hochbogan. I was at Grand Central train station trying to ask in broken English how to get to Hochbogan. Strangely enough, nobody knew where Hochbogan was, until a clever taxi driver finally figured out where I wanted to go.

In six weeks being in America I had wonderful experiences. I made a lot of friends, many of them friends of Rasa's. I became lovers with one of those friends of Rasa. Rasa had recently graduated from Hampshire College, near to Northampton. His college friend Brian impressed me immediately with his brilliant mind. He impressed most everyone. Some people had a hard time following his illuminating thoughts because they were at first so taken by his intense enthusiasm. Brian was at the time just starting a study of neuroscience at MIT in nearby Cambridge. Brian and I talked for long hours about neuroscience and philosophy, introducing each other to many people with many powerful ideas. Over the years Brian and I have met again and again, not as lovers, but as very good friends. Always I am delighted to hear him talk about nearly anything, as his soft heart and dazzling intellect are always charming.

One afternoon while walking down the street in Northampton, I met an interesting Kashmiri man who owned a rug shop in town. I invited him to Rasa's house. I thought Rasa might enjoy meeting him as he came from a part of the world that was not too far from where Rasa studied sitar. As Rasa and Bashir talked for a while we were all surprised to realize that the two of them were born on the exact same day and year, January 7, 1952. At the age of seventeen both of them left on journeys that would take Bashir from India to

American, and Rasa from America to India. This was the beginning of a long friendship for the three of us.

I rescheduled my flight two times just to keep staying a little longer in America, but I returned to Germany in the end of the summer of 1982. About a month later, Rasa and Rebecca came to Germany, and stayed with us for six weeks in the beginning part of a two and a half year journey they made traveling once around the globe. They had amazing experiences together in Europe, Africa and Asia, but they learned during that time that they would not stay together as a married couple after they returned to America. After he left Wesel with his young bride in 1982, I didn't see Rasa again in the next ten years.

In September 1982, Timothy Leary came to Hamburg to speak to a large crowd at the University. A friend of mine, Tom Sperlich, who had brought Tim to Europe, invited me and Joachim to come to a small dinner after the speech. At that time Tim was experiencing a new wave of popularity, largely from the philosophy in his latest publications, but also from his outspoken social commentaries. He had been touring on the lecture circuit with notorious Watergate burglar G. Gordon Liddy. They were debating the topic, *the soul of America*. As we drove away from the restaurant later, we talked about his theories on our relationship to our DNA, a major theme in his work, and coincidently, I had with me a small painting I had painted for Tim. When we parted, I gave him the painting, watercolors on silk, rolled up like a small Tibetan *thangka*. He unrolled the painting and held it in the air. In his famous spirited manner, he excitedly pointed out an abstract DNA spiral he saw in the painting - DNA floating in a vibrant sea of color.

This was the year after his book *Exo-Psychology* was published in German, where he first wrote about his *Eight Circuits of the Brain* theory. I was using his theories about how the brain functions in a lot of my thinking after reading *Exo-Psychology*. Tim talked about how consciousness has traveled from east to west. He was speaking about the wisdom and philosophy of Asia coming to the West, and the great western movement to the Americas during Europe's rise to power. Now he felt America, and especially California, was the current western edge of yet another new consciousness in the world. He invented the phrase SMI^{2}LE which is an acronym for Space Migration, Intelligence Increase, and Life Extension. These and other exciting ideas led me to the plan that I would move to California sometime before the end of the next ten years. Exactly ten years later, I moved to California with my husband Bastian.

Chapter 12

Becoming an Artist

Art does not reproduce what we see; rather, it makes us see.
                                                            - Paul Klee

*J*oachim had an old friend, Rigo F. Schmidt, one of Germany's great portrait painters. Joachim had a few of Rigo's early abstract paintings hanging in the house. In school I learned something about the most famous artists in history, but I really didn't know about art itself at all. Before meeting Joachim I had never been in an art gallery or museum. All of that changed quickly, but most especially because of Rigo's paintings. When I first saw the paintings, I didn't see anything in them. One day I was sitting in the living room with one of Rigo's paintings in front of me, and suddenly the whole painting transformed into a scene of beings dancing around a fire in the forest. With that experience I saw that we had to connect to a piece of art, not only with our intellect, but on another level. I experienced Rigo's painting while in a different state of consciousness, without my mind interfering. From this point on I understood what I could call the way of abstract art.

Joachim had started painting in 1971, and I watched him produce his powerful impressions of dynamic elemental forms. He used mostly dark blues, strong reds, and mixtures of blue and black. I was fascinated to see the dance of colors as they played across the canvas. In my life I had created artful forms in music and on the stage, but aside from creating jewelry from flowers, I never had the experience of playing with color. I soon started to create my own abstract impressions of nature - silver, gray, light green and indigo on paper or silk.

I was very excited when the Kellergalerie in the nearby city of

163

Kleve exhibited my early paintings. At this first exhibition, I remember enjoying the opportunity for feedback - hearing for the first time the comments from strangers looking deeply at my simple creations. I joined a team of artists who created an art installation inspired by the land art of Christo. This was the beginning of my career in art. In 1971 I became a founding member of Germany's first artist's union, BBK (Bund Bildener Künstler). My first paintings, abstracts using soft watercolors, came from my response to the landscapes of the Niederrhein. Through my sitting so often in nature, I absorbed hours of impressions that I later brought to the canvas. In 1971 I met Rigo for the first time. We talked for hours and hours over the question, "What is the meaning of art?" When he saw my abstract landscapes, he told me, "Ma, just paint what comes out of you without controlling it, because the controlling part is anyway there. You control the paper, the brushes, the paints. That is controlling enough." Rigo became my first teacher of art.

From this point on my peaceful abstract landscapes disappeared. Now, as if coming organically out of the canvas, I began to paint with fast simple strokes totally without thinking. These appeared as calligraphic landscapes. I realized from the very start that I was conscious of painting some of the most basic forms in nature, particles and waves.

When examining the smallest parts of our universe in a laboratory, scientists discovered that when looking at a single photon, wave measuring machines always see a wave, while particle measuring machines always see a particle. Someone looking at my art with their particular lens alternately sees matter forming or energy moving in the abstract calligraphy of particles and waves.

At my first exhibitions many people didn't understand these early works. Sometimes looking at abstract art is like listening to someone speak to you in an unfamiliar language. You have no idea what the symbols represent, and yet your brain in its hunger for meaning keeps working.

When abstract art forces the viewer's rational mind to give up, the viewer's insightful mind can start making connections. At this point the abstract expression on the canvas can be seen as a message from the artist's insightful mind. When that communication is made, the artist's expression creates a resonating impression within the mind of the viewer. That vibration does what all vibrations do. In triggering its sympathetic overtones, it seeks to create harmony. It vibrates the parts of you that are sympathetic to the message. If those parts of you are not in tune in themselves, the message from a powerful piece of art can vibrate so strongly that you become tuned by the experience.

So what is the message in a powerful piece of art? I think that depends on the intention of the artist. In the presence of danger and suffering in my life, my actions have usually followed my optimism. My optimism rises from my curiosity, and my intention to understand and transform the world around me. My message, as an artist, is this healing intention of transformation.

After a while I developed a relatively set ritual before painting. I arranged all my materials in the studio, types of brushes, colors I would use, types of paints (watercolors, oil, acrylics, pigments), and what I was painting on, canvas, silk or paper. I would then sit quietly in front of a candle and think about the theme that would inspire the work. I created a special mantra for my artwork which I can not share in this book, as the nature of some mantras require that they remain only for one person to know. My special art mantra would disconnect me from the outside world. I would enter an ego-less state of mind where my hand seemed to move by itself across the canvas.

My healing intention rides like words on a melody as the brush creates movements of color on the canvas. The intention communicates its message wordlessly in color and form, but evidence of that intention is always reflected in the painting's title.

The following titles come from four different series named, Nature Spirits, Joy for Peace, Activate Your DNA, and Gratitude:

The Time Has Come To Lose Your Gravity

Sailing from Universe to Universe

Visualize Your Health

Infinite Joy

No Spiritual Requirements

Listen to Your Higher Self

The Blueprint of Knowing

From One to Eight

Rhythm of Creation

Talk to Your DNA

Language of Light

Meeting one of you

Surrounded by Ascended Masters

Stepping Weightless Into Color

Energy and Consciousness Walking Around the Corner

Here and You

Genetic Whisper

Programming Rejuvenation

See My True Self

Moon Goddess

Isis in ihrem Mondenschiff

Surrounded by Lightworkers

DNA Seeding The Planet

Invisible Being Holding Flowers

See yourself in this Painting, I Don't Mind

You Have The Power Inside You To Be Completely Relaxed

Meeting the Spirit Within You

The Light of Ananda

Restructuring Water

Formula for the Relief of Minor Aches and Pains

Just Add You

Appreciation for the Planet

If You Look Closely You Can See The Flowers Breathing

Peace Rising

They Can Become Immortal And Go To The Stars

Over the years, mostly in Germany and America, I've visited many galleries and museums. I was mostly attracted to Kandinsky, Klee, Miro, Kiefer, and most especially Beuys. I loved the American Avant Garde, Agnes Martin, Barnett Newman, Jackson Pollock, Mark Rothko, and, and, and . . .

I developed a wonderful friendship with a German photographer and painter, Claus. He was also from Wesel, but growing up ten years apart in generation (he's ten years younger) gave us together a wide perspective on many subjects, especially on art. We spoke with each other from the beginning like the two old friends we have since become. He left Wesel around 1976, and we lost contact with one another for a while. We met again years later in my home in Berlin, continuing our lifelong conversation about nature and art. It was always delightful whenever he visited. We usually always went to galleries together and then talked for hours afterwards about, as we say, *God and the World*. In describing his deep and textured understanding of my art, Claus gave me a great amount of confidence.

I have been fortunate enough to show my art in many exhbitions over the years, and I am extremely grateful for the success and recognition I have achieved as an abstract painter, but the way of the artist is not easy in the world. There are plenty of walls where paintings could hang, but in fine art, and especially abstract art, the artist must navigate through the commercial world of galleries and sales. There are a great many artists, and that commercial world is very small. I am so fortunate to have a small number of collectors who again and again support my art year after year. In return they have art on their walls, and an investment in keeping art in all of our lives.

My art, like my Self, has evolved over the years, reflecting the events and ideas that have influenced me. I always create paintings in a series following a theme, sometimes a major theme that includes paintings from several months of work. I painted over twenty years in Europe before leaving for America. In Europe I painted with watercolors and oils, sometimes pure pigments. Sometimes I applied sand as a textured layer of color. For years while traveling I collected different sands from deserts and beaches all over the world. Several friends who knew I used sand in my art, would often bring me sand from exotic places they visited. I liked to use as well sand and earth from sacred places in the world - the Hopi land in America, the Pyramids in Egypt, a temple in Sri Lanka. At one point I had at least fifty different bottles of sand on wooden shelves. I sometimes meditated on this amazing vision of subtle earthen colors all radiating the energy from their different sources.

In America, perhaps because everything is faster in America, I have mostly painted with acrylics. They dry so much faster than oils, but also have that vivid saturation of color that seems so typical of American culture. Early on in America I created a series called Nature Spirits. Compared to little Europe, in the American continent I found vast open spaces of only nature, and then in many places bombastic natural structures dominating the landscape. The cities too were often bombastic in dimension and in depth of diversity. And of course America defines materialism for the world. Shopping is on everyone's top ten To Do list. In the series Nature Spirits I created large canvases exploding with natural and created objects. In one painting I used all these materials: sand from the Pyramids, sand from Death Valley, silicon chips, dried flowers, birch bark, gold and silver leaves, gold and silver powder, and acrylics.

When I look at my paintings I get a connection to my soul and my heart. The materials on the canvas perform an energy dance of form and color, all responding to whatever theme I invoke in my meditation, and the energy I carry into the now of creation.

In one series from 2001 called Activate Your DNA, all large bright and dynamic one meter by a meter and a half paintings, many people at the exhibition asked me, "What do you mean, *Activate Your DNA?*"

For me the DNA is like a living being. At this stage in its evolution we could say that it is not fully activated. Recent studies in the effect of consciousness on structures of the brain show that we can consciously build custom neurons for our needs. Actively influencing your DNA means the ability to reprogram the DNA and your entire physical being, cell by cell. If this is possible, we would be entering directly into the web of life as agents of consciousness.

Chapter 13

Prisoner of the State

Auch wenn Mauern mich umgeben Ich bin frei.
Even when surrounded by walls I am free.

- Marlis Jermutus

*I*n December of 1982 I drove to Berlin to see Claudia Susanna on her seventeenth birthday. I stayed at Peter's apartment on the Seeling Strasse. One evening he introduced me to his friend Bastian. I immediately felt within him a calm and deep harmonious energy. He sat up very straight in lotus posture on the floor. With his father's Huguenot French dark hair and the striking lines of his face, Bastian looked to me like the Indian yogi Babaji of Haidakhan.

Bastian was twenty-four years old when I met him. He was studying meteorology at the Freie Universität Berlin. He had been reading since he was very young in any subject leading to deeper understandings of nature and spirit. He read physics and metaphysics. His interest in the study of weather came from his interest in chaos theory, and its relationship to quantum physics. We immediately found we had a lot to talk about together. However, most of that talking came later, over the many years of our lives we have lived together.

On that first day that I met him, Bastian left to go home and I thought to myself, "What a kind and intelligent, really wonderful young man." Some days later I was happy to see him again. In those first few meetings we were simply mutual friends of our friend Peter, but from the beginning we both felt within our hearts a similar harmonious resonance. Bastian helped to open up a new part of my life. It is perhaps ironic that just as I found this new beginning, I

173

would be just as quickly separated from everyone I knew. On that trip to Berlin, I was arrested, soon to be convicted and put in prison for three years.

I was caught in a drug raid in downtown Berlin. An undercover American narcotics detective working with the German government had said he was my friend. When my lawyer talked to the District Attorney later that night, they fairly quickly came to the understanding that I was not a *player* in the Berlin drug scene. I didn't even live in Berlin. My lawyer told me he was confident that I would be treated very lightly. On my day in court it happened that the District Attorney who knew both my case and my lawyer quite well never showed up. He was ill and replaced by a District Attorney who came in the court room and immediately saw a gallery full of school children who had come on a school trip to see a real German courtroom in action. When my case came up, the new DA felt he had to set an example for the impression of the children. My lawyer had agreed with the first DA that I would come immediately out on parole after the trial. Within half an hour, however, the judge gave me a sentence of three years. My lawyer at once filed for an appeal, but the appeal process would go on for the next six months as I sat in Prison Lehrter Strasse, the main prison for women in Berlin.

It was a well built old prison building. During World War II Lehrter Strasse held Nazi officers who for whatever reason disobeyed the Reich. The lower floor where I stayed for four weeks when I first came in, darker and not as well kept as the upper floors, must have terrified the least fortunate of wartime criminals. The upper floors had been for high ranking officers, and now for prisoners with long sentences. There was a lot of sunlight with polished wooden floors in places - an acknowledgement of upper classes even in the prison system. This was, however, still a prison, and as soon as I first came through the large entranceway of the Lehrter Strasse Prison and heard first one large set of iron doors close heavily behind me, and then another set soon after, I knew that everything in my life would soon change. And yet, I was curious. I have always been extremely interested in every detail of every new place I encounter. Prison had a lot of very interesting details. My first thought as I entered was, "This is another world. A world with its own laws."

In my first days, like with every new prisoner, the guards rudely taught me my place in the prison structure. All prisoners first enter the clothing room. I had to stand in front of the guards and remove all my clothing. They purposely made me stand naked for a while, trying to embarrass me, but I honestly felt no embarrassment. I like my body, and I like the way it looks. I was more interested in that moment in their efforts at intimidation. I was of course at their mercy, exposed in my nakedness, but my nakedness meant something different to me than nakedness meant to them. I enjoyed the freedom. They had probably seen bravado and defiance before many times, but I didn't feel defiant. I didn't act defiant. I was curious, and a little amused. One guard brought me a pair of underpants to put on that was made for a woman about 150 pounds heavier than me. They were ridiculously large, and I'm sure the guards were intending humiliation. I just smiled and complied. I lifted the huge underwear up over my legs, and pulled them around my waist. As soon as I let go of my hands, the underpants fell immediately to the floor. I laughed out of sheer amusement at the whole situation. Even the guards then laughed a little. I saw quickly that these guards were also day after day in prison. I was free, in as much as my spirit never left me. They had to go every day to work in a prison. I grew up in crowded rooms, and lived for years inside a van. I very quickly adapted to the fact that I was going to live in a small space again for a while. The poor guards had the job of making the confinement of prison feel oppressive. They seemed to think more about being in a prison than I did. As I say, I was very actively learning about my new environment. Prisons hold not only prisoners convicted by the state, they also hold the raw emotions of both the prisoners and the guards who watch over them.

I never considered myself a criminal. In my first few days I asked the guard for some paper and a pen. I wrote, "Auch wenn Mauern mich umgeben Ich bin frei. Gott ist überall." *Even when walls surround me I am free. God is everywhere.*

175

I came to prison in the late afternoon. The next day I went out, for our one hour a day outside, to a courtyard that had one tree in the middle surrounded by stone plates. Now leafless in the winter cold, in the spring and summer a small area of grass and clover would appear on one side. I came into the courtyard that first day with about twenty other women, and because I was new, no one talked to me. They all watched to see something about who I was. When I walked in, I went directly to the tree and sat down with my back leaning against the trunk. I closed my eyes and quietly observed a ritual of taking in the energy of the tree. I could feel the tree's energy adding strength and power to the energy in my spine. I had for a long time made many rituals to help me connect to nature. This tree would be the best connection I could make for a long time to come.

From very early on I gained the trust of both prisoners and guards. I felt compassion for everyone, and they understood that very quickly. In my fascination with this new experience, I honestly felt the enthusiasm for life that I always have. I was cheerful and good natured. I was eager to talk to people. I was a good listener, being genuinely interested in people's stories and feelings. I was also fair. I had no problem taking the side of a guard against a prisoner, or a prisoner against a guard, defending whomever I thought was right. Information travels very fast in that closed environment. I had a reputation after my first day.

At first I lived in the lower floor of the prison reserved for non-convicted prisoners awaiting trial. I was lucky to have a cell for myself, but these cells were less cared for than in the upper part of the prison. The walls had not been painted for years. The furniture and fixtures were old and poorly maintained. After four weeks I asked for a piece of letter paper and a pen. I wrote a polite letter to the warden asking if I might have some white paint and a paint brush to paint my cell. I didn't think of this as a provocative act. I always like to very openly and honestly express myself. With genuine sincerity I wanted to change my environment. My punishment was not to suffer in bad conditions, but simply be isolated from normal society. Near the end of the letter I added that I didn't want to live in such a dark environment. The next day I was told to gather all my belongings, and I was led by elevator to the upper floor where I was given a very light room with a south facing window, a comfortable bed, a well-made wooden chair and desk, a tall wooden clothes closet, a clean porcelain sink, and a toilet with a lid.

During the six months of the appeal process I was not required to work in the prison like almost all the other prisoners. They asked me if I wanted to work, but I said no. They told me then that I had to be in my cell with the heavy wooden door closed the whole time while the other women were working. A tiny peep hole in the door was the only way to see into the cell, but you could always hear when someone turned the little cover on the outside before they looked in. I liked being alone in my cell. I had a lot to read, like Paramahansa Yogananda's great autobiography, Fritjof Capra, Heinrich Boll, Hermann Hesse. When I wasn't reading I was just sitting, thinking and meditating. Later on I was painting.

Our breakfast was always brought to us at seven o'clock in the morning. The guards would always open and close the doors for us. After my first month most of the guards were friendly or at least polite. There was a small shop where we could buy coffee, cigarettes, sugar, soap, milk, yogurt, or heavy cream. With so much time to myself I began to feel as if I was living in solitude in a cloister.

I made one very good friend in prison. Claudia R. was also convicted on a drug offense. She was my same age, had two children like me, and had a strong intellect and spirit. When she first saw me she asked, "Do you believe in God?" I said, "Yes, of course, but not the normal idea of God. I believe God is in everything, and vibrates as a kind of universal energy." She was delighted to hear a description of God like that. We started a conversation then that still continues today. Of course then, half of our conversations were spoken softly through the bars of our cell's windows. Each cell had a window high up on the wall. I would put my chair on my bed, climb up onto the chair and then lift myself onto the thin window sill. We would each hold a mirror out of the window to catch a glimpse of one another while we talked. The guards never liked that, and eventually they would stop us. We didn't care if we got caught. We so enjoyed those precious moments. We laughed once about how our conditions were so good in prison compared to what we imagined existed in other parts of the world, even in other parts of Germany. I was surprised when I first arrived when I was told I had a choice of "Normal, Muslim, or Vegetarian" meals. With our good spirits lifting each other, we were better off than most around us. Of course, we all had our stories.

One woman tried to kill her husband. An older woman killed her mother. Two other women killed their children. Another woman tried to kill her week old baby. One young woman was involved in a robbery where a person was killed. Two women were in jail because of their illegal political actions against America's involvement in Iran. There was one woman about sixty years old who was homeless and had been in and out of Lehrter Strasse Prison thirteen times. Especially in winter she would steal something, or commit some other small crime, and she would get some months in a warm dry room, with regular hot meals.

Ulla was a young woman, already seven years in jail, who told me that she checked me out when I first came. She told me she saw that I wouldn't let anyone put me down, but I always defended myself or someone else with a good heart, with good intentions. She liked that, and she liked also my open spirituality, my meditations and rituals. The prisoners and guards were always aware of who was on top of whom. Who had dominance or cunning or trustworthiness.

In those six hours that the other prisoners were working and I was in my cell alone, I often rang the *Schalla*, the bell that would summon a guard. We called the guards *Schlusen*. That was a slang word that combined two words that pretty much summed up our idea of the guard's job. The word came from *Schlüssel* and *Schloss* - *key* and *keyhole* mixed together. A wonderful combination. Schluse, pronounced in English like *schlooz-ah*.

I don't mean to reduce the guards to this narrow idea we developed as prisoners. Women in prison are very emotional, feeling the separation from family. This was especially hard for those who had young children. The guards not only kept the doors under control, they were helpful in keeping some emotional balance in the prison as well. At night many women would hear the key turn in the lock and instantly become very afraid, isolated, and often struck with the terror of their fears closing in on them in the unyielding darkness. They would sometimes ring for the Schluse, and the guard would open the door, and lead the prisoner to the guard's room where the guard would make coffee, and sit and talk, or even play cards, sometimes for hours and hours. I rang the bell for the Schluse often, but only during the day. I didn't really want the interruption. I was always happy when the door was closed. I appreciated the time I could take for myself, but with my options so limited in my cell, I often needed the Schluse. Around nine-thirty in the morning I would ring the bell. The Schluse would unlock the door, and politely ask, "Frau Jermutus, what do you want?" I would say, "Can I please have a shower?" They at first always laughed and asked why I didn't take a shower at seven like all the others. I just laughed with them, and they let me go. While going for my shower I could talk with Claudia R., who was every day cleaning the floors around our cells, or secretly talk to the two women who were in prison for political crimes. Their cells were in the isolation section. We would talk through a closed door for a while, but sometimes the Schluse would hear, and a precise and official voice would say, "Frau Jermutus, it is forbidden to speak to the inmates in the isolation ward. Please return to your cell at once."

I also rang for the Schluse about an hour after my shower. I asked for hot water so I could brew coffee in my cell. Often after the first cup, I would ring again for water for a second cup. I enjoyed the short conversation I usually had with the Schluse. Most of the prisoners had the pattern deep in their heads that all the Schlusen were by design against them. From the beginning I didn't participate in that thought pattern. I gave a lot of good energy to the guards and to the prisoners. The guards saw this as quickly as the prisoners.

All the nice favors they gave me were expressions of my good will towards them. They became very generous over time, but of course always joking a little whenever I rang. "Ah, Frau Jermutus, what is it you would like now?" reminding me always that I was receiving special treatment. The Schluse were not always so nice. When they had to be, they could be very tough. Some of the prisoners were not easy to guard. Many of the prisoners looked for opportunities to break the rules.

Mostly, in prison, I was invisible. Visible but invisible. That was an art. I was neutral most of the time. When I had to be dominant I was briefly very forceful in expression, but always careful not to be hostile. Any hostile expression immediately generated punishment from the guards. I was always carefully examining my observations, and prudent in my reactions.

A little like in Breiter Weg, after a long time being in prison, I began to meet with and talk to a lot of different women, giving advice, or just discussing life. Later on I was teaching women individually about meditation and yoga. I wanted to start classes in a small room that was used for Father Longard who came in to conduct Mass on some Sundays. Before that happened, I was transferred to another prison.

While still at Lehrter Strasse, I asked the warden if I could get materials from outside - paper, paint, brushes - and continue to be an artist. He denied my request to get materials from outside, but he said I could paint if I could get my materials from inside the prison system. Our social worker from the Catholic Church, who came in twice a week, showed great kindness to all of us. For me, she spent the church's money on buying the best paper, watercolor paint, and brushes. She was not allowed to buy oil paint. Too many prisoners would get high by sniffing the turpentine used with oil paints. With the best materials, and in a sunny studio, I painted a series entitled *Particle and Wave*. The inspiration for the theme of the series came from reading Fritjof Capra's *The Tao of Physics*. In a prison cell I invoked the quantum world, a world of potential time and space. I imagined the art I would create would instantly be everywhere in the universe in the moment I created it.

After creating about twenty paintings, I asked for permission to arrange for an exhibition in Bücherei Weigel, a famous bookstore at Bahnhof Zoo, downtown Berlin. My new friend Claudia had a lot of connections in the Berlin art scene, and she made the connection to Bücherei Weigel for me. I'm sure many people in the prison administration discussed my plans. After a week, a guard I knew well came to me and said that I had permission to arrange the exhibition. I could even go to the exhibition opening, but she would accompany me during the entire trip there and back. At the exhibition I had a prison guard in uniform at my side the whole time, but I was humorously thinking, "how nice, I have a bodyguard with me." Of course this was more than strange for a number of people who attended the exhibition. Many people didn't know I was in prison. Some were instantly paranoid just seeing someone in uniform. I put most people at ease when I politely introduced Frau X, explaining that she was accompanying me while I was on leave from Lehrter Strasse. Everyone in Berlin knows what Lehrter Strasse means. I think most were still surprised, unaware that someone could be *on leave* from Lehrter Strasse.

Rasa sent me a letter when I was first in prison. The letter began, "So, now you are a guest of the German government." At the exhibition, addressing the room, I explained to everyone that I was currently a guest of the German government at Lehrter Strasse, and Frau X was kind enough to escort me for the evening.

Of course Lehrter Strasse Prison was not like staying in a comfortable room at the Hotel Berlin. I spent many hours asking myself why I was there. I asked that question in many different ways, getting many different possible answers, but I really didn't know the answer at first. I was always looking outside myself at what others had done to me, or what I had done to others, or how life simply became hard, but then I realized that the whole key was inside myself. I realized that it was a blessing for me, sitting in a cell, being alone with myself, with plenty of time to look within.

I spent a lot of time looking within, but I was always conscious of my stark environment. I felt that all the walls of the prison around me were holding all the negative energy of all the years of prisoners suffering. I thought that if I gave out a positive energy that I could transform some of the energy around me. Especially in the night time when everything was more quiet, I could feel the heavy emotions of years of imprisonment and fear. I sometimes added my own emotions to all the others.

I had written my mother just before the trial that I would be given parole immediately. My whole family was shocked when they heard the verdict. My first night in prison, after the verdict came, my body burned the low emotions I felt by giving me a high fever. I was taken to the hospital for my first five days after the verdict. This was actually a nice way to start. My daughter could come to visit me every day, and even bring flowers to my room. I could relax in bed and watch the prison hospital routines. As soon as I returned to my regular cell I started thinking. I had thoughts of what my mother must be feeling. She came the long distance from Wesel to visit me twice while I was in prison. I also thought a lot about Claudia Susanna, without her mother available when ever she needed her. I knew that she was old enough to be independent, and she had a lot of friends near by, but I also knew that her mother was taken away from her. We both had a lot of compassion for each other at that time.

With my son Ralf, I never worried. I knew he could trust his own strong positive nature, and he was also in good hands with his father and step-mother.

With Claudia Susanna living in Berlin, she came regularly to see me, usually a half an hour every two weeks. Later she was allowed to visit once a week. This was all carefully controlled by the various offices that oversaw the lives of prisoners. Claudia Susanna always brought me coffee and cigarettes. We talked in that half hour over *God and the World*. I always wanted to take her in my arms, but that was not allowed. I felt bad for my family, but I was mostly concerned with Claudia Susanna's welfare. At age seventeen, then eighteen, then nineteen, she was having many key experiences in her life while I was in prison, but week after week in every visit I could see that she had the strength and good balance to make good decisions. In that weekly half hour we became closer than many times in the past when we were free to move. I was much more fortunate than most in prison. My faith that all would end well for me, my own positive energy, made my stay in prison into an opportunity. I had three years to myself, and all the time I needed to look at that Self.

In the spring of 1983, after three months being in prison, Bastian gave Father Langard some books and music tapes to bring to me. He knew my passion for new information, and heard all the news Claudia Susanna brought to our circle of friends. He had a feeling that I would really like those particular books, scientific and mystical, and he was exactly right. Even the music was perfect for my state of mind and heart. My favorite tape was Fripp and Eno playing a new form of music unlike anything in the world, minimalistic and powerfully electric. The record was called *Let the Power Fall*.

In the summer of 1983 Bastian visited me in Prison. I was of course very excited. When I entered the room with the guard, my heart pounded as I saw Bastian sitting there. We immediately felt the same strong connection to each other. This was not a sexual attraction. On a deeper level we felt a resonance within one another. He didn't tell me until a year later that he had been having dreams about meeting a woman dressed all in white. She appeared as a Goddess. As it happened, on that first day we met in prison I was wearing a white summer dress. I had every day in prison never missed our one hour outside. I would lay in the sun as long as possible. On that summer day Bastian watched me come into the visitor's room, all in white, glowing with tanned skin healthy with sunlight. He looked at me and said, "My God, it's hard to believe you are in prison!"

When I returned to my cell, holding that thirty minutes with Bastian close to me, I sat at my desk and looked over my orderly collection of paints, brushes, two candles, a small painting hanging in front of me. I looked up and focused on nothing for a moment, and then said to myself, "My God, I'm in love with Bastian." Then I had in my mind Bastian's hands. I could see his hands while we talked. They were as expressive as his words. Bastian's hands looked to me like fine filigree.

In September 1983, I was transferred to Berlin Lichterfelde, a prison around twenty kilometers from Lehrter Strasse. After my appeal failed, I was required to work in a small factory setting within the prison system. At Lichterfelde, the state had contracted prison labor to work for private companies. I had the pleasure of sewing threads onto price tags for six hours a day, five days a week. This was not the worst job in the prison system. I was able to sit comfortably in a small room with three other women, and talk about our lives while we slipped thin white threads through tiny holes, and then tied a tiny knot, again and again and again . . .

After our workday, for a while we were free to be in the prison yard until four o'clock when the guards would bring us back to our cells. On one warm summer day I went to the back of the yard where the grass was uncut and about a half a meter high. I laid down in the grass and looked up at the free sky above me. For everyone else in the small courtyard I had simply disappeared, at least no one noticed that I was hidden by the tall grass. After a while I drifted off to sleep. When I awoke I realized that the sun was too low in the sky. I sat up and looked around. The yard was empty. The guards had come for all the prisoners, but they had overlooked me. I stood up and looked around. There was the wall, not too high, and behind it a way to the church grounds, and then to the street. I turned back to the prison and walked over to the heavy iron bars of the locked gate that stood before the heavy wooden prison door. In the summer the door was left open so air could flow through the iron bars. I stood in front of the bars and rattled the heavy gate as best I could until a guard came around the hallway corner and saw me. She looked at me like she saw a ghost. She said laughing, "Frau Jermutus, what are you doing there?" I said, also laughing,

"You forgot me. I slept in the meadow and you forgot me!" As she opened the gate and let me back in she looked at me skeptically, but relieved, and perhaps embarrassed that all her prisoners were now back in prison.

After I was in prison for one year, I was able to receive some lenient treatment. I was eligible to take a twenty-four hour leave on my own to see my daughter. I couldn't leave the city of Berlin, but I was out of prison, free for one day. Claudia Susanna and Bastian met me in front of the prison, and we drove Bastian's VW bus together to Seeling Strasse. Claudia Susanna had moved out of the Seeling Strasse household soon after Joachim and his new girlfriend Anna Zee had moved in. Our friend Peter was still paying the rent, but the place had been becoming more and more Joachim's domain.

When I walked out of the prison, and the door closed behind me, I suddenly felt myself breathing free air. It felt like silk. I didn't feel free, as the clock was ticking away my twenty-four hours, but I was breathing free air. It was as if the clock had a chain attached to me, always reminding me that I would be pulled back into the prison after one day, and during that twenty-four hours I was conscious of every minute. I had crossed into another dimension of both time and space by passing through the prison doors. I felt as if I were a visitor in another world.

A small group of friends were waiting at Peter's apartment, Peter, Michael, Joachim, and Anna Zee. I felt immediately that the energy was different than when I was last there, a full year before. All the joy and genuine excitement was missing. No one was talking except Joachim, and he was still talking like in Wesel, all his ideas pointing to his belief that we are the elite. I felt like going immediately. Soon Peter, Claudia Susanna, Bastian and I left. We went to a friend's apartment that was empty where Claudia Susanna and I could stay the night. We four talked for long hours into the morning. I had the thought that perhaps Bastian was in love with Claudia Susanna, but I was surprised to hear him tell me later that he had no romantic interest in her, which was in itself remarkable because most of the young men who knew her were on various levels in love with

Claudia Susanna. A beautifully stylish, intelligent and independent eighteen year old girl, some years wiser than her age - Claudia Susanna came easily into everyone's heart. After getting some hours of sleep, the morning sun woke me. We all went to a cafe for breakfast. Claudia Susanna and I drove to the Tiergarten, the city park, and sat quietly in nature. Five minutes before six o'clock we arrived by bus back in front of the prison. I was sure to be punctual.

Three months later they allowed me to leave again, this time for forty-eight hours. Claudia Susanna and Bastian picked me up and we drove to where Claudia Susanna was living, with a friend Katja who was a devotee of the Indian saint Babaji. We all joyfully said "Namaste" as we arrived. I met for the first time Claudia Susanna's new friend, Jutta, who had recently moved into the Seeling Strasse commune. Shortly after Joachim had left Seeling Strasse, Jutta became Peter's girlfriend, and had moved into that chaotic atmosphere, bringing with her a strong grounding energy everyone certainly needed.

After a short visit, Bastian and I drove off to his apartment. As soon as I entered, very quickly I saw key after key - clues about Bastian's life, and how they resonated with my own. He used the same natural soap I used. He had brown rice and tahini in the kitchen. There was a wonderful palm tree in the living room, a large white Berber carpet, a colorful Buddhist Tankha on the wall. He had many books on subjects of which I had great interest. He made us both a cup of tea. The apartment was very clean. I had the feeling that Bastian lived like a monk in this environment.

I was sitting on the floor under the palm tree listening to the German Avant Garde music group Between. Bastian had an unbelievable timing for finding the best new music just as it became available. With my eyes closed, listening to the music, suddenly my heart opened up to Bastian sitting in front of me. We looked in each other's eyes, and then slowly our hands moved across the carpet and tenderly our fingers embraced. We both felt our senses racing ahead of our hearts, but we so enjoyed just being in each other's presence, that our hearts kept us suspended in love under the palm tree. When we kissed, we merged together and made love to the rhythms of Between. He was so lovely in love, soft and caring; this was my best experience in so many years of trying but not really knowing truly compassionate sensual pleasures. We fell into blissful sleep gazing into each other's eyes. The next morning Bastian made a wonderful simple breakfast for us, muesli and coffee. We spent the entire day and that night in Bastian's apartment. The next morning I began to feel the clock was ticking. In the afternoon time we had remaining, we sat over coffee after coffee and discussed philosophy and physics. Over the years I had begun to developed a tremendous curiosity to know how the universe works. After just reading Capra's mixture of Eastern and Western science and philosophy, I was eager to discuss these ideas, and figure out ways in which they applied to my life, from now to now. After talking and talking, Bastian then brought me back to Lichterfelde, and before six I was back in prison.

I was sitting in my cell, drunken in love, thinking about the wonderful hours in the most recent now. Suddenly the voice of my mother from years ago came into my thoughts. "Orgasms? Women don't have orgasms!" I carried my mother's comment within me for years. My night with Bastian erased an old pattern.

A month later I could again go out for forty-eight hours. Claudia Susanna and Bastian picked me up, and the three of us went for a leisurely coffee and cake in a cafe. Later alone with Bastian at his apartment we sat facing each other, talking and talking. Suddenly, spontaneously, I looked at Bastian and asked him if he would marry me. He said nothing. I think we were both in shock. I had no intention to ask that question. Bastian looked at me in disbelief. This was too much information for a quick response. When I came down a little from my own surprise, I suggested tenderly to him, "You can think about it."

For the ten years since my divorce from Joachim, I promised myself that I would not get married again. That was a promise made in self defense. Now in love with Bastian, a flower in my heart was fully open. I had no need to protect myself. I could just be happy, and let that flower open and grow.

Some days later Bastian had a family reunion in Bonn, the birth-place of Beethoven, one of my favorite composers. Bonn was only two hours from my hometown of Wesel. Instead of driving directly to Bonn, Bastian drove instead to Wesel, and sitting on the banks of the Rhein river he wrote me a card. A week later I was sitting in my cell, day dreaming about Bastian, and a guard came in and said, "Frau Jermutus, Sie haben Post." She handed me an envelope. The postmark said *Wesel.* There was a card inside with a painting of Lakshmi, the Goddess of love and abundance. Inside the card was written one sentence in English, "Yes, my lady love." I was in awe. At first I didn't even realize that he had written to me in English, and so I didn't think at the time that his note in English was a sign of something to come.

Eight weeks later, on June 4, 1984, we were married in a small government office in Berlin. Bastian loved my name, and according to a new German law, a woman could keep her name when mar-ried, and a husband, if he chose, could take his wife's name. Bastian wanted to change his last name to Jermutus, but I suggested he keep his last name, and use both. He liked the idea, and became Bastian Stäuber-Jermutus.

I had a three day leave from Prison. Two days before the wed-ding I had an exhibition opening in a new gallery downtown. A reporter for the *Bitd Zeitung Berlin*, one of the city's three large newspapers, came with a photographer for the unusual artist on leave from prison, and the new gallery, called 4D. 4D was an abbre-viation of the names of family members of the owners of the gallery, but I thought of it as the fourth dimension, presenting art known for expression beyond boundaries. The next art page in the city's newspaper had a photo and a large headline. I was seen hugging a famous Berlin stage actor, and the text read,

"Marlis Jermutus, presently sitting for three years in prison, ap-peared at the new 4D gallery with a show of her art painted in prison entitled *Der Kosmische Tanz* (The Cosmic Dance). On Mon-day Jermutus, 42, inmate at Lichterfelde Prison, will marry Freie Universitaet physics student Bastian Stäuber, 25. She will the next day return to prison for another one and a half years."

Shortly after our simple wedding ceremony, Bastian and I drove by ourselves to the Buddhist temple in Frohnau, a short distance away, for a private spiritual ceremony. Das Buddhistische Haus was built by a German Buddhist in the 1920s. The temple community was persecuted during the war. Sacred texts translated into German were destroyed, and after the war the temple and buildings were looted. In 1957 the temple was restored by Buddhist missionaries who had come to Germany from Sri Lanka. After five hundred years of receiving Christian missionaries, the Sri Lankan monks liked the idea of returning the favor. At the entrance to the temple, an elephant and lotus adorned gateway leads to a stairway of seventy-three steps and eight landings. The steps represent the stages required for one to become a Buddha. The landings serve as a reminder of the Eightfold Path, the fourth of the Buddha's Noble Truths. As Bastian and I walked up the long stairway, we paused on each landing, honoring each element of the path, representing the ideal forms of Perception, Intention, Speech, Action, Livelihood, Effort, Mindfulness, and Concentration. When we entered the temple, we sat in meditation, quietly observing the peaceful energy we shared. For the last part of our spiritual ceremony, we simply walked slowly through the temple gardens.

Bastian had spoken about me a lot to his mother, Gisela. She knew that I was in prison. She knew that I was sixteen years older than her son. She gave Bastian all the different logical reasons why he should not marry me. For Bastian, the spiritual connection we found together sounded deeper than any well offered advice.

After visiting the Buddhist temple we went for a little celebration at Bastian's mother's house to introduce me to his family. Bastian's father had died unexpectedly of heart failure when Bastian was twelve years old. His mother found love and comfort with another partner, Heinz, many years after her husband's death. At our celebration we were joined by Bastian's older brother Rainhard. His mother and brother were both still a little shocked by the whole situation. They were polite, but they really didn't know what to think.

Over time we overcame the preconceptions a lot of people had, not only Gisela and Rainhard, about my marriage to Bastian. Good behavior over time can do that.

On my wedding day I felt like the Goddess Bastian saw within me. I wore a white dress that I had knitted myself in prison. I had soft exquisite yellow shoes from Italy. My dark brown hair fell long over my shoulders. I was forty-two years old but I felt like twenty-four. Bastian's mother was expecting a forty year old inmate on a short leave from prison, but what walked into her house was the Goddess in her son's heart, and she saw that immediately in my smile and the joy in my being.

On the day after my wedding I wrote Bastian a love letter from prison. The next day I received a love letter from him, and a bouquet of sweet fragrant oriental lilies. Nearly every day for the next several months we wrote love letters, and nearly every day I received a bouquet of flowers. My cell was filled with flowers. Most of the women were speechless just from the idea of me marrying a handsome young man while I was in prison, but as every day flowers arrived, everyone talked about Marlis' charming true love. Many women would honestly congratulate me on my good fortune.

In moments throughout my life I have been a charming woman, easily warming people's hearts. I could also be stubborn and angry, sometimes aggressively stuck in old patterns. Fortunately I am fast in everything I do. I was quick to get angry, but also quick to get over it. Even so, those short intense moments of anger always hurt someone. Those patterns changed after many years of struggling with them, years later in America. Claudia Susanna experienced that angry side of my personality as we clashed over the many aspects of a mother and daughter's balance of holding on and letting go. In prison, my fiery moments amazed and intimidated - most everyone surprised to see such intense focus coming from such a petite and normally agreeable woman. Perhaps as a response to the intense fear I experienced growing up, I developed the confidence to defend myself quickly with words, but with that equally important ability to then let go completely of my anger. Perhaps during the war I learned that things change too quickly to ever hold on to one reality for long. I've always been known for my passionate expressions of outrage or delight. Sometimes people don't know what has happened. They meet a pleasant unassuming woman, and then suddenly I am strongly criticizing something they said or did, or something I notice about their environment. They are usually shocked at my quick fury, but my words carry compassion within my convictions. I am always with the person I am confronting, never against them. Almost always people have to smile at my intensity, seeing the genuine devotion to truth in my concern. Bastian loved the power of my attitude and aesthetics. He tolerated with understanding and love the ego struggles when my righteousness slipped into impatience. In Bastian, I had a partner who understood the personal pain of evolution, the effort I have made my entire life to observe everything in detail, feel and understand, and then transform. I was trained to be a professional housekeeper. I learned to clean a house starting from the top so the dust would always fall below me. I learned to always clean the corners first, a place people commonly forget, the corners of rooms and the corners of windows. I learned that windows should always be clean so we can see the outside world clearly from inside. Everyday of the year I open the windows in my house to let old energy and air out and fresh energy and air in. Bacteria, viruses and germs love old stale air. Old patterns in our heads love old stale energy. Everything in the universe changes or moves constantly, from now to now. Every object in my house is sitting in its own place. I can find anything in the dark. But I move everything at least a little when I dust. My fresh flowers are always closely cared for, snipping stems or trimming leaves and then arranging them in small zen temples on tabletops. Nothing remains stuck in place in my environment. I care deeply for all the little details. Open the windows, clear the dust. Small refinements lead to large improvements, and with consciousness, transformation.

Unlike many prison systems in the world, in the German system there was still an effort at rehabilitation. After a year and a half I was required by law to find a job in the city. My social worker would then evaluate my ability to reenter society. At that time there were very few companies that would hire a prisoner. I sat for several weeks in an office at the prison calling by telephone various companies who might hire me as a secretary. Most were of course a little shocked to hear that I was in prison, but I communicated my intentions well over the phone, and was invited for interviews. I had gone to a school for secretaries, but I had no experience. I went on over thirty interviews, but no one would hire a prisoner with no experience. After more than a month of looking, I turned my expectations around and thought that since I had little choice, I would look for work in a factory. The first company I called hired me immediately after my interview. By curious chance, this was Krone GmbH, a famous old company that manufactured security locks and keys. The locks and keys used by every guard at Lichterfelde prison came from this factory from Krone.

Every day I would go to work and the prison knew exactly my work hours and how long it took to travel by bus. After nine months cutting keys for Krone, I looked for a change. Bastian had worked for a summer while at university for Scheering Pharmaceuticals, and I got the idea to ask them for work. They had never hired prison labor before, but after my interview they hired me. In the first weeks I packed birth control pills into boxes for shipping. Then they trained me to control a computerized assembly line, and make sure that every package had the correct amount of pills, and that nothing was broken. I got along really well with all the employees, but they often had parties or simply met together after work. Only a couple people at Sheering knew I was in prison. My coworkers sometimes wondered why I was so friendly during the work day, but always disappeared so quickly after work. After Sheering knew I was a good worker, I spoke many times to a social worker in the company's worker's health office, a division of the personnel office, about Sheering hiring more inmates. After my six months at Sheering they opened up for the first time to regularly hiring female workers from prisons in Berlin.

By 1985 the number of female inmates in Germany grew to a level where the government built a new maximum security prison in Berlin. We were all moved to this cold modern building complex. My good fortune was that as a *Freigänger*, someone who could go free to work outside every day, I was housed in a small separate building with about twenty rooms. These were not cells. Within the building we could walk around freely. When I was there we had only five to seven women. One guard worked in the building, but the doors were open for us to come and go. Every night I had to be in by ten p.m. Every day after work, Bastian would pick me up and take me to his apartment. I would cook us a dinner, and we would sit together for as long as we could afterwards. Sometimes we went to a movie, or a concert or lecture, but always nine o'clock would come, and Bastian would take me back to prison.

Normally when released after serving three years, I should have gotten five years of probation. Five years of not leaving Berlin. Five years of always reporting any changes in where I worked or where I lived. Five years of monthly coming to a probation office to be approved again and again. For reasons I still do not know, in an act of mercy, four weeks before I was to be released, the highest ranking justice official in Berlin, Justizminister Oxford, issued me a pardon. There was no petition to ask for the pardon, and there was no explanation given by the Justizminister. A paper arrived at the prison stating that I had received a pardon for the rest of my sentence. I would not be required to have probation, and I could leave prison within a week. As quickly as I was sent to prison, abducted in a police raid in Berlin, through another swift swing of the justice system, I was just as unexpectedly released.

Chapter 14

Coming into Balance

As soon as you trust yourself, you will know how to live.
- Johann Wolfgang von Goethe

*I*n the last days in prison I quit my job at Sheering. When I got out I was free to move in with Bastian in his one bedroom apartment at Biebricher Strasse. He had a top floor apartment in that typical Berlin four story *Altbau*. I felt like I was on the top of the world. Suddenly I was free, but it took me some weeks to come out of the conditioning of prison routine. I woke up in the morning and had to remind myself that I could do what I wished to do.

Claudia Susanna had met a new boyfriend, Klaus, and I was happy to see her so in love. Four years later she would get married to Klaus, and then have a son. My grandson Demian would be born.

Bastian had been rethinking his study of meteorology. As we sat discussing his options and desires, I started talking about computers. We could see from everything around us that computers would soon be important tools for everyone. We talked about new ideas in science, technology and art, and how computers would transform all these fields. Bastian left the study of the chaotic formation of weather patterns, and started taking classes in the orderly form of binary patterns. Some years later he was working as a computer programmer at Siemens corporation where his father had worked as an engineer. Among other projects, he designed the first voice recognition program for a prototype Mercedes voice activated automobile. He was beginning a long career in computer software design.

In spring of 1986 we moved to the Kantstrasse in downtown

Berlin. We had a much bigger apartment, also on the fourth floor. I had a large art studio space for myself. In this studio I created the largest paintings so far in my career. With my new studio and so much freedom to express, I needed large canvases. The series I worked on was titled *Spuren*, or *Tracks* in English. My theme was the Spuren in my life. Some of the painting titles were *An Der Quelle Der Weisheit* (*On the Spring of Wisdom*), *Im Garten der Evolution* (*In the Garden of Evolution*), and the mythical bird reborn from the ashes, *Phoenix*.

In the next seven years I had eight exhibitions in Berlin. All art expresses the consciousness of the artist, and my art evolved along with my personal growth. Living with a calm and kind husband in a calm and secure environment, I began to feel that I could let go of some of the effects of abuse I received from men through nearly my entire life. Bastian was working full time as a creative programmer in the corporate world, but gradually feeling the increasing pleasure in programming his music synthesizers in his free time. Often in the evenings and weekends we played music together, tamboura and synthesizers, weaving a new kind of minimalistic, soft and meditative sound. We were laying the ground for what would later in America with Rasa become the music group Starseed. Thomas, a friend, built us a copper tube frame shape of a pyramid in the exact proportions of the Great Pyramid in Giza, but a comfortable two meters tall. We set up the pyramid in my studio and often sat inside to meditate and play music.

We were so excited about new information and new techniques for applying that information into our lives. So that we both didn't have to read the same books, we got into the habit of me reading a book out loud. We would discuss the information as we sat there, drinking coffee and listening to our expanding library of new musics.

One day I was cleaning the house, with the radio playing music in the background. At one point the program changed, and I began to hear women talking to a psychologist about their experiences of sexual abuse. As I listened to the women's stories, images of my own abuse suddenly flooded my mind. I stood in shock for a second, and then fell into a chair overwhelmed with emotions. As I sat there, confused and horribly sad, I heard the voice of the psychologist describing patterns arising from guilt and shame that were similar to what I saw in myself. I listened intently to this female psychologist bring some clarity to the mixture of pain and confusing images I was experiencing.

The next night, while making love with Bastian, a joyful moment shattered when a horrifying flashback of abuse came upon me. Suddenly, triggered by a simple kiss from Bastian, I was in the past, experiencing a moment of horror in vivid detail. I sat up in the bed with my eyes wide open, but staring at nothing, only looking deeply within.

After some days of thinking and thinking about my situation, and not finding any peace, I had the thought that I should take training in psychotherapy, and heal myself, and perhaps learn something about psychology to offer to others.

A friend told me about a school in Berlin that offered a one and a half year certification program. I enrolled. Four times a week I took the U-Bahn to the institute in Schöneberg for classes. The instructors were four therapists, two married couples. For nearly three months I tried to apply what we were learning to what I knew from life experience. They were able to describe the symptoms, but we never came to any solutions. I could feel the reason for this in the first days of classes. One therapist would make a comment, and then his or her spouse would comment on the comment. In subtle ways I could see the comments were shaded with the therapist's own unresolved conflicts. In trying to explain how people are caught in destructive patterns, they were actually just demonstrating the patterns themselves. These were very intelligent people. They were really good at analyzing each other's words, but then they simply responded with even more clever words. After three months of watching them going in circles, I left the program. I realized they would never turn their circle into a spiral, and pull the whole teaching up to a higher level of understanding. This was an interesting realization, but not very useful. In the end I felt no closer to a deeper understanding of my own psychology.

In these old Berlin *Altbau* apartments the ceilings were nearly four meters high, high enough that we had a loft over our living room. The loft for Bastian and me was a sacred space. Every morning I would sit there and meditate. There was really only enough space for two to sit in meditation. We had always many people visiting us for evenings in the living room, but only a handful of people would sit with us in the loft. My grandson Demian, when he could walk, loved to go up and down the stairs to visit our sacred place. He loved to sit for a moment with me in front of the Buddha statue. One of his first words was "Bud-dha" with a hard "d" sound given to the Buddha's name. Demian was a earnest curious child, but he loved to hear me sing children's songs and giggle in joy. We were both giggling in joy.

Demian was born two months after the Wall came down. He was born a child riding on that wave of change. On November 9, 1989 we joined thousands of others who danced on and around the Wall near the Brandenburger Tor. We watched as West Berliners helped East Berliners over the wall to join the party in the West. No one could be certain if the East German soldiers would start shooting, but no one could stop the excitement. Germans from East and West dancing on the top of the Wall. Who would a German soldier shoot? On the morning of November tenth, after the celebrations grew more quiet, we walked around the Wall and could feel a peacefulness we had never felt in Berlin. The city had always had that exciting tension from being an island in the middle of a Communist Empire. That reality made the already vibrant city of Berlin vibrate with an urgency, living-for-the-moment feeling that most cities are too peaceful to ever experience. The nations around us were in a mostly quiet cold war, where West Berliners served as an example of Western success, and West Berliners wore that success with enthusiasm. On that November tenth, I painted a series of forty canvases, each of them in the shape of a large brick. Years later through a special digital printing process, I had the bricks arranged as if built into a wall and printed onto one large 68" x 30" canvas. Each of the bricks vibrates with color and abstract calligraphy, just as the western side of the Berlin Wall was covered with art and poetry. With these small paintings sitting one on top of the other, the feeling of a wall is there, but a wall transformed by passion and art, eventually, in reality, to be dismantled by a peaceful revolution, dancing in the transformation.

In the spring of 1991, I was hired to oversee the decoration for an international peace festival at the former summer palace of Frederick the Great at Potsdam, just outside Berlin. *The Festival Kraft der Visionen*, the *Power of Vision Festival*, celebrated the unification of the East and West Germanys, and brought religious representatives from across the world to promote peace. Because I had a pass to go anywhere in the festival, I was able to talk with most of the representatives. I videotaped many presentations as well. I had a particular fondness for the Tibetan teacher Sogyal Rinpoche. He was presenting in the grand golden theater of the Sanssouci palace. I sat in front of him as he led a guided meditation. I was transported to a space of infinite compassion where I experienced a vision of the Rinpoche transformed into the living Buddha. Later in that same day I mistakenly videotaped for a few moments in an area where Native Americans were performing a ceremony. Normally cameras were not allowed. At some point after that I put the camera down, and before I realized what had happened, the camera disappeared. I thought for hours after that about the camera, the many wonderful moments from the festival as well as those few forbidden moments. Very early in the morning after a sleepless night, I closed my eyes and my thoughts went immediately to Sogyal Rinpoche. I asked the Rinpoche if he might help me find the camera. Some hours later I saw the busy Rinpoche passing in a nearby hallway.

He looked over to me and called out, "Did you call me?" I turned around and said, "Yes, I called you in the morning." He said, "On the phone so early?" I said, "No, not on the phone. I called out for help." We both paused and smiled for a moment, perhaps both of us wondering for a second about the meaning of the other's words. He went on his busy way. It was a passing conversation. I don't think I the Rinpoche helped me find the camera. I was just thinking of him when I needed some peace of mind. But, nonetheless, soon after that the camera reappeared.

Claudia Susanna and Klaus and young Demian visited us often. After Demian was about a year old, Klaus became the house-father, and Claudia Susanna worked as an organizer for a social service project to help young East Germans learn about environmental issues. The Berlin Wall had just come down the year before, and a West German environmental awareness group was concerned with the East German lack of environmental awareness over the decades of Soviet control. Claudia Susanna organized a theater troupe that entertained children and at the same time taught them important lessons about chemicals, plastics, and also the types of foods and drinks they consumed. Klaus cooked meals for Demian, took him into nature often, and he often came to our house where Demian would run around the apartment or play with his favorite gold painted wooden toy deer. Some years later he would be petting real wild deer in my back yard in California. Even though Demian lived in a big city, his parents took him often into natural settings. They visited Klaus' parents as often as they could, who lived in Westerwald, seven hours drive from Berlin, in beautiful rolling hills and forests.

In a private midwife's office, Claudia Susanna gave birth to Demian. Klaus cut the umbilical cord. As the midwife made Claudia Susanna more comfortable, Demian laid on a blanket with a heat lamp shining down above him. I was sitting next to Demian, his tiny fingers wrapped around one of mine. We looked deep into each other's eyes and I had the sense that we knew one another from past lives. In the first two years of his life, before Bastian and I left Germany, Demian and I grew very closely together.

Chapter 15

Decision in Denmark

The world is but a canvas to the imagination.
                                        - Henry David Thoreau

In the summer of 1992, Bastian and I took a vacation for four weeks in Denmark. We rented a small house on the beach. I painted using Japanese ink and brush. I collected flat stones from the beach. I painted them all black and then with gold paint I drew the Sanskrit Aum on one face, and on the opposite side I wrote the word Love.

We took long walks on the beach, enjoying the sun and calm vibration. Nothing was happening, and we were happy when we could be doing nothing as well, in tune with a simple peaceful silence. After two weeks in Denmark, one night we were sitting on the couch, candles and wild flowers arranged in front of us. Suddenly I realized this was 1992, and I had promised myself exactly ten years earlier that I wanted before the end of 1992 to be in America. I turned to Bastian and cried out, "Bastian! Guess what! We have to go to California!" Bastian was speechless. Then I told him of the vision I had where I knew, without knowing the details, that I would have a major transformation in my life in America. I told Bastian that I knew that I would go. I told him that if he felt within himself to also go that we would go together, but either way, I must go to America to find what I must find, *whatever it is.*

Some days later Bastian had a dream where he very happily left Germany for an English speaking country. The next day he described his dream to me, and I knew then that we would go together to California. As the vision became more anchored in the planning of how to actually leave our families and friends and move to a distant land, my first thought was of Demian. How could I leave that wonderful little child, not knowing how much of his early life I would miss?

We decided to keep our decision a secret for a while until closer to our departure date. I called Claudia Susanna and told her I wanted to have Demian with us for the last week of our vacation in Denmark. We drove south, while Klaus and Claudia Susanna drove Demian from Berlin to Hamburg, where we picked up Demian and drove back to our house on the beach. We spent a blissful week with two and a half year old Demian, giving him many loving prints and patterns in his mind with the background of the beach, the ocean, and the warmth of our small cottage.

On December 1, 1992, Bastian and I flew Lufthansa Airlines from Berlin to New York. Four weeks before, an old friend from America who knew Rasa for a long time, visited us. He was still in touch with Rasa, and he gave me Rasa's new phone number in Northampton, Massachusetts. With an accent thicker than I have now, I left a message on Rasa's answering machine, "Rasa! Here iss Ma! From Germany! I vhant to fisit you!" I left our number and Rasa called back the next day. I told him I was coming to America with Bastian, my new husband. Remembering all the times Sweet Smoke arrived at my house late at night in Wesel and I always offered tea, Rasa joked, "I'll make tea!"

We arrived in America without a lot of thought about my legal status. Many years later, when I made an inquiry, I would learn from the Berlin Ministry of Justice that all records of my conviction and incarceration had been routinely deleted - a humane practice in Germany as part of an effort to let people get on with their lives. When we arrived in New York City we were given three month visas. I didn't know at the time that in America court records are never deleted, and since my arrest in Berlin was recorded in American records, the American Immigration and Naturalization Service would soon be receiving those records from the FBI, records about a case in Germany that no longer existed.

Just before the end of our visa, we left the cold northeast of the United States and traveled in the Caribbean for a few weeks of very sunny weather. When we returned to the U. S., we again received three month visas. At the end of those three months, and finding good prospects for work in California, we started looking for a good place to live in the San Francisco Bay Area, and then we returned to Germany with the idea of organizing our affairs and possessions for a long stay in America. One of our first tasks in Berlin was visiting the American consulate to apply for longer visas. Bastian, overnight, received a six month visa. I did not. The American Consulate's reaction to my visa application was quite different, and took a lot more time. So much more time that we decided that Bastian should return to California to continue looking for work, while I straightened out my visa situation.

We arrived at the consulate in Dahlem, in the former American occupied part of Berlin, one of the nicest parts of the city. We came into the reception area. Every visitor speaks with a member of the consul staff separated by a glass window. We went to the window to ask for visas, and were cheerfully told that we had to leave our passports overnight, and that German citizens normally get six month tourist visas that are good for ten years. We filled out the paperwork and left our passports with a friendly woman behind the glass. A couple hours later at home the phone rang. A nice man at the consulate said that he was sorry, but because of my criminal record, I would never be allowed into the United States again, for the rest of my life.

In that moment I thought and felt "die Welt geht unter!" "the world has fallen out from under me!"

The next day we went to the consulate to pick up our passports. One with a visa, one without. I knew that the consulate staff were shocked when they saw this handsome, dark-haired husband with a polite and nicely dressed wife, a wife who had spent three years in prison. Still, people were sympathetic. Some of the staff were Germans. I asked a young man who was from Berlin if I could speak to the Consul General, Frau Schulz. He walked back a few steps to her office, but came back and told me that she refused to speak with me.

I communicated with the Consulate several times in the next month, always trying to get a different answer. One day I was speaking to a woman behind the glass who I could see listened with an open mind and kind heart. She listened, but said there was nothing she could do. I told her that I had spent three years in prison, and instead of paying off my debt, the punishment is now going on forever. I told her that according to German law, the law under which I was convicted, I no longer have a criminal record. She paused for a very short diplomatic moment, and then turned and walked a few steps back to the Consul General's office. She returned a few minutes later, and said, "The Consul General says that over time all things can change. She suggests you wait a few years, and then apply again for a visa." I had the thought that I was in a mystical palace asking for a favor from an officer of the court of the emperor. "All things can change." She didn't say that one of those things would be Frau Schulz leaving Berlin and being replaced by a new Consul General.

I waited four years. Able to travel anywhere except America, from the time I left America and until I returned, Bastian and Rasa were working to navigate the immigration laws and regulations, while I was looking for anyone anywhere who could offer any kind of help. I was also talking often on the phone to California and Massachusetts. Over those four years we hired two different immigration attorneys. Over the network of our friends, we received letters of support that we forwarded to the INS. Letters came from people in many fields - business, law, politics, education, the arts. I knew I would be a wonderful immigrant to America. People who knew me knew that, but there was another belief system working.

I was sitting in Berlin. The Wall had come down. All of Europe, from the eastern borders to the Atlantic in the west, felt the fall of barriers and the new movement of people and ideas. I was sitting in Berlin, looking west, wanting to move west, but my Berlin still had a wall. My wall, however, was bureaucratically surrounding Tegel Airport, where flights left everyday that could take me to America. On this side of that wall was, of course, all the rest of the world, and although I visited friends in Germany, Holland and Ireland, I spent most of my time in Berlin. I spent a lot of time in galleries and museums. The Pergamon Museum became a favorite place to sit quietly, meditating before the giant 6th century Ishtar Gate of Babylon, transported in fragments and reconstructed to its full fourteen meters tall, covered in blue glazed tiles and bas-relief dragons and aurochs (ancient cattle). I also often went to the National Gallery Berlin, the old gardens at the Charlottenburg Palace, and of course, Das Buddhistische Haus, the site of my private marriage with Bastian. I also spent time in nature, mostly in Berlin's large Tiergarten park, but I once traveled to Bergen aan Zee, in Holland, where I sat on the beach for hours, looking out over the North Sea.

During this time, I shared a smile with His Holiness The 14th Dalai Lama. A few years before I had bought one of the first *brain machines*, an electronic meditation device that used certain notes and patterns of sound and light to change the frequency of brain states. I had been doing the most modern meditation technique just in from California, but essentially trying to reach a place described for centuries in beautiful paintings and in poetry in the ancient Buddhist tradition. Commemorating the fall of the Berlin Wall, the Dalai Lama spoke to a large group in the center of the city. I was standing behind him before he walked to the stage, and at one point I gently touched his back. He turned and we looked into each other's eyes and the two of us smiled in joy.

In spring of 1997, Bastian visited me in Germany, and we went together to the American Consulate to apply again for a visa. I immediately asked at the window if I may speak to Frau Schulz, but was told she had been replaced by the new Consul General, Herr Kaiser. In English his name would be Mr. Emperor. When I first heard that name, I immediately felt that this emperor would help me.

Still behind glass, but now in a small private room, we spoke with the new Consul General Herr Kaiser. He was friendly, elegant in manner, and he listened politely. At first he was puzzled when he saw both Bastian and I, as polite as himself, and yet extremely earnest about our immigration problem. He left the room for a moment, and then returned smiling, holding a thick pile of papers in his arms - my file. He looked through my record as I told him my story. He could see all the inquiries and reports made by the INS that led to Frau Schulz's refusal. He also looked at us closely, and listened even more closely. At last he said, "Let me see what I can do. I will have to write to the Embassy in Frankfurt. They need to make the final decision." He said he would send a letter to me when he had received a reply. As Bastian and I walked out of the embassy, I knew that I would get my visa.

Two weeks later Bastian returned to his work in California. I was waiting for word from the embassy. In the beginning of May I received a letter from Mr. Kaiser. He said he was sorry, but that Frankfurt denied his request. However, he wrote that he would try again. He wrote again to Frankfurt, and a week after that, exactly on my fifty-fifth birthday, another letter from Mr. Kaiser arrived. Frankfurt had agreed to let me visit my husband in America. They gave me a visa for an eight day visit. Only eight days, but they had said yes. They had granted me an exception to the rule. I thought that if they gave me eight days, then there was no reason to think they would not give me more.

Chapter 16

In the Land of Liberty

There is one breath that connects all of us.
There is one light that shines in all of us.
There is one love that flows through all of us.
- Bastian Stäuber-Jermutus

I flew to Boston a week later. When I gave my passport to the Immigration agent at the airport he looked at the new American visa, and then looked at the string of codes typed onto the bottom of the page. He cried out in a loud voice, "My goodness!" He went off to get the head agent on duty. The head agent took me into an interrogation room. Over the next three hours, he asked me about my arrest, and I told him the whole story. I told him that my husband now worked in Silicon Valley, and I was on my way to see him. He called Bastian in California and asked him several questions that only he could know, things the agent had just asked me. Bastian confirmed to the agent that I had a husband waiting for me in California. The agent then stamped my passport and said, "I'm going to give you a six month visa. When you get to California, get yourself a good immigration lawyer and try to get this all straightened out." He wished me a lot of luck, smiling warmly the whole time. We shook hands, and he welcomed me to America.

Meanwhile Rasa had been waiting at the airport for those three hours, unable to get any information about what had happened to me. He called Bastian, but for the first two hours Bastian knew nothing also. When I finally came through the security gates, I told Rasa that I had just received a miracle.

A few days later I flew to San Francisco. Bastian had an apartment in Mountain View, the heart of Silicon Valley. For four years he had been working for CIC, Communications Intelligence Corporation, beginning his career as an engineer designing high end security and handwriting recognition software. His company's lawyers had easily arranged a normal work visa for him. My lawyer would have a more challenging task.

My new lawyer, Beth, asked me many questions about my life and my legal history, but she asked me one important question that offered the possibility of opening a door. She asked if I was well known as an artist in Germany. From my whole history in art, she was especially interested in my exhibitions arranged from prison, and how the press in Berlin enthusiastically followed my achievements. Beth told me that if I could provide the documentation, then she would apply for an O-1 visa. The Immigration and Naturalization Service called the O-1 a "visa for an artist of extraordinary ability," usually reserved for noteworthy artists wishing to live in America for some time while working and exhibiting their art. The visa lasts for twelve months, but can be renewed each year. This is a type of work visa, a green card, but unlike a normal green card, this visa can not lead to a residency visa, or citizenship.

Beth told me the O-1 is not an easy visa to get. I would have to show evidence of being a successful enough artist to merit that special O-1 status the American government required. This is an unusual situation for an artist. Many artists live their whole lives without critical or financial success. I now had to prove to the United States Government that I was recognized as a successful artist. Measuring the success of an artist is something I think gallerists, critics, and philosophers can more easily do. In any case, if I received the O-1 visa, I was not getting the U. S. government's judgement on the value or quality of my art. At the least, I was getting their judgement that they could believe someone else's judgement. At the best, I was getting a visa to the United States. I could stay in California with my husband, and I could paint with an inspiration from a land where the frontiers of Western and Eastern civilizations meet.

Four years earlier, when Rasa picked Bastian and me up at New York's Kennedy airport in December 1992, we were just beginning our odyssey in America. We had no idea my legal history would soon become a major focus in all of our lives. We arrived in late afternoon, and drove on the Belt Parkway along the southern Atlantic coast of Brooklyn and into Manhattan. This was a return trip to New York for both Bastian and me. When Bastian was seventeen he traveled by himself to America. He took buses and visited mostly the East Coast. Bastian's father, before he unexpectedly died, was scheduled to leave the next day for America and work on an engineering project for the Siemens Corporation at their New York offices. At seventeen Bastian was mindful of the steps his father wanted to take.

Now, with Rasa, we looked up at the tops of tall buildings as we drove through downtown Manhattan. We drove into New Jersey and visited Rasa's oldest friend Pat Patterson. He lived with his wife Cyndi and son Andrew in a split-level ranch style house in the suburbs. I had become friends with Pat and Cyndi ten years earlier when I came for Rasa's wedding. Pat and Cyndi's warm welcome to America started our journey with a good feeling. It was in their living room with all of us laughing and remembering the time we shared ten years earlier, that I pointed to Rasa's belly and said, "Rasa, you are too fat! Ve vill take care of zat." After Rasa's divorce from Rebecca he had gone through a dark period, and I soon realized that a lot of Americans eat their way out of dark times. I knew that I could help Rasa change a few habits.

The next day we again drove through Manhattan, this time the Upper West Side. We stopped for lunch in Rasa's favorite bagel shop, and then with huge cream cheese stuffed bagels and cups of hot coffee, we drove north to the hills of Western Massachusetts.

We arrived in Northampton in the early evening. We came into

Rasa's very small one bedroom apartment. I was surprised at the size, but saw Rasa's sensitivity in the way he used the space. He had only a small living room which turned into a bedroom at night. He slept on a thin futon on the floor. On one side of the living room, through a doorway, was the kitchen, with its nice, rounded dining area surrounded by glass. On the other side of the living room, closed off by an Indian cloth hanging, was Rasa's office. The office was only the size of the desk pushed up against a window, and the little piece of floor in front where Rasa had a large comfortable office chair. Bastian and I planned on staying a week with Rasa, perhaps a little longer if the energy was right. When we came in that tiny apartment in tiny Northampton, we never thought that we three would share that space for the next three months.

After we had been in Northampton for two months, I so missed Demian that I called Berlin, and arranged with our friend Peter to fly with Demian to New York. This was the first of many trips Demian would make to America. Bastian and I drove from Massachusetts to pick them up and bring them to Northampton. They stayed for one week with us at Rasa's apartment. In heavy snow, Rasa took three year old Demian out to build his first snowman. We all walked through the snow drifts of New England, all a winter fantasy for Demian. The year before, at the Festival Kraft der Visionen in Berlin, Demian had been amazed to meet an authentic Native American, Manitonquát, a Wampanoag elder. It is curious that Demian in Germany would meet a Native American whose tribe was from the part of America where Rasa lived. It was even more curious that the week Demian was in America, Manitonquat was in Northampton speaking at a Whole Health Expo. Demian was so excited to be in America meeting his Native American hero once again. In Manitonquat's Prayer, written in 1971, he says,

Above all,

let us set the children free,

break the traps of fear that history has fashioned for them.

Free to grow, to seek and question, to dance and sing,

to be dreamers of tomorrow's rainbows
and if we but give them our trust,
they will guide us to a New Creation,
for love is life believing in itself.

On our second day in America, our first day in Northampton, we sat long into the morning talking, drinking lots of strong coffee. Bastian was normally quiet with strangers. Even so, Rasa immediately liked Bastian, and Bastian liked Rasa. Rasa told me later that night that he had a very good feeling about Bastian. On his travels both east and west, Rasa was used to the long nights with many long quiet meditations that we shared so many times in Breiter Weg, and Kirchplatz. In those quiet moments that first night in America, while Bastian was learning the ways of a new friend, while beginning his journey in a new land, Rasa understood something of what Bastian was feeling.

Over the next two weeks many friends came to visit, mostly people I had met at Rasa's wedding, ten years before. We celebrated Bastian's thirty-fourth birthday on the thirteenth of December. Northampton was having one of its strong winters, and some days we would look out the window in the morning and see white drifts of snow, only parts of the houses rising out of the white on white. Still, many friends came and Rasa's small living room carried conversations about years past in Europe and America, and the years we had in front of us. For us, discussions of the future were mostly conversations about California, new technologies, and new ideas.

My good friend Brian Marasca came for a weekend with his wife Eva and their young daughter Jobie. Jobie was nearly three at the time. I immediately had a strong connection to this young girl. During that weekend Jobie gave me a thick piece of red yarn as a spontaneous present. Later I used that thread in a large painting that I titled, *Jobie's Roter Faden, Jobie's Red Thread*. All of my paintings have threads in them, although they are usually metaphorical. Years later Brian bought *Jobie's Roter Faden*, and it now hangs in his living room.

On December twenty-third we drove south. First we went to Washington, DC and arrived for a nice evening with Rasa's family. The next morning we went to the Vietnam War Memorial, that long dark V-shaped scar in the center of the capitol. We also visited the Smithsonian Air and Space Museum, and of course the National Gallery of Art. Later that afternoon, December twenty-fourth, we drove from the historic city center, and then through some of the poor ghettos of Washington on our way to the Atlantic Coast of Maryland. Rasa's parents have for many years owned an apartment overlooking the ocean in Washington's nearest ocean-front city. We could sit comfortably up on the fourth floor and day and night watch, hear, and smell the waves of the Atlantic.

Every morning I woke up early, before Bastian and Rasa were awake, and I took the elevator down to the beach. I would walk south along the ocean, barefoot even on those icy December days. I collected shells, smiled at the birds who followed me as I walked, and again and again I stepped in and out of the cold ocean.

We spent about a week at the beach, celebrating Christmas, Hanukkah, and every day the miracle of Nature with its non-stop rhythm of the waves. On the last morning, as we were cleaning the apartment, I gave both men a hug, first Bastian, then Rasa. While holding Rasa, I suddenly had this old feeling I had years before in Wesel, and again at his wedding, but a feeling I always kept under control. This time, I thought, let's see what happens.

On the drive back to Northampton, I was thinking about that old feeling, and how I always felt so easily close to Rasa over the years. As I rode along in the front seat of the car, I thought, "My God. I just came with my wonderful young husband to America, and that old feeling for Rasa comes up. What do I do?"

Over the next days I spoke with Bastian and Rasa, both separately and together. They were both remarkably calm and loving, listening closely to my thoughts. I told them what I felt in my heart. I told them what my intuition told me. We spoke about one another tenderly. We talked about love, what we all believed love to be. We talked about the nature of being and consciousness. We talked about freedom, freedom to be ourselves, and grow in the ways we needed. In the end, I told them that I was in love with both men.

In the weeks that came, Rasa and I acted like the young lovers we could have been twenty years earlier. In 1972 in Wesel we shared precious moments of wordless communication, singing a melody with our hearts. Our deep love for each other always vibrated with that unforgettable melody. Now, after all these years, we finally gave voice to that melody. There was the glow of attraction and sensation, but all of it growing with our deep and long friendship we had for one another. Rasa gave to me the passion I had heard so many times in his sitar playing. I had never experienced such an intense sensitivity in sex. Bastian had to laugh at us. I was ten years older than Rasa. Rasa was six years older than Bastian, but of the three of us, Bastian acted the most like the adult. Rasa and I explored the new world of an unfamiliar and joyful possibility in our friendship. With the tenderness of long familiarity, but the eagerness of teen-agers, we fully released our sexual passion. Bastian was laughing a lot of the time, laughing with us and at us. These days were also a strong test for him. While Rasa was at work, Bastian and I talked for hours about love and freedom, experimentation and evolution. These were familiar conversations for us. That we had already spent years describing the nature of our relationship made this time easier to understand. We both agreed that we would support each other in any sound evolution. Both of us agreed that Rasa was our most important and closest friend in this new land. Bastian had the choice of seeing Rasa as a threat, a typical lower circuit response, or seeing Rasa as an old friend who has always been in the family. Bastian took all the energy in his heart to live up to his ideals of how a conscious non-emotional, loving and generous human should act. He took Rasa into the family.

Rasa had an easy schedule at his work at that time of year. He was doing public relations and admissions work for Hampshire College, and spent the fall and spring traveling all across America.

The other months he worked part time. While Rasa was working, Bastian and I prepared for our journey to California. Bashir sold us a Toyota van that he had used to carry oriental rugs for his shop. Bastian, the engineer, drew plans for how to turn the van into a camping car. With Rasa's help, we spent several days shopping for lumber, bedding and kitchen supplies. Watching Rasa figure out what store has what and where to go to get all the things we needed, both Bastian and I were impressed at the complexity and depth of the consumer culture we had just entered. Rasa, of course, like most Americans, was a master at shopping.

With Bashir's van cleaned out, and with Rasa's tools and carport, Bastian started the transformation. Rasa and I had both lived in vans and traveled as couples sharing that small space for long periods of time. Now Bastian and I would drive across America in a van and begin a new life in a foreign and exotic California.

All three of us were enjoying being together, and we spent a lot of time in Rasa's living room, sitting, talking, listening to Rasa play sitar. We were also having adventures with old friends who came to visit and with new friends we made in the area. The culture of the small town of Northampton blends old New England traditions with the influence of five colleges, lots of young people, and what is probably America's largest lesbian community - with a lot of Massachusetts liberal and progressive values.

As I promised, on the first day we were all in Northampton, our second day in America, I started to help Rasa change his lifestyle. He wanted to lose weight, but had developed the habit of eating too much, too often, and at the wrong times of the day. Over the three months Bastian and I stayed with Rasa, except for when we tried a few restaurants, I cooked every meal for the three of us. We ate very simple but tasty vegetarian food. We all three followed Rasa's new diet, but this was the normal diet for Bastian and me - actually even more than we normally ate. Rasa's new smaller diet was still, for us, a lot of food. Every trip we made to the giant health food supermarket amazed us. America had so much food for sale, and such variety that we imagined everyone spent the day just thinking about food. I think for many Americans, this is not far from the truth.

In the morning we only had juice or fruit. At noon or so we would eat our first meal, either a breakfast or a lunch, whatever we were in the mood for. At dinner we ate well, but not too much and always very fresh organic foods. We always ate dinner before eight p.m., and ate nothing but tea, coffee, juice or fruit after eight. Rasa had been in the habit of eating big breakfasts, small lunches, normal dinners, and almost always snacking on something, often ice cream, at night. The human body likes to have a regular digestive pattern. Rasa, like most people in the West, certainly, was never giving his system the time it needed to work. The body likes to eliminate waste in the morning. Water and juices, or fruits, help that process. Eating any other food slows down the elimination, as the body will put its energy into beginning new digestion. Elimination ends by noon, so we can start eating for the day. The body begins the heaviest part of its digestion after dinner, and so if we don't eat anything after eight, we give the body the full time it needs, all night long, to digest the day's food. If we eat a hard to digest snack late at night, digestion slows down. All of this slowing down of digestion in most people means that a lot of waste never leaves the body. Overly fatty diets and poor digestion added to no exercise means a lot of extra weight. We changed Rasa's diet over night.

As the van came close to being finished, Rasa and I drove to his parent's place at the beach in Maryland for a long weekend. While standing in the cold winter ocean we held hands and declared our love for each other. In a ceremony at the edge of land and sea we came together as lover and lover. I later joked with Bastian that now he had a brother from another mother. I think we three could never have started this unique relationship without a lot of love and respect for one another. A lot of people have wondered about us, sometimes even asking one of us how we can manage and not be jealous. For all three of us, the answer always comes back to love, honesty, and freedom.

When men stop thinking of women as their property, then two men don't have to think of themselves as competitors. Both Bastian and Rasa loved me, but neither one wanted to possess me. From the beginning of our relationship, Bastian and I understood our path as a kind of spiritual quest. Sex was not our main attraction. With my old friend Rasa I developed a compassionate love with passionate sex and always the rhythms of our deep understanding of one another's soul.

Even so, in the beginning I was shocked that I had that strong attraction to Rasa. At the same time I had no desire to leave Bastian. I didn't want to hide these feelings, not for myself, not for Bastian, and not for the world. I talked to Bastian. I talked to Rasa. I talked with all three of us together. Even with non-possessive men, I realized, these were two men who were different in many ways, and I wanted to be sensitive enough to balance this dance we were beginning. Over the coming years I would travel back and forth many times from West Coast to East Coast. While I was in Germany, both Bastian and Rasa came to visit me. Rasa came many times to California. Bastian came as often as he could to Massachusetts where the three of us would sit in the tower and play the music that became Starseed. There was a lot of motion in our relationships. We were all busy in our lives, but with no pressure we gave ourselves a lot of space, and a lot of care and understanding. We didn't see ourselves as doing anything particularly extraordinary. We three all felt strongly about conscious evolution. Now we had an opportunity to see if we could consciously evolve. We carefully watched our egos, the ways in which the ego protects its patterns. We were careful to be honest in our words and actions. We learned in time, by disuse, to simply let go of the old patterns. Both men were happy when I arrived at the airport, but in truth, both men were happy to have some time in their homes by themselves when I was gone. Both Bastian and Rasa have a great love of quiet contemplation, or activities, like music, that creatively elevates one's consciousness. I too loved the travel and the two different environments, but in time I realized that we needed a third home. That would come.

Both men are very loving in many details, and both men are very clean, especially important to a housewife. When I arrive at

Rasa's, he has the house full of fresh flowers, and Bastian does the same. Both men love women, meaning they respect women. They honor the Shakti, the divine female energy. Both men respect the Shakti in me. When the three of us are together we move freely in any of our homes - all equal members of the household. Over the years Bastian and Rasa have become very close friends. In all these years, they never had an argument. In all the years Demian has been coming to America, he sometimes stays with Rasa and me in Massachusetts, and sometimes with Bastian and me in California. Sometimes he is with all three of us. He has grown up fully enjoying the energy from the three of us, and the two compassionate and responsible male role models in Bastian and Rasa.

In many ways it was easier for Bastian and Rasa to come together as friends than it was for me to be both wife and lover. In the first years of our unusual relationship, we struggled with issues that sometimes took painful lessons to resolve. With Rasa, we knew each other so deeply over so many years. As lovers we could be very sensitive. As partners, sometimes stubborn, and sometimes impatient, we sometimes struggled with great difficulty over the painful truths in our pasts that brought out our worst behavior. Perhaps only with Rasa, and he with me, could we have been so rude at times, and then immediately so deeply regretful as we began to understand the dynamics of our attachment to old patterns.

With Bastian we also had our stress, and in some ways it looked similar to the struggles Rasa and I worked through. While Bastian was learning to adapt to the high pressures experienced by all of Silicon Valley's programmers, while also learning to communicate in a foreign language, we were both learning to be husband and wife with those pressures in this foreign land. As long work hours, and issues with money began to be the focus of so much energy, our insecurities led to more and more moments of frustration. I've never been very good with money. Because of the war, my family was very poor. I remember being hungry many times during and after the war. Throughout my early childhood we struggled for all of life's essentials. In the years after the war, I was often hungry during the day. We had dinner every night, but when I came home from school, we usually had nothing to eat until dinner. Sometimes we had bread, and if I was lucky, we had margarine. When we didn't have margarine, and I was lucky enough to find some brown sugar, I had a little trick. I would sprinkle the sugar over the bread, and then sprinkle some water on top of the sugar. The water crystallizes the sugar, and I loved the taste of that moist sweet bread. I remember when I was nine years old, during our summer school holiday, I would walk with my friends to the city's public swimming pool. We walked for about six kilometers, and on the way we passed two farms. When we were really hungry, and had the courage, we would knock on the back door of one of the farm houses. We would ask the farmer's wife if we could please have some bread. The farmer's wife was sometimes in a bad mood, and she would tell us to go away, but sometimes she would invite us in and give us all a slice of fresh home-baked bread with real butter and marmalade. In the winter months, we went often to a place outside of town on the side of the road where a fruit shop would dump the fruit that was too old to sell. My first taste of an orange in my life came after we peeled away the moldy half, and each of us bit into the still good side of that incredibly sweet and juicy fruit. The next Christmas I was delighted with my family's new addition to the tradition of everyone at the table receiving some sweeties on the *Weihnachtsteller*, the Christmas Plate. That year everyone received an apple and a large navel orange.

I seldom say I am hungry. I am never hungry anymore, except perhaps when I fast, and then I am only hungry for a short while. As a child I went day after day feeling that my stomach was never full enough.

Years after the war, my family was not poor, but still working class, and I realize now that I was always ashamed of that lower class status in society. When I was humiliated as a ten year old by my friend's condescending mother, and again when I was fourteen and an upper class boy would not associate with me - these incidents, and others, brought out a defensive reaction. I didn't consciously choose a strategy to deal with shame, but I did develop a pattern. I simply acted and looked as if I were wealthy. I believe it was in my nature and training to dress well and speak well. Somewhere I discovered the added benefit of making people think that I was wealthy, simply because I wore an old but elegant dress well, and I could carry myself with confidence. I didn't care if there was no wealth behind my apparently wealthy appearance. I enjoyed feeling wealthy, and along with my wartime consciousness of living only for the moment, I usually spent all my money with that idea in mind. Why not spend it while I have it? In times when I have needed to seriously focus on my expenses, my discipline has given me the needed awareness, but mostly, I prefer to be spontaneous and follow my heart, and so I usually don't hesitate in spending or giving my money away. In America we were introduced to a credit economy. Confronting the obvious financial results of overextending our credit added to the obstacles Bastian and I needed to overcome in America. It took us a while to balance that part of our American experience.

We had come to America on a spiritual journey. I believe that in Bastian's mind, he probably never thought about marriage as part of his life's plan. He would have been happy as an adventurous monk, but for both of us on a spiritual quest in California, being married had many advantages. Perhaps the difference is that I had a model of marriage, after three previous attempts, that I wanted to improve. I wanted my marriage with Bastian to work because of our devotion to love, honesty and freedom. I didn't want to make again the mistakes I had made in the past, but the speed and intensity of America gave added pressure to all our decisions. I guess I would be surprised if Bastian, Rasa and myself had come together so nicely without some pain, a lot of reflection, and just the right amount of compassionate adjustment. Everyone has triggers from their past that can instantly ignite our insecurities, often without our control. Through compassion and detachment, and hours of effort, we have learned to recognize our triggers. We have changed our behavior. We have learned to disarm ourselves, and live in harmony.

When I am with Bastian, we are in our German language together, with all the subtle cues and phrases so familiar to our culture, and all the quick connections we can make as we share similar perspectives on our journey in a foreign culture. When I am with Rasa I am learning about American culture. I experience the American language through Rasa, and often through misunderstandings, in the beginning, I improved my vocabulary and grammar. I also began to understand the meaning and importance of all the phrases in English that exist, not to get the meaning across, but to be polite in the process. In German, to a friend, we would informally say, "Give me the water." In America, "Would you pass the water, please?" I came to America and as I translated my German culture into American English, I often sounded too abrupt. American English, for me, seemed to go too far in the other direction. Then I began to see the complexity of the culture here, all the different immigrants from the entire world, and I saw the importance of being polite. I still often felt that people would too easily use politeness as a way of avoiding the truth of a situation, but I've come to see the wisdom in always using kindness with every communication. As Rasa was making his German better, listening often over days and days to Bastian and me talk to one another, Bastian had improved his English, and I had with the loving help of a friend, found many unexpected insights about my new home.

When I am with Bastian, we spend many hours on spiritual practices, either sitting in meditation, or making pilgrimages to holy people and places. Bastian likes to get away from his work as a software engineer when we are together so that we can share our time away from the heavy routines of the work world, experiencing the bliss of our spiritual quest in so many of our actions. When I am with Rasa, we also make experiences to take ourselves into the bliss of higher consciousness, most often in the music we play together, but also in the innocent life play we have always so easily shared. We have never stopped our occasional spontaneous eruptions into song, or our moments of dropping in laughter over some shared absurd realization. Sometimes in the kitchen we will dance the tango. We dance with such a dedicated pretend seriousness, we inevitably end up laughing and tripping over our feet.

All three of us have a strong connection to Nature - walking silently through the woods of the Berkshire Mountains, or over the cliffs on the Pacific coast, or on the slopes of Mt. Shasta.

With both Bastian and Rasa I have a very strong connection through music. We live together with an unrehearsed respect and love for one another. This reality is expressed in many ways, but when we sit without words, with our hands on our musical instruments, we come together as if we are one instrument able to play many notes. Our three instruments share equally the soundscape. Our improvisations blend without any one of us dominating the others. We play not for the ego, but only for the sound of sensitive, joyful and compassionate harmony.

Some years ago, I found that my instrument in our relationship, my physical body, was undergoing a transformation. This resulted in a retuning of the entire being. When I came into my menopause, I suddenly didn't like to have sex anymore. I talked to my doctor and she said, "Marlis, you have had so much sex in your life. Maybe your body has had enough. When you have had enough ice cream, you don't want anymore." So I thought, okay. I have to talk to Bastian and Rasa. I told them that I would not have sex anymore. I didn't mind if they masturbated, or became involved with other women. The men are free to explore as they wish. That was up to them. And they respected that. We continued to have the same love. That never changed. It actually became a deeper spiritual love in the years after. I don't mean to say you can't have as deep a spiritual love with sex. You could practice Tantric sex, or in some other way overcome attachment. But I feel I went through sex, and arrived on the other side. On the other side I found my energy moving up and into my heart.

About a month before we left Northampton in March of 1993, a friend offered me a small house to stay in for two weeks. I took the opportunity to have some time by myself, leaving Bastian and Rasa alone together. Bastian and Rasa visited me in the tiny house, but mostly I sat alone, enjoying the warm cottage, meditating, and then beginning my first paintings in America. I used pigments, gold and silver leaves and sand. A couple of the titles were *Eve Was Right*, and *Shiva's Dance*.

Chapter 17

California

Imagination is more important than knowledge.
For knowledge is limited,
whereas imagination embraces the entire world,
stimulating progress, giving birth to evolution.

- Albert Einstein

In Hindu mythology, Shiva dances and the world is transformed. We didn't know how our personal transformations would change us, but we knew that our dance would soon take us across the vast landscape of America. Still in our first months in America, on March 18, 1993, with snow still covering Northampton, Bastian and I began our journey to California. Everywhere along the way I collected sand and flowers.

We traveled at first south to get out of the cold weather as quickly as possible. We spent one very cold night sleeping in the van in New Jersey. When we came to the Gulf Coast of Mississippi, we visited NASA's Stennis Space Center. We toured the grounds, looking up at rockets designed to take humans into space.

While in Texas we visited Andy Dershin, Sweet Smoke's bass player. He was in the process of getting a divorce at the time, and we were with him for a week, giving him our thoughts and good energy. He had lived with his wife in Germany during the Sweet Smoke days, and I believe he enjoyed talking with us, and reflecting on happier times.

We drove into the American Southwest. I loved the natural landscape. I loved the architecture. In Santa Fe we visited the Institute of American Indian Arts Museum. In front of the museum on the ground were Native Americans selling handmade crafts. We bought some jewelry before going into the museum. As I walked through the exhibits and saw the bitter history of the native Hopi and Navaho, I could only think of their children on the ground in front of the museum selling little pieces of their culture to tourists. I felt like nothing much had changed for the Native Americans.

We drove up to the Grand Canyon, arriving in the late afternoon, and we stayed the night in a camping ground. The next morning we found a parking space just on the canyon's edge, and frigid with frost, we sat in the van with the sliding door open and watched the vivid colors of sunrise on the canyon's walls. When I looked to the bottom of the Grand Canyon, my mind could not conceive of its depth. No matter how long I looked, I could not adjust to the idea that the raging Colorado river was that thin wandering line I saw on the canyon floor.

After leaving the Grand Canyon, we drove into the Hopi lands. We drove for miles and miles. The countryside was beautiful and stark, and all the rock and sand in shades of reds and browns. I was happy that we lived in our van and could cook a meal later on the butane stove, when we stopped to sleep for the night. I was happy about our independence because we drove for hours and didn't see another car, or a billboard, or even a gas station. We drove to the Hopi Mesas, a village in stone over eight hundred years old. This area is often closed to visitors, especially during religious ceremonies. While walking through the village, I was shocked at how this poor village exists in this rich America. I stopped to talk to a young woman for a while. She was very friendly and invited me into her small house. She had only one room with a bed, a table, a chair, a refrigerator and over the refrigerator in a large dark frame was a picture of the King, Elvis Presley. It was a big photo of the older Elvis on stage with a guitar and a microphone. Printed on the photo was simply The King. My English was not so good, and her English was not so good, and as we both smiled realizing this, we had the feeling of sharing another kind of energy different and more honest than words. Before we left, I went to the car and brought the young woman some of our candles as a small gift.

We arrived in Southern California and at first visited Steve Rosenstein, one of the guitar players in Sweet Smoke. With his wife Inga, from Holland, Steve had moved to Los Angeles to become a lawyer. We talked for hours about the early 1970s and Steve's days as a rock 'n' roller. We left Los Angeles by driving north on the old coast road Highway 1. We parked on the beach for two nights on the way. When we arrived in San Francisco, we pretty much left right away because we wanted to go over the Golden Gate Bridge, which leaves the city. We drove over the bridge out of the city, then walked over the bridge, once and back. For me, this walk was a symbolic gesture, an honoring of the golden gateway into California. Then we drove into San Francisco again and directly to the Whole Earth Expo. Timothy Leary gave a speech at the expo that night, and afterwards we talked with him. He remembered our dinner in Hamburg ten years earlier. and he told me that the painting I gave him has been hanging in his house ever since. I told him his writing in those days brought me to my meeting him again ten years later on the western-most coast of America.

Later that night we arrived in San Jose. While in Northampton, Bashir had arranged for us to stay with his friend Kamal, who was a computer programmer. Kamal was also a sitar player, and he was sharing a house with Ashish Khan, one of the son's of India's most famous classical sarod players, Ali Akbar Khan. Kamal and Ashish suggested that we stay in their garage for as long as we wanted while Bastian looked for a job in Silicon Valley. The garage was very large. There had never been a car in it, and since it was cleanable, we decided to move in for a while.

We drove around the Bay Area for some days, just looking at our new home, then Bastian started working - working on getting work. Kamal gave Bastian a computer and a line to the internet. Bastian started filling out many applications with *headhunters*, the brokers who had connections, hopefully, with the high tech companies. Bastian would spend about a month filling out forms and sending e-mails, before meeting up with a Danish headhunter who had moved to California to help, in his way, with the computer revolution. In the middle of Bastian's search for work we had our shocking trip together to Germany where I got stuck for four years. Bastian returned to California by himself, and some weeks later he was offered a position writing code for CIC. At the time CIC was beginning to become famous for making writing in your own hand-writing onto a computer screen nearly as natural as using paper. Bastian jumped right into that competitive high tech world, and has worked for CIC ever since.

When I finally returned to America in 1997 with my six month visa and lots of optimism, I stayed with Rasa for some days, and then flew across the continent to begin my journey in California. I very soon met my attorney Beth and began my immigration jour-ney - my efforts to obtain an O-1 visa. At the same time, I was finally in California, and an inner journey was also beginning, a journey that I could only find in the mixture of old and new wisdom on this edge of Western civilization.

Bastian had a one bedroom apartment in a typically California flower and sunshine environment, just two blocks from the penin-sula's busy main artery, El Camino Real. The apartment complex was surrounded by thousands of other houses and apartments, roads and cars, and the expansive campuses of the high tech companies. I created there my first California influenced paintings.

I explored the area in and around Mountain View by foot, bi-cycle and car. I often had a lunch salad at a popular sidewalk cafe. I met our diverse neighbors, the local silicon residents - program-mers, writers, artists, intellectuals - some of them spiritual aspirants.

Bastian and I drove very often to San Francisco, around 30 miles north, to visit many friends we had in the city. Bastian had for many years programmed his synthesizers, creating meditative ambient music, and we both became friends with many musicians, as well as other artists in the Bay Area. Early on we met Peter Siegelmeier, keyboard artist, who created Ciber Records, and owns a hip shop in Haight-Ashbury. Through Peter, we met Monika, a German concert producer from Berlin. We went to many parties at her place where we continued to meet more and more interesting people.

Through Monika, I met Olympia Rosenblum, an Australian film maker and fashion photographer. With Olympia I have a very deep friendship. She lives now again in Australia, but she is one of those friends I see again and again as she travels around the world. The last time we were together was in Berlin.

Through my German friend Tom Sperlich, European agent for Terrance McKenna, Timothy Leary and Robert Anton Wilson, we met another group of interesting people in California. Tom introduced us to Peter Meyer, an Australian we met first when he was working as a programmer in Texas. Later in California he worked with Terrance McKenna, creating the program that computed Terrance's Time Wave Zero theory. With Tom and Peter, Bastian and I met Terrance at his house up in the northern woods of Marin county. Terrance was always brilliant and wonderful to hear. He spoke about long expanses of time and marvelous changes in our world, always honoring the patterns he saw in the seeming chaos of history. In his way, he was one of the most radical proponents of conscious evolution in our time.

Tom also introduced us to Bob Wilson (Robert Anton Wilson), author and philosopher, and husband to a wonderful spirit, his wife of many years, Arlen. Rasa, Bastian and I became very close friends with the Wilson's. Rasa was especially close to Bob in his last years, after Arlen died. Rasa created the graphics Bob used in his last published book, *Email to the Universe*, and the two of them enjoyed a deep and warm friendship, sitting together many hours on Bob's balcony overlooking Monterey Bay.

In one of his books, Bob wrote what has become a treasured philosophic slogan, *Keep the Lasagna Flying*. Bob used the flight of the lasagna as a metaphor for the human brain, and his lifelong effort to encourage people to keep their brains in use. Once we were eating dinner with Bob and Arlen, sitting around the dinner table at their house in Capitola, just south of Santa Cruz. Arlen was serving lasagna. At one point during the serving process, Bob's lasagna flew from his plate. All of us laughing, I'm sure we all had the same optimistic thought, "Keep the lasagna flying!"

In the end of 1997, with a lot of help from many open hearts, I was granted a two year O-1 visa. After that first visa and through the time I am now writing, I have been granted a new O-1 visa every year - now ten times.

I am so grateful to so many people who wrote letters supporting me and my art, and to all the immigration agents who were so sympathetic, and most especially to Mr. Kaiser of the American Consulate in Berlin. I must also thank my lawyers in America, Beth, and now Rhoda Wilkinson-Domingo who is looking for ways for me to have a more permanent visa. I am so thankful.

During the next few years we would move several times, living in very different parts of the Bay Area. Both Bastian and I were exploring this wonderful land on the Pacific, but we were exploring, far more, places inside our own minds and hearts. In our inner explorations, we were also exploring, along with many others, our continuing expansion of consciousness.

We lived for a while in a comfortable tiny wooden-frame house with a wonderful small but lush garden in Fairfax, a town in Marin County, a half hour north of San Francisco over the Golden Gate bridge. From there we moved closer to Bastian's work in Silicon

Valley. We rented a condominium high up on a mountain side overlooking the Pacific Ocean in the town of Pacifica, just south of San Francisco. I say *overlooking the Pacific Ocean*, but Pacifica is so often covered in thick clouds that it can be difficult to see your house from your own driveway. Even so, on those many foggy days, the sky would often clear in the late afternoon and we could see magnificent sunsets as the sun appeared to sail over the blue horizon.

One day a friend asked me if I knew Stewart Springs, near Mt. Shasta, in the far northern part of California. We learned about its history as a Native American mineral springs that had been converted in the 1800s to a healing center, with heated mineral baths, a sauna, a wonderful fresh mountain water bathing creek, and an authentic weekly Native American sweat lodge led by Karuk Spiritual Leader, Walking Eagle Hün-Na-îtch. Bastian and I loved the waters and atmosphere of Stewart Springs, but we were even more fascinated by Mt. Shasta, the dormant volcano, and one of the highest mountain peaks in California.

Over the years I have often hiked high up on the side of Mt. Shasta, on and off the trails. I will make the twenty minute drive from Mt. Shasta City up to the end of the state park's road, and park the car at about eight thousand feet. I sometimes come alone, but often with Bastian or Rasa, or all three of us. We take the trail through the rocky mountainside until we reach the first high ridge. From here we can climb a nearby peak just for the view, or we can hike further along the trail down to South Gate where beautiful streams bring green meadows and millions of spring flowers. Mt. Shasta is so stark with its endless broken rubble of beautifully colored volcanic rock - thrown across the mountain side during major eruptions. The last eruption was only two hundred and twenty-two years ago, but geologists think the mountain, at this stage of its growth, only erupts every six hundred years or so. It is likely we are experiencing one of Shasta's meditative periods. We will walk through this dry landscape and then suddenly come upon South Gate, so lush and green and alive with Nature Spirits. In this divine natural environment my soul can feel at blissful rest.

In the summer of 1999, Rasa, Bastian and I invited Joachim for a six week stay in America. We all had known Joachim for many years. I thought of our years together in the Breiter Weg, how I was seeing more and more while Joachim was closing a world in on himself. I wanted to give something to Joachim that I found and he lost on the Breiter Weg - a wider view of the world. Since the demise of the Seeling Strasse commune, he had lived with our friend Ananto in Berlin. In 1998 he had an exhibition of his newly created hand-colored black and white photographs. He was entering the art world again after many years mostly out of normal society altogether. In America he absorbed all he saw with fascination. Rasa tested his appetite by bringing us to a pancake house for breakfast one day. Joachim ordered a giant apple waffle, so big that it made its giant plate look small. Joachim ate as much as he could, but he gave up with a smile, just appreciating the wonder of a country that would make such a large breakfast. I wanted to give a gift to Joachim, something both practical and symbolic. He usually wore conservative leather shoes, mostly because he had a hard time finding shoes in his large shoe size. Rasa found a store that sold only large shoes, and we found a men's size seventeen running shoes. Joachim loved them. He stayed with Rasa and me for three weeks, visiting New York and Washington D.C., and seeing many old friends again at a Sweet Smoke reunion in Andy Dershin's new house in Pennsylvania. Joachim and I flew to California and the Bay Area, and with Bastian, we drove to Mt. Shasta where we climbed high up the side of the mountain. Before he flew back to Germany, Joachim thanked us deeply from his heart for giving him the opportunity to experience, as he said, "the land of liberty." While he was in America, none of us, even him, knew about the cancer spreading in his body. He passed away in Berlin a year and a half later. Through low and high times, I learned so much and changed so much from having Joachim in my life. With his death, I felt that, for me, an era had ended.

We had gone many times on the mountain when one day we talked with Jessica and Otto, the owners of the city's well known esoteric bookstore, the Golden Bough. Jessica asked me if I had ever been to St. Germain's Living Room. She told us it was a beautiful small meadow high up on the side of the mountain, somewhere above the tree line. She said that from where we parked the car, we should head up the trail, and then walk up further for a while, and then we would find it, or not. We looked again and again for St. Germain's Living Room, always walking along the slightest trail, but never finding it. Finally we just gave up. Then one day we walked up and up along an unfamiliar side of rough rocks, far from the nearest trail. We passed through a wide flat treeless clearing with very large boulders laid out like chess pieces on a giant board. Then after climbing a short distance further we were there. A small stream came out of the rocks, and all around us were wild flowers coming out of soft spongy moss and grass. We took our shoes off, and walked into the small meadow. We sat and meditated in this high place, so far above so much of the world.

For many months Bastian and I drove to Mt. Shasta, and would spend the weekends, staying sometimes at a cabin in the woods at Stewart Springs, sometimes renting a chalet on the edge of Lake Siskiyou at the Mt. Shasta resort just outside the town. One time I stayed in a chalet for ten days by myself, walking the three miles into town on some days. I enjoyed the thought of having my own house in such a beautiful area. During that time I met Kolona, a shaman who lived in Mt. Shasta. I had several deeply effective shamanistic sessions with her. Some time later she moved to a house on the shore of nearby Lake Shastina. Bastian and I visited her there several times, and I told her from first seeing her place that if she moved out that I would buy the property from the owner. I was strongly attracted to the energy of the land. The well-built cedar house was surrounded by large pine and juniper trees. The house was built in the shape of a cross, with large two story windows in the cathedral shaped living room that overlooked the small woods that led to the lake at the edge of the property.

For many years Mt. Shasta has attracted spiritual seekers with many different traditions. The Native Americans have always considered the mountain sacred. Guy Ballard had his vision of St. Germain on the mountain which began the world renown *I AM Movement*. There are now many temples and retreats on and around the mountain, all anchored by the tiny city of Mt. Shasta. There is a Buddhist monastery, with bald-headed monks in practice, and seen regularly shopping like all of us at the local community favorite, the Berryvale health food store and deli. The city's two small health food stores, Berryvale and Mountain Song, truly enrich the growing health conscious community. Berryvale's kitchen uses the best of California's wonderful fresh foods and creative cooks to make sure we often see our friends again and again in the dining area. Tara's Refuge, a Tibetan Buddhist temple and gardens, regularly hosts open ceremonies, and visits from Tibetan luminaries like Lama Wangdor Rimpoche. Our friends Sharon and Purusha sponsor some of those special occasions at Tara's Refuge, and have for years in many ways worked to help keep Tibetan culture alive. In their own smaller temple closer in town they offer a simple weekly meditation. Sunday mornings at ten a group of people enter the small temple and sit with meditation chairs or pillows on one of several oriental carpets. Many statues of Eastern and Western deities and saints sit in silk and flower arrangements, but the overall atmosphere is of a simple elegance, and the meditation gatherings mirror that simplicity. The people enter in silence, and when all are seated, Purusha begins to play the soft drone repetition of the stings on a large resonant tamboura. After about five minutes, he stops, and for the next hour everyone sits in quiet meditation. At the end of the hour Purusha simply rings the penetrating tone of a Tibetan singing bowl three times, and then people slowly leave, sometimes talking quietly. Sharon and Purusha always leave the doors of the temple unlocked, and over the years many individuals and groups have been invited to come and sit in stillness.

For Starseed music, their energetically powerful temple is one of our favorite places in Mt. Shasta to perform. Another favorite place is Graell, Tony and Shasta Corsini's Flying Lotus, a healing space for theater, dance, music and mystical rituals.

Over the last seven years my art has been shown in nearly thirty exhibitions in and around Northern California. Amorah Quan Yin's Dolphin Star Temple in Mt. Shasta City kept a permanent selection of my art on their walls while the temple was on Main Street. Amorah helped present me as an artist, but she also helped me personally years ago in a psychic reading. Her inner view of my inner world was for me like looking at a map of my life, and seeing details from an unfamiliar perspective. She didn't know me at the time. She gave the reading over the phone, but in some details she saw me perfectly. She said that when I come into a room I immediately feel the energy in the room and I observe every detail, she said, "like a laser." This is true. I have always been curious about all the details. I almost always notice immediately what people and objects are around me, what plants are blooming, what emotions are turning, and what hearts are closed or open.

In 2000 we purchased the shaman's house on the shore of Lake Shastina, in the valley under Mt. Shasta. The house is sitting in the least populated part of the state, some five hours north of San Francisco by car, and about an hour south of Ashland, Oregon. On most days, if I don't drive the twenty miles into tiny Mt. Shasta City, I usually only have the wild deer, and other wildlife, for company. When not in Rasa's tower, I have been writing parts of this book while sitting on a bench overlooking Lake Shastina. Eva, my deer friend, will often lay down in the dry desert soil beside me as I write. I think she prefers to sit with me on days when I sit on the soft clover and grass lawn next to the house. If I would ever let her, she would probably most prefer to lay down on the oriental carpet in the living room, gazing out of the large glass windows at the backyard, just as we do. Eva's mother Lisa has become famous on the internet (in deer circles) for a photograph of her laying down in the small frame pyramid that sits in the middle of the lawn. That's the same pyramid Bastian and I sat under so many times in Berlin. Now Eva has taken to laying down in the pyramid as well. There is a family of Blue Jays that we've gotten to know. Otto, the father, will come several times a day, land on my hand and pluck two or three almonds into his beak. Now his son, we call him Hansi, sits on a tree branch just next to me as I write every day.

The first few times that Otto landed on my hand to grab an almond, his tiny but powerful claws nervously dug deeply into my skin. The next time I fed him, he was a bit more gentle. Now when he lands on my hand he simply stands, relaxed on my fingertips, not gripping at all. This trust came only through my calm and kind intentions. The deer have more to fear in the wild, and so even with my years of kind behavior, they still remain very wild. The deer who know us well will trust Rasa, Bastian, me and some of our friends, but they are always wary of anything strange or suspicious. Rasa made a gallery on his website for photos we had taken of our unusually close relationship to wild deer. He sent the page link to several friends, who sent it on to others. After six weeks, more than half a million people had visited the page. The web site's small internet provider couldn't handle the volume of traffic and had to shut down the site. Rasa switched to a larger provider, and then the e-mails started to pour in. Rasa received over a thousand e-mails within a couple of months from all over the world. We realized that with all that is ugly, painful or distressing on the internet, people were responding deeply to these simple scenes of peace. Most of the letters were filled with heart-touched appreciation. Some told us of their remarkable experiences with deer, and we could feel in those letters the same respect we have for these majestic creatures. They appear to be soft and gentle, and most of the time they are, but with sharp hooves, muscular legs and lightening fast instincts, these wonderful beings can summon a frightening display of power. We see this in the way they defend their territory, or in the strength of two giant sets of antlers interlocked in battles over male domination.

I had watched Eva deliver two sets of fawns over two seasons. I knew Eva from when she was the fawn of Lisa. I met Lisa when I met her mother, Mama Rose, who was the first deer to approach us after we bought the property. Eva trusted me with her babies, and I watched closely as she brought her newborn fawns to different locations around the property, hiding them under a sage bush or a young pine tree. She would keep them separated so that she could more easily defend against predators. She would walk from one to the other, giving each a little attention. She would always push her giant nose up under a baby to help it get to its feet, and then she'd lead the baby to another hiding place, some meters away. I could watch this habit from the balcony of the house, but Eva didn't mind if I sometimes walked along with her to visit the babies.

When Eva was pregnant in her third year of adulthood, I was walking in the back yard one day and found a newborn fawn alone under a sage bush. I looked around for Eva, but she seemed to be nowhere near. I went to the baby, and stroked her head, a little the way Eva might lick the baby's head. The little fawn didn't open its eyes. It didn't move at all, only breathing softly. Perhaps Eva was off giving birth to another baby. I didn't know. I had to drive into town, and when I returned two hours later, the fawn was gone. I looked around the woods and found another newborn, perhaps it was the same one. The fawn was more awake, but clearly still getting used to being on the planet. I gently stroked her head and she spoke a soft little cry. In an instant I heard for the first time a deer running through the woods. Usually they are completely silent as they run away from danger. Only a second later I saw Eva galloping directly towards me. The deer have an amazing sense of hearing, but their eyesight is not as precise. I could not be sure that she would know who I was immediately. As she was almost before me I calmly said, "Hi Eva. What a nice baby you have." She slammed her back hooves into the ground just before me, stopping in an instant her enormous weight and speed. A cloud of dust flew up around us. As quickly as she had been alarmed, she was now as calm as if I were simply another deer she knew well. I scratched her between her giant ears, and then she went to attend to her baby.

I have seen over time that Eva is the smartest deer in the herd. Her aunt Rosie is older, and so the most dominant female, but Rosie is getting old, and Eva looks over the entire herd as if she is in charge. I think Eva may see me as the dominant female in my backyard. After years of seeing her every day as I work and relax in the yard, we have grown quite close to each other. Deer are naturally curious, and Eva particularly so. I often talk to her when I see her, telling her how nice she looks, or telling her not to eat certain flowers or trees, or sometimes I tell her to be nicer to an injured deer who comes through the yard. Often I am sitting in the back yard in a lounge chair and Eva will lay down next to me. She is very used to my voice, and over time has demonstrated again and again that she knows exactly what I am saying. She understands a lot of words in both English and German, simple words like *come, nice, "don't do that," go away, babies, water, flowers, trees,* and she seems to understand the meaning of simple and complex sentences. She also seems to understand when I tell her I am going away for some months. I will tell her that, and she will instantly become a little agitated, as if not liking the news. When I drive into town for some hours, Eva will often arrive at my house just when I return. She will be walking across the street and into the front yard as I come into the driveway. Deer migrate daily through their territory, and so I know there is no reason for her to be so often there when I spontaneously arrive. Perhaps she knows the sound of my car, and can run to the house before I get there, but it was really a mystery for me to see her there so often. Then a remarkable thing happened. I was on the East Coast and calling Bastian staying at our house in Lake Shastina, and every time I would call, Eva would walk up onto the back porch and look into the living room where Bastian was on the phone. At first Bastian was simply amused to see Eva on the porch staring into the window. He would laugh and tell me, "and Eva is again looking in the window," but after a couple of weeks of Eva always quietly showing up on the porch just when I called, both Bastian and I were really surprised. He would often not see Eva all day, the phone would ring many times, but just when I would call, Eva would appear on the porch.

As I first walked around our new property, I practiced an old habit from my childhood. I have always been curious to taste nature. I can use all my senses easily when I walk in the woods, but we are always cautious about what we are tasting, as the consequences can be dangerous. Even so, I have always wanted to taste pollen, seeds, flowers, leaves, and nearly anything else from the plant world. Lake Shastina's giant evergreens produce rich veins of amber sap that collect in large abstract forms on the tree's trunk. A little piece of that fresh resin sticks tenaciously to the teeth, and strangely has very little taste at all. I once broke open the seed from an oak tree. I bit into the light colored center and immediately spit it out. It was so powerfully bitter and tart, I felt like I had tasted in an instant the entire tree. I am very careful to only put a tiny amount of some things on my tongue, and for good reason. I once rescued a giant eight foot cactus that was sad and lonely, used as decoration in the dark corner of a shop. We borrowed a truck to bring the guy into my sunny living room. At one point the cactus was scraped, and a small amount of sap began to flow. I touched the sap with my finger, and then touched my finger to my tongue. Then I ran to the kitchen to wash my mouth with warm water. For the whole day, my tongue was numb and swollen. These small adventures in taste deepen my understanding of nature. From that understanding I have a deeper respect. That big cactus, now fifteen feet tall and dominating my living room, normally in nature bravely dominating a dry desert landscape, every time I see him I can remember the taste of his power.

We have parties at the house on special occasions, and friends regularly visit. Soon after we bought the house, I was surprised to meet a German woman about my age who lives in Mt. Shasta. Omanasa has been for many years a spiritual seeker. We have discussed our experiences on the spiritual path, but more important for both of us, I believe, is having the simple comfort of being in a foreign land, but talking in our native language. When I first visited Lake Shastina, I met another German speaker who became a good friend. Neera moved to America from Austria, bringing with her the strong hands and intensity of purpose required for being a master in deep tissue massage. Perhaps the most penetrating body work one can experience, but as Neera loosens parts of muscles that normally never receive a direct touch, even tiny hidden parts of body armor can be dismantled. Neera lives more remotely than I, in a part of this California valley that gets many feet of snow in the winter. She lives with her British husband, painter and photographer Pan Paine in a house Pan lovingly crafted by hand. You can buy Pan's astoundingly luminous photographs of Mt. Shasta in bookstores and gift shops. Without filters or special editing techniques, Pan is able to capture Mt. Shasta with a clarity and vividness of color that normally only the eye can see.

One new friend, a petit energetic woman named Gitangili, shares my love of nature, and in this part of California with so few people but so many pathways in the forests, Gitangili and I explored hidden waterfalls and small pristine alpine lakes. Sometimes we would walk through trails for hours and come across a creek that filled a little natural pond in the space between giant boulders. We would sit in these secluded places with no purpose in mind, we simply followed our spirits drawn to nature.

Most people will drive some distance through this large valley to get to Lake Shastina, others are much closer. My friend and fellow artist Todd Friedlander lives just on the other side of the lake. We visit each other's studios and discuss fine aspects of art and spirit. Jack and Abigail, also close neighbors, live at the end of a long dirt road in a nearby flat part of the valley about a ten minute drive away. They have a majestic view of Mt. Shasta with the valley spread out before them. They moved here from Hawaii where they had over the years developed together a unique and powerful type of healing energy ritual. They still offer their work, but now from their remote location. Jack and Abigail show great compassion in their struggle to grow fruits and vegetables in this desert environment. There are so many small animals who are very clever in eating all the food before it can be harvested. They have built elaborate fences, and other non-lethal ways of keeping the animals away, but they had one strange problem with the desert wood rats. Jack came out to start his car one morning and it was completely dead. He opened the hood and found a family of wood rats huddled in a pile. To make their new home more comfortable, or perhaps just because they were hungry, they had chewed through most of the car's electrical wires. Jack scared them off, and ordered new parts and fixed the car. Some days later the wood rats returned, their teeth just as sharp as the last time. Jack fixed the car again, but this time he decided to work more creatively with the laws of nature. Now Jack and Abigail have three cats who love their new home, and their new responsibilities.

Near to Jack and Abigail lives a remarkable scientist. Rollin Rose calls himself the Wizard of Weed, taking the name from our surprisingly named village on the western side of Mt. Shasta. Rollin is a Stanford trained clinical psychologist who worked most of his life as a therapist in California's prison system. Now he devotes most of his time to his wizardry. Rollin will come to visit from time to time, and at every visit he will energetically examine objects in my house, or even the land itself. When he first moved to this desert landscape, he needed to find the right place to dig for a water well. White Bear, a Sioux friend, taught him how to douse for water on his property, and in time Rollin became an expert in the art of dousing. Since he was so successful in finding water through the energy affecting the movement of his copper dousing rods, he wondered if perhaps dousing might locate more than just water. Rollin's house is filled with odd and fascinating machines, all experiments in focusing or increasing different waves of energy. His dousing rods, in their simplicity, are probably his most elegant tools, but Rollin's dousing led him to an even more ancient energy art. Rollin started to collect conch shells. He carefully learned the technique for cutting their ends and turning them into horns - a tradition in cultures all over the planet. The conch shell horn is even a sacred object in Tibet, a landlocked nation far from the nearest ocean and surrounded by the tallest mountains in the world. Even there the conch shell has been blown to release the energy of its powerful sound and *frighten the demons*. In his research and dousing of many conch shells, Rollin collected twenty-three shells whose notes, he believed, corresponded to the vibrations of the seven traditional chakras and the sixteen minor energy centers of the human body. I picked up one of the larger conch shells in Rollin's house once, a huge abstract orange and white crown of calcium - previously a sea creature's impervious home. I imagined this giant conch shell could have been used to announce the entrance of a Hawaiian queen. Rollin took the conch in his hands, straightened his posture, and took a deep breath before releasing a long bottomless note that could have been used to signal ships at sea. Rollin said this was the left knee conch, and then Rasa, amazed, said that while the note was sounding he had felt a soft but steady vibration in his left knee. Rollin had recordings of him blowing all twenty-three conches, and Rasa offered to engineer and produce a CD of what Rollin calls *The Wizard of Weed's Conch Shell Magic*. Rasa digitally enhanced an image of Rollin blowing a conch shell for the cover of the CD. He gave Rollin a fanciful wizard's hat and robe. When you don't see Rollin on the cover of the CD, or while he is dousing in a wizard-like trance, you would never think of him as a wizard. Under his old baseball cap and in comfortable casual clothes, The Wizard of Weed looks more like he just drove in from the ranch. This wizard never calls attention to himself. I don't know if that is a wizard's strategy, but Rollin Rose periodically emerges from his desert home, and if I see him, I know he will be happy to humbly offer the power of his talents.

There is a lot of open land and vast spaces here, but the Mt. Shasta community comes together in many ways. So many people come to my mind as I think of my time at Lake Shastina. Even when I don't write about so many of the memorable moments, those moments are still a part of me, and never forgotten. Spiritual teachers and seekers come to Mt. Shasta, some coming for a short time, others staying and living here for many years. Mystics, healers, therapists, writers, artists, musicians, dancers - all living harmoniously with the local descendants of the area's old cattle and lumber industries, and all in California with a kind of *edge of the Western world consciousness*.

Of course, this is the material world, *the world of illusion*, and so some people inevitably become lost in the illusion. And this is California, *The Golden State*, the destination of dreamers and deceivers, all looking for a pot of gold. During the gold rush of the 1840s the San Francisco neighborhood on the bay at the end of Pacific Avenue became known as the Barbary Coast, named after the pirate-infested coast of North Africa. While miners walked out of the hills with gold dust and gold nuggets, a lot of that gold ended up in the pockets of thieves of all types in the streets and saloons of the Barbary Coast. In the New Age, the gold is still golden, but much lighter. People hunger for spiritual gold - good health, clear minds, bliss, and enlightenment. In that optimistic search for higher truth, many become lost along the way, and sometimes some are led astray. Critics of the New Age point to charlatans, naive believers, and an incoherent jumble of diverse philosophies stolen or poorly invented. When you only look at some aspects of the New Age, aspects that any movement may have, then the critics are right. The New Age has its problems. Perhaps the label gets in the way.

I never liked the term New Age. I liked the idea behind it, that we are entering a new age more enlightened than the previous, but that is not a new phenomenon. We are always entering a new age. We are always experiencing more and learning more, and as a result we become more conscious. Many people credit the start of the so-called New Age with Madame Blavatsky and the Theosophical Society in the late 1880s. Perhaps we need a newer New Age.

Physical power defined the Industrial Age. In the Information Age we are learning the power of words, ideas, and the extraordinary secrets of the quantum world. The new force in the New Age is supposed to be light - the light of enlightenment. I doubt the Hindus believe this is a new idea. The news, I believe, is that this ancient idea, the power of light, is now so popular in the East and the West. Perhaps we could call this new stage the Light Age.

In the Light Age, my vision has not always been so clear. I chose to live in Lake Shastina, in part, because of the solitude. I wanted to be a member of a vibrant spiritual community, but I also wanted a private retreat, a place of peace in nature, away from all distraction. I am, however, again and again in the Mt. Shasta community, both taking and giving, and sometimes, not fully aware of the dynamics. In my optimism I have mistaken empty claims for honest intentions. Some people seemingly deceive unconsciously, or at least their motives are complicated by ego or self-deception - people who claim to have powers they do not possess, or people who claim to be teachers without any grounding in experience or compassion, or sometimes people who seem to have little control at all over their reality.

One fellow, Gerald, a follower of metaphysical teachings, attended a concert of Starseed in Mt. Shasta. After the concert, he told Rasa that he had purposely found a seat on the side of the stage, so that he could more easily see Bastian playing his synthesizers, but when the concert started, Gerald realized that from the angle he now had, Rasa was blocking his view of Bastian. He said to Rasa, "You were right in my view, and then you dematerialized. For a while I could watch everything Bastian was playing, and then you re-materialized." Rasa said, "That's interesting." Rasa looked at Gerald for a moment and then asked, "So do you think I really dematerialized and reappeared? Did that really happen, or did you imagine that? Did it happen and only you saw it? I'm curious when someone experiences something unusual."

Gerald replied, "No, it was not my imagination. I think we were both vibrating at a higher synchronous frequency. I have manifested invisibility on occasion when needed."

When Rasa told me this story, my immediate question was simple. "Is that guy nuts? Why didn't he just move over a seat?"

Rasa laughed, but later as we all watched the video tape of the concert, and we noticed that the camera never lost sight of Rasa, we discussed a quick list of all the possibilities available in an examination of Gerald and his power to *manifest invisibility*. Rasa said, "Even if Gerald could manifest invisibility, you're right. What's the point? Why use such an astounding power so frivolously?"

We all were wondering about the telling of mystical events in the stories of esoteric teachings. I can't argue with Gerald about his belief system. That's his reality. But when Gerald likes his version of the story, and tells the story again and again, in time a myth may be born.

A fascinating blend of belief systems merge in the region around the mountain of Mt. Shasta. The Ajumawi Pit River Native Americans believe a powerful spirit, called Mis Misa, lives inside the mountain. Her presence keeps the universe in balance. The Karuk tribe believes the mountain has healing powers. The College of the Siskiyous reports:

> *The Shasta Indian name for Mt. Shasta, Waka-nunee-Tuki-wuki, is the same as the name for the Shasta Creator. This name, meaning to "walk around and around, but never on top," should be repeated twice anytime the mountain comes into a Shasta person's vision. The area above the tree line on Shasta has been reserved for the "Gods," and therefore, is not a place a Shasta person would travel except under special circumstances.*

Ascended Masters Teachings speak of wise and compassionate St Germain appearing on the mountain, offering humanity many gifts, among them the *Violet Consuming Flame*. Believers in UFOs regularly come to the mountain as sightseers, hoping to make contact. The strangely round lenticular clouds that often float over the mountain are sometimes described as motherships of benevolent aliens. Christian settlers in the region brought the miracles in the message of Jesus. Buddhists *settlers*, following a search for enlightment built a monestary next to the mountain. Some people believe the ancient Lemurian race is secretly living under the mountain, benevolently aiding in planetary advancement. Some environmentalists believe the mountain to be sacred for the precious water flowing and filtering through its mineral rich interior. Other people believe an alien race of reptiles are living among us, disguised as humans, and manipulating individuals and governments. I believe in my own experiences, and the reality I have perceived, but I can not dismiss other realities just because of my inexperience. Modern scientists believe we coexist with multiple universes. Perhaps some of us perceive realities beyond the normal borders. We live in a time where change occurs so quickly that it can be hard to know what to believe. In an open-hearted community, we would like to believe that everyone is acting from the heart. The con-artist loves that environment.

I met a healer while eating in Berryvale one day - small, intense, well-mannered - and he gave me the impression that he was a master in his field. He was a master outstanding in his field. Actually a little too outstanding. Police in two other states were looking for him. He claimed to be a chiropractor who practiced applied kinesiology, acupuncture, and sold herbal remedies. He was so persuasive and confident, and that is part of why I missed so many clues about his real intentions. He often talked to me about his clients, and many other people in town. Perhaps because I have been used to listening to other people tell me about their lives, I didn't think too deeply about it at the time. However I remember a strange incident. He had been telling me about a negative encounter he had had with someone I too knew in town. He ended his thoughts by saying, "That guy is a reptile." Almost immediately after that conversation, Rasa was eating lunch at Berryvale and he saw the *reptile* the con-artist had been talking about. He mentioned that I had been at the con-artist's office, and the *reptile* replied, "I wouldn't trust that guy. He's actually a reptile." I don't believe in the reptile theory, but the con-artist acted like one. When Rasa later told me what the second reptile said about the first, we were both laughing at the absurdity. I was beginning to see beneath the surface, and I realized sharply the difference between my judgement and my discernment. With my open-heart I had felt insecure about making a negative judgement about the con-artist. I wanted to believe in him. I gave him my trust. When his actions betrayed him, I woke up. I could see the reality behind the illusion. I am thankful to the con-artist. This was a lesson I had to learn about overcoming the idea that I was judging, or being judged. I needed to learn to simply discern the truth.

I sit on the bench in my back yard in Lake Shastina, looking over the lake at the sunset. I wonder how to navigate living within the world, and being at peace within myself. Fortunately, there are many honest seekers and teachers in the world, and many more every day. Even in a troubled world, this Western optimism, this sunny California spirit prevails.

Both of Claudia Susanna's children, Demian, and her younger son Cosma, have visited me in Lake Shastina. Even these young kids were excited to tell their friends that they were going to California. Cosma celebrated his 6th birthday in Lake Shastina. A week later he was there to celebrate my 60th birthday.

Lake Shastina is in the municipality of the very small city of Weed, California. I like the seclusion of living nine miles from the center of Weed, but while Mt. Shasta City is the center of the spiritual community in the region, Weed is the closest urban area. Weed's downtown architecture looks pretty much the way it did just a few years after 1897 when Abner Weed paid four hundred dollars for the Siskiyou Lumber and Mercantile Mill and the surrounding two hundred and eighty acres. The mill created a small town with those typical wooden frame buildings you see in every Western movie. The bakery on Main Street is still in operation since it put in its oven in 1906. The present owner told us about a ghost that sometimes appears. I've had exhibitions in the three galleries now on Main Street. More and more artists are moving to Weed, and very quickly an art community is developing. One of the galleries was started by our friends Brenda and Shannon who created Weed's Village Oracle and the Buddha Belly Kitchen - great organic food and an exhibition space for artists, and musical and spiritual events. Brenda and Shannon's daughter Trinity, now seven, loves to come to my house, pretend to be a faery or a princess, and feed the bluejays and play with the deer. I so enjoy her company.

She reminds me so much of myself when I was a child.

I came to America with my mind on California, a place I knew was famous for creative people who were not afraid of new ideas and transformation. I did move to California, but with regular journeys with Rasa I had the opportunity to visit many parts of America. Every year I have lived with Rasa for several months in his Victorian mansion in the western woods of New England. Rasa bought a condominium in the top of the one hundred and thirty year old mansion. He had the large tower renovated, and with a painting studio on a lower floor, I have a secluded studio and a tower with views of the surrounding woods and mountains where I can meditate, play music, read, and write this book.

As a sensitive musician, over the last ten years Rasa has used his talents as a graphic artist to compose, like creating music, beautifully crafted websites and videos. In the care and extra details he adds, I think his web clients feel a small part of the unconditional generosity he has always shown to me and all our friends. While in America, Bastian has risen to the top of his field in Information Technology, while also composing innovative electronic music influenced by the newest ideas in sound healing. For several years he has attended conferences and classes at San Francisco's revolutionary Globe Institute for Sound Therapy and Healing. Both Rasa and Bastian visit Lake Shastina often. Bastian drives up from Silicon Valley most weekends, and Rasa flies across the country two or three times a year for extended stays. Both of them feel a part of the Mt. Shasta community.

When the three of us are together in California we have given concerts, always looking for environments where the audience has an appreciation for a journey within. When people come into the hall or temple the three of us are in meditation, sitting in lotus posture with our instruments before us. People usually sit in meditation with us until the concert begins. Many people stay in a meditative pose throughout the performance. With the vibration of meditation, and the astounding resonance of sitar, tamboura and synthesizers, the music creates a mesmerizing field of sound. We silently move from piece to piece and in those short moments of silence in between the room is perfectly quiet. People become so relaxed and elevated that I sometimes think they even forget they are at a concert. We receive a lot of words of appreciation after a performance is over, but more rewarding for us is that silence, and the transformation we feel in the room as the music gently brings everyone into the peace we all have within.

I have adjusted in many ways to life in America, but even with Rasa's help, Bastian and I took some years to begin to understand a lot of everyday aspects of American culture. I was first overwhelmed by food. Everywhere was food, and everywhere people were eating, and eating a lot. I once heard someone say, "I want it all, and I want it now!" In grocery stores, my eyes simply couldn't take in the variety of every kind of food. We would eat breakfast in a restaurant and so much food would arrive that I would lose my appetite. I could eat some of everything, but I certainly couldn't eat it all. As vegetarians, we eventually enjoyed these restaurant meals after we figured out how to pick what we wanted from the menu.

I also had to get used to Hollywood and television. There is an enormous amount of discussion about the latest movie or what just appeared this week on the TV. A lot of references in people's conversations included something from *Seinfeld* or *24* or *The Daily Show*. I came to realize that some, maybe many, Americans come home and turn their TVs on, and then leave them on all the time whether they are watching them or not. Everyone seems to know when a commercial is coming and everyone seems to know exactly how much time they have to go to the bathroom or the kitchen before the commercial is over. I still can't figure that out. I realized that some people would watch most of their television or video on rented DVDs. One time I watched hours and hours of a serial TV program on DVD non-stop simply because I wanted to know the final outcome. Usually that happens in two hours in a movie, or you have to watch the TV show in weekly one hour mini-dramas. I didn't want to wait to find out what happened at the end of the last episode. *I wanted it all, and I wanted it then!*

Most everything in America is so big, but most especially America itself. A city block seems big to me, but I drive often from Mt. Shasta to the San Francisco Bay Area, and after years with those regular trips, those thousands of miles in my car have made me adapt to America's car culture. The German autobahn has speed limits, but also places where you can go as fast as you like. On those very long parts of Interstate 5 in the Sacramento Valley, I drive and drive in a straight line for miles and miles. At first I felt like an autobahn driver. I simply kept getting faster and faster, until I saw the flashing red lights behind me. Maybe it is common for Germans in America to get speeding tickets. The officer in my traffic school taught me how to break the rules in moderation. He said that he knew of no officer who would give a ticket when a driver goes only five miles over the speed limit.

I have figured out how to eat well and in a healthy manner in America. I usually don't watch television. I watch a good movie on DVD sometimes. I drive more conservatively, but I am still amazed at the size of everything. I am still adjusting to that aspect of America, but like all who find their way in America, I slowly stopped making comparisons to my native land. I found that I could very quickly be comfortable in America, and sometimes too comfortable. In this extremely busy culture I was searching for a way to become calm and peaceful. Perhaps in a very busy place, I began to realize, there can be a greater appreciation for calm.

I mentioned my friend Sharon, and her and Purusha's temple in Mt. Shasta. Like myself, Sharon has a great appreciation for calm. For about a year we have sponsored a Monday afternoon women's group, for just the two of us. I will make us a lunch, and then we sit in the living room for coffee with German chocolate or cake. Then we listen to ambient, minimalistic or spiritual music - Snatam Kaur, Hildegarrd von Bingen, O. S. Arun, Tony Scott, Michael Vetter, Starseed. Then we meditate for about an hour in the silence of Lake Shastina. For two hours while listening to music and meditating we say nothing. Sharon is one of the few people I have met who seems completely at ease in silence. Perhaps our common sensitivities help to make the space between us uncluttered with unnecessary things to discuss. We have both played the meditative Indian tamboura for many years. We like to play together sometimes, but mostly we like to sit in our silence, or simply in a calm vibration. Often the deer sit outside the living room window as we meditate. We both have a great love for nature and animals. Sharon has worked for many years as an animal communicator, using her love and psychic abilities to understand the pain of animals. She has created a line of pure organic herbal remedies, and she spends long work days on the phone in sessions advising humans about pets, farm animals and wild animals who need assistance. Her telephone sits not in her office, but in a small exquisite temple nearby. In front of colorful arrangements of orchids and countless images of Goddesses, Gods, saints and animal spirits, she advises humans and sometimes communicates directly to an ailing animal. We have a wonderful short video of Sharon with my deer friend Eva. The deer who visit us are normally afraid of strangers. When they know we trust the people, then they become calm, but still ready to run in an instant. In this video with Sharon, Eva shows a remarkable moment of intimacy as she calmly rests her head on Sharon's arm for a moment. The deer are known for their silence and their ability to swiftly and gracefully run through the forest. When Sharon comes to visit Lake Shastina, the deer immediately appreciate, as do I, her deep love and calm.

There is also a deep love, but the opposite of calm, in several of my close friends in Mt. Shasta. Zephyr, son of Joanna, I have known since I felt him kicking against his mother's belly before he was born. He is now six years old and is always eager to talk to me, and nearly everyone else, with excitement about what has just happened to him in his life in the last ten minutes. Nöel's two young boys, Lotus Moon and Sapphire, are always a delight to see where ever we may meet. Usually I see them running up and down the aisles at Berryvale, their mother calmly shopping, knowing the kids are well looked after since most of the people in the store at any one time probably know Lotus Moon and Sapphire. Julianna, granddaughter of my friend Karen Rogers, comes to visit sometimes with Karen.

Karen and I, in recent years, have been traveling on a similar spiritual path. Some years before she met me, she bought one of my paintings at an exhibition, but while still in the gallery, she stood for a long time staring at the painting. She told me that the painting gave her, for the first time, an understanding of abstract art. She said she could see the joyful energy of the movement in the abstract lines and shapes, and that when she looked away, and then back again, she would see things she previously didn't see. While Karen and I are talking in the living room, Juliana is slowly moving from object to object in my house, examining everything as if in a museum. Sitting on tabletops, hanging on the walls, and behind glass cases are objects from all over the world. Musical instruments from India, faeries and elves from Germany, river stones from Ireland, all the gifts and objects that came to me over many years. Juliana will come up to a table and stare for a while, and then she will carefully rearrange the objects according to her inner aesthetic. I have my own way of arranging all these objects, but Juliana is so concentrated and careful with her imagination, I enjoy watching her sensitivity, and seeing the new designs she creates.

For ten years Rasa had a job working for Hampshire College, an unusual progressive institution. Rasa would travel around the country and some other parts of the world, explaining this new idea in education to young students beginning their look at colleges, and to professionals who needed to learn something new about how a college could be. I traveled with Rasa on some of these trips, visiting states on the West and East Coasts. While Rasa was opening eyes about a serious challenging academic program, I was in the background, observing this young generation of American youth. At Hampshire College students have a lot of freedom. They are required to design their own programs. If they succeed they can learn some valuable lessons about managing their lives in a chaotic world.

I came to America, and California in particular, and found myself facing a similar challenge. I had no set program to follow, but I knew that in America I could find the freedom to create my own program of transformation.

Chapter 18

Healing

The art of healing comes from nature,
not from the physician.
Therefore the physician must start from nature,
with an open mind.

- Paracelsus

S ome of my familiarity with freedom in transformation came to me during workshops I attended in Holland and Germany in 1990 to 1992. Many followers of the Indian spiritual teacher Bhagwan Shree Rajneesh, later known as Osho, lived in what Osho himself called Das Dörfchen, a section of Charlottenburg, part of the center of West Berlin. Osho's devotees, called Sanyassin, were often successful at many yogic and Western styled methods of therapy - all of them in some way challenging the control of the ego. My massage therapist Vikalpo was a devotee of Osho. He told me that the armor built into my body and consciousness over many years was too tough for his hands. He suggested I attend a workshop held by Veeresh, a Sanyassin in Egmond ann Zee, Holland, and the founder of the Humaniversity. On that same day I sold a painting, and suddenly having the money, and finding out that the next workshop would be starting in two days, I left the next day by train to Amsterdam. On the following day I went to Egmond and began a ten day workshop with about three hundred people on healing childhood traumas. All to challenge the ego and clean out the being, we played games, role-playing, we fasted for several days, only drinking tea and water, we chanted, we danced, we had twenty-four hours of silence. We had long meditations. We also walked along the beach of the North Sea. In one game I played, I was the little girl Marlis. I had a nice partner, a young guy, who played my father. That was a pleasant experience for me. Other games were much more intense. In one exercise your partner would sit on top of you, and you would simply say, "Give it to me." They would simply reply, "No." You are pinned under them and asking a primal question over and over with always the same response. This goes on for hours. There are many therapists in the hall with so many people, always watching the process. Sometimes the therapists would have to restrain a participant because that simple game would so extremely challenge the ego and release the intense emotions of our childhood traumas.

After the workshop in Egmond, I went to the Osho Multiversity in Berlin and met the founders Sakino and Prabhat. We talked about my experiences in Egmond. They learned that I had a video camera, and asked if I would document their workshops. In Berlin, Bastian attended many of their sessions as a workshop participant. I too attended, always observing from behind the lens, but always feeling the transformative energy of the sessions. In one workshop Bastian attended, the workshop leader announced that if you liked your current workshop partner, you would be spending an intimate evening with them, otherwise you could look for another partner. All participants were required to be AIDS tested before beginning the workshop, and although sex was not required during this intimate night time session of the workshop, it was certainly allowed. During a pause in the afternoon program, Bastian, feeling a little embarrassed, asked me what I thought he should do. His partner was a good looking free spirited young woman named Shaki. Bastian liked Shaki. I told him immediately that he should take her to our home tonight. I would stay the night with friends, and he should feel free to explore this liberating intimacy, without guilt or embarrassment. That night we both had the opportunity to experience different aspects of freedom.

The greatest help I found in conscious personal transformation came through Dr. Zaida Rivene, chiropractor and applied kinesiologist. At one time chiropractors were considered the quacks of the medical profession, but now most insurance companies recognize their expertise, and every day, people receive relief from the pain of improperly aligned muscles and bones. One day we may find that applied kinesiology will gain the same respectability, perhaps following a similar difficult path. Applied kinesiology, also called muscle testing, is a natural feedback system that allows the body to communicate directly to a practitioner. Any new medical art will have those doctors who excel at the practice, and those who do not. Zaida had long years of experience, and a special spiritual sensitivity that I immediately trusted. I began to have weekly sessions with her. She loved my artwork as much as I loved her healing abilities, and after a while I traded paintings for all the work she did with me.

With her help I could heal the effects of sexual abuse in my life, realizing that I must forgive in order to move on. Through that forgiveness I learned to appreciate men. Separate from the pain of abuse, I could now see what I had learned from all these men. I could for the first time appreciate men, and what they had to offer to me, and not just be afraid of what they could take *from* me. After forgiving the abusive men in my life, I could overcome the reflex of pain. I could be free of that distraction pain creates. Without pain, without the hurt, I could see everything more clearly, not only the frail egos of scary men, but also the powerful spirit of a little girl abused by war and patriarchy. I was taught to accept my abuse, to know my place in society was below everyone else, but my little soul could not accept seeing such a worthless version of the child Marlis. At an early age the little ego cleverly used intelligence and humor as ego armor against the insanity of injustice. In the 1960s even the title of housewife lost respectability as feminism fought against the depreciation of traditional female roles. My intelligence helped me to see my situation, but my situation did not appreciate my intelligence. Arrogant men wanted a dumb little girl. I gave them a girl proud of her intelligence, but I had to play that proud game so often that I later had trouble dismantling that part of my armor. My humor helped me to open my heart to my situation, but while my humor by nature is joyful, it was often out of necessity sarcastic in those many moments of defending myself.

With Zaida's help I went through my whole life. We followed every path, and examined every turning. When I would come in for an appointment I would lay down on a chiropractor's table in a small comfortable private consulting room. Zaida would come in and ask how I was feeling. Sometimes I went to see her because of back or muscle pain, the result of some injury or stressful situation, but mostly I would ask her help in dealing with far deeper issues. Once I told her that throughout my whole life I felt low self-esteem. Through muscle testing, she asked about my low self-esteem. I would raise my arm up, keeping it level some inches above the table. With each question she asked she would gently push down on my arm, measuring the resistance I was able to maintain. The practitioner learns a lot from this simple test. It is a subtle art that responds as much to the phrasing of the questions, as to the response of the client. She said to me, "Let's go back to when it started. Was it in the womb?" She would push down on my arm with a very precise appreciation for my muscle's resistance. She could feel that she was years off in her question, so she next asked, "Was it at six years old?" My arm responded. "Was it eleven or twelve years?" "Yes." was the response. Zaida asked me, "What was going on at that time?" I knew immediately this was the time when my friend's mother decided I was not good enough to play with her daughter. Zaida told me to go back and feel that low self-esteem, that feeling of humiliation. I went back to those moments and felt that pain. Zaida said, "Now consciously erase that feeling of low self-esteem. Visualize yourself rubbing it out." I took myself to that part of my memories and watched myself erase that information, not the memory, just the pain of the memory. Then she said, "Coming from love and light, fill that space now with . . ." She paused, letting me finish her sentence and fill the space. I said, "I am a divine being, in love with myself and all others."

Every time I had this kind of session, I asked similar kinds of questions, going always deeper into the traumas of my past, always seeing how they crippled me as a child and young woman. My body, mind and soul never forget the experiences of my life. Working with Zaida, I saw how every scar from the past left some kind of corresponding sensitivity or pain in the present. Re-living and consciously reprogramming each of these kinds of experiences through many sessions over several years, I gradually became healthier and younger.

Nearly every time after a session, I would come home and lay down on my bed and relive the experience. I would repeat what Zaida and I did in the session in my mind. I had sometimes a kind of breakdown. I experienced echos from the past. Something like flashbacks. My body would hurt. I would experience all the sensations of the memory. Often my body would shiver in revulsion. And then the pain would gradually disappear.

During this time I learned something about the meaning of detachment. Spiritual teachers speak of detachment as a way of limiting the ego's presence in our actions. They speak of being detached from desire, desire for people and things, fame and wealth. Detachment also describes a state of living in the now, not holding onto events and ideas in the past or worrying about the future. This last definition came to me naturally as a child in wartime. I was compelled to live in the moment. I was always moving, leaving possessions behind, and never really knowing what the future would hold. I can still live my life with very little attachment to the past and future. Desire has been a much greater challenge. Not desire for fame or wealth, but my desire to be a good mother. How could I detach myself from that basic maternal instinct when I had felt so guilty about not being a good mother. Through the work of healing myself I came to realize that my thinking was wrong. I was a good mother. I had to agree that my children were better cared for with their fathers at those times. This was a decision from my heart. However, the ego was still holding on to my guilt. It was a way to keep me attached to my old programming. The ego eagerly reminded me of my guilt. That sneaky little bastard. So conveniently reinforcing my low self-esteem. With the guilt removed, I could see the compassion in my decisions. My decisions from my heart, so long hidden by guilt, could now become a part of my whole being.

As I have described myself in this book, Rasa has often suggested using adjectives that made me feel uncomfortable, words like beautiful or lovely. He advised me, "Don't let low self-esteem influence your descriptions, even if that has now been mostly transformed. Remember that modesty is not always honesty." To be honest, I admit that I have always been viewed by others as physically attractive. However, while physical beauty attracts a lot of attention, it brings little to nourish the heart. In my life, my appearance has brought a lot of unwanted, and sometimes dangerous, attention. At the same time, my need for approval always compelled me to accentuate my appearance. I have always loved beauty in nature, and though I knew I looked good, and I enhanced the effect by dressing well and smiling a lot, still, I didn't feel like I looked good. On the outside I appeared attractive, but on the inside, the beauty of my true nature was hidden by fear and doubt. My beauty on the outside mostly attracted men who never bothered to look beyond the surface, and so the ego believed my outside appearance was more important than that radiant being hidden deep behind a complex web of insecurity.

One day Zaida said to me, "I think it would be good for your personal power to participate in a fire walk." She explained that a fire walk was an ancient healing and initiation ceremony, a way to experience conquering one's fear. At about three in the afternoon Bastian and I arrived at Half Moon Bay and parked next to a large field near the ocean. We joined a group of forty people. I noticed the large pile of wood off to one side, as we all formed a circle. One by one we each went into the center of the circle and spoke our names and a few words to describe ourselves. After this we formed two lines, facing the person across from us, and holding tightly onto their arms. One person would stand on a two meter high platform with eyes closed, and simply fall backwards into the interlocked arms. Then they would take their place at the end of the line, to help catch the next person ready to fall. Some people had a great fear of this short but total free fall. I totally enjoyed it. Just to fall back without any care, landing in the arms of nice people.

There were two of these exercises for the group before we came to the fire walk itself. After everyone had fallen into other's arms one time, we all assembled before the ceremony leader, Heidi, for an introduction to the second exercise - a alarming challenge to the mind in the world of matter. We each were given a wooden arrow, a regular metal tipped feathered wooden arrow. After listening with some fear at the instructions, I took my arrow over to a nearby tree. I placed the feathered end of the arrow against the tree. The metal point of the arrow I placed in the center of my throat at that spot just above where the top of the rib cage ends. You can feel with your fingers the hard muscle of the throat all the way from the bottom of your chin down to just above the rib cage. At that place where the throat muscle ends and the ribs begin, there is a small very soft, very sensitive spot. With the arrow on this spot, I was to break the arrow by pushing my throat into its point, the heavy tree keeping the arrow in place. With legs planted into the ground, my arms down, and only the pressure of my body weight pushing the arrow up against the tree, I cried out in my loudest voice and quickly pushed my neck against the arrow point. The arrow snapped in two.

After several hours the sun had set and the pile of wood had burned down to look like a round red glowing carpet. Everyone gathered in a circle around the burning embers. I stood with Zaida at one end when she simply entered the embers, and walked across. I was about to follow when I saw Bastian coming from the other side. He walked confidently across. I didn't need to look down at the coals to know how hot they were. I could feel the intense heat. Then thinking nothing, I crossed the fiery red carpet and on my last step I thought to myself, "Is that hot!" and then I immediately felt the bottom of my foot begin to burn. In the next second I was on solid cool ground again and I felt an ecstatic sense of being. The small burn on my foot healed remarkably fast, but even more remarkable was my fear of water had gone. Ever since nearly drowning as a child I had a fear of being under water. The next day after the fire walk I went to the pool at our apartment complex, and with eyes wide open, I took a breath and lowered myself below the surface of the water. I thought to myself, "if I can walk on fire, I can go under water." For the first time in my life, I felt confident swimming around the pool, completely under water.

Through Zaida, I met a shaman woman named Aven Air. She lived near the Russian River north of San Francisco in a quiet wooded area alone with her pet white wolf named Dihna. Dihna was a beautiful animal, with a full thick white coat and penetrating blue eyes. Dihna was usually with us during our healing ceremonies, but she always was laying down quietly near by. Over some months I would drive the three hours to Aven Air's house once a week for a shamanistic session. With Aven Air I worked on a different level than the work I had with Zaida. Aven Air worked more in the elemental realms. Through her variety of healing rituals connected to air, fire, water and earth, I was able to consciously ground myself to Mother Earth. Sometimes the experiences during these sessions were so powerful that I felt a blissful oneness with all beings. Other times I felt the depth of sadness within me. Once she asked me to make a drawing on paper of a table with all my family members sitting at dinner. I drew the table, and then everyone who would be there. I drew a simple circle and simple figures around it. She then asked me who everyone was in the drawing. After I named them all, she asked me if I noticed anything particular about what I had drawn. At first I didn't, but then I saw that all my relatives were sitting on the top part of the circle, and I was alone on the bottom of the circle, small and insignificant. On the three hour drive home that day I was thinking and thinking about the implications of that simple drawing.

Around this same time Bastian read about the founder of the Rebirthing Movement, Leonard Orr. Leonard created a new kind of pranayama, a breathing exercise, that became known as Rebirthing. Bastian went with Rasa to a week long workshop Leonard held at Stewart Springs. They went with our friend Peter, who lived in San Francisco with his wife Santo Shima, a devotee of Ammaji. I thought all three of the men would have a good experience of a week in the woods with the fiery philosophy of Leonard Orr. They did.

The three men shared a cabin for the week. They lived an austere lifestyle for that week in the woods at Stewart Springs' remote mountain location. It's a beautiful alpine setting thick with tall evergreen trees, and always the sound of the creek that flows through the grounds. About ten people gathered to work with Leonard for that week. Everyone would have partners while learning Leonard's breathing technique, and everyone would experience several two hour sessions of *conscious breathing*. There were workshops on most of Leonard's major themes - all concerning care for the whole being. He uses the concepts of air, fire, water and earth, to teach basic principles of health and awareness. In a simple way, you could say that Earth represents an awareness of diet, both the food we eat and even the ideas our minds consume. Leonard is most famous for his theories on Air, as his circular breathing has been taught to millions. With Water, aside from the importance of drinking enough good water, Leonard believes daily bathing does more than simply wash away dust from the day. Water, like Fire, Leonard says, can wash or burn away many deep impressions we have experienced in our lives. One whole day at the retreat was spent in silence before a ritual fire, a Dunhi. Stewart Springs has authentic teepees constructed in the woods, and Bastian, Rasa and Peter sat silent for a day of tending the fire in the middle of the teepee, meditating on the flames. Rasa said six days of Leonard's disciplined and varied practices helped him break out of a lot of old patterns. All of us have benefited from Leonard's conscious circular breathing.

Some months later Leonard and his wife Isabelle stayed with us at Rasa's house in Massachusetts. Leonard offered a lecture at a nearby college. Before Leonard spoke, Rasa and I played sitar and tamboura for the gathering. Rasa composed a lovely melody he entitled *Introducing Young Raja*. The title refers to Leonard's spiritual name, as well as his thoughts on longevity and immortality. Many of his thoughts were inspired by the famous yogi, Babaji of Haidakhan.

While Leonard offers an extensive philosophy tantalizing to the Western imagination and spirit, one Indian saint who embodies the essence of those teachings has many times come from India to California. Bastian and I stood in the long lines of thousands of people touched by her presence, as we waited for a hug from Amma. Her unconditional love flows, as she says, as simply and as naturally as a river.

Bastian had been reading about an Australian housewife who had a major yogic transformation in her life, and had become a well known metaphysical teacher. She changed her name to Jasmuheen, and tours the world talking about her experiences, and offering yogic exercises. She claims to have lived only on light, no food, for seven years. She became the world's most famous supporter of the philosophy called *Breatharianism*. I resonated deeply with their fundamental idea. We are already living on light. It is Prana or Chi or life force that sustains us. The legends of Indian philosophy speak of many masters who could live only on Prana, never eating for many many years. Why not a Australian yogic housewife master? Jasmuheen didn't just stop eating. She says that over a long time she slowly changed her diet, eating first vegetarian food, then eating lighter and lighter vegan foods altogether. She also had a strict practice of yoga and meditation. She says that at one point she just realized that she didn't need to eat, and so she stopped. She admitted that every so often she had a small taste of ice cream, but just because she liked the wonderful sensual taste.

When I first met her she was doing a workshop for about forty people in a private home in Northern California. Our music group

Starseed played at the event, but Rasa, Bastian and I wanted to attend even if we were not playing. We were all very curious to see this woman we had read and heard so much about. I liked her immediately, because of her kindness and humor. She spoke very clearly, and I had the feeling I could trust her.

I liked the idea of living on light. I thought about it for weeks and weeks, even the idea of turning our kitchen into a sauna after we didn't need it anymore, but I figured out that it was not the right time for me to do this. I was, emotionally, not stable enough. My green card situation was unresolved. I was still in various ways uncovering the emotions of my past. After the fall of the tech stock market at the end of the century, we had a new house in Mount Shasta and a hole in our financial portfolio. We had to be very conscious and attentive of how to manage our money. This would have been a perfect time to live on light, saving so much money and time on getting, preparing, eating and digesting all that food every day, but living on light is both easier and more difficult than you think.

One time when we were living in Fairfax, just north of San Francisco, I was sitting in meditation, letting my thoughts freely flow, when an amusing image came to my mind. I was suddenly standing in a great temple in India. There were hundreds of people all looking on as an illustrious guru spoke. I was shyly standing behind a large column, a little afraid the guru might see me and call me up. Suddenly I heard his voice, "Marlis, come up here. Do not hide. I see you anyway." So I went to him, and he said, "Let us dance a waltz!" I was so shy in front of all those people, but I had no choice. He was suddenly standing before me in the classic waltz position, his arms waiting for me. So we danced the waltz. For some months after that every time I sat at my puja table I closed my eyes and I was instantly back in India dancing the waltz with a great teacher.

Chapter 19

Journey to my Self

Become a butterfly of eternity
and fly away to the shores of immortality.

- Paramahansa Yogananda

I am living in a world of mirrors. Everything reflects back to me - what I am thinking, what I feel. I figured out over the years, that I always meet the right people at the right time, to show me, like a mirror, what I need to work on.

I believe the work, the reason why I am here, is to shift myself to a higher consciousness, and act from that consciousness in ways that help to bring the world to peace and harmony.

Sometimes when sitting at my puja table, I experience that peace and harmony, and a vision arrives in my consciousness. I perceive the world and all its creatures, plants and minerals as connected, all part of a magnificent harmonic creation.

Puja is a Sanskrit word that means reverence or honor. Puja is the ritual of honoring God within your Self and the universe. I have a puja table at one side of my living room. My living room is filled with art and artistic creations I have made, received or found from around the world. The puja table takes up an entire wall of the room. The table itself has several levels with paintings, murtis, statues, candles, small bottles and containers, all sitting on soft red and gold silks and tiny woolen carpets. There is a strong female presence on my puja table, anchored in Eastern and Western traditions and represented by large statues of Quan Yin and Mother Mary, and a tanka of the White Tara. Everywhere around the table are old stones, very old stones. These are rocks I've collected from different parts of the world, some are ancient creations with fossils, and others are even older.

I am surrounded by holy images representing unconditional love and light. I have not simply collected these paintings and statues and made an interesting tableau. Each one came to me through a direct contact to the energy that object radiates or represents. Every time I meditate, I sit before this puja table and enter the sacred space created by all my experiences with these sacred energies.

When I first created the puja table, I sat in front of it and had the idea that I wished I could be in India, sitting in the presence of a great spiritual teacher, what the Indian's would informally but reverently call *Babaji* for a male teacher, or *Mataji* for a female. Suddenly a thought came into my head. The thought said, "You don't have to go anymore to India. The spiritual teachers are coming to you." It is interesting that I had the intuition to move to the furthest point west on the planet in order to connect to the most progressive ideas and people, and so many of those ideas and people I've met traveled here as well, and from even further east than myself. It is as if all the world is moving west, following the sun as it illuminates the most exciting ideas.

Just before I sit in front of my puja table, I clean my aura. I take some drops of *Aura-Soma White Pomander* into my palm and rub my hands together. I then clean the space around my body by stretching my arms above my head and then letting the fragrance of the pomander swirl around me as I swing my arms down and around my body. After reaching my feet, I lift my hands to my face and breathe in the purifying essence three times.

I then light the fifteen candles that sit in different places on and around the puja table. I say Aum to the flame of each candle I light. When the last candle is lit I put the special long necked candle lighter on its holder, and I kneel before the center of the table. I lower my head to the floor in devotion to the magnificent mystery of all of creation. The Hindus believe before doing a ceremony in honor of Lord Shiva one should first honor the elephant god Lord Ganesh, son of Shiva and Parvati. In the same way, everyday I offer my love to all the deities, and then I honor the highest energy, the source of everything. Aum.

I sit in lotus position, back straight, legs folded, eyes closed. I sing Aum sixteen times. I imagine the Aums as they come out of me, floating and then flying off to all parts of creation. I do these chants to the rhythm of my breath. Throughout my puja, I am performing several different mudras. These are mostly ritual hand positions and movements that help to center me and promote a proper flow of prana. I then visualize my Self connected to the highest Source. Once connected, I begin the Brain Illumination Meditation. One should learn this meditation from original materials to be as exact as possible, but in a brief description, I can say, one consciously brings light into all the components of the brain, and then all the parts of the body from the energy centers to the organs and cells down to the DNA and RNA. Now that we know a lot more about all the parts of the brain and body, what they do, and how they do what they do, we can create a meditation that more effectively illuminates. After flooding the brain and body with light, I then consciously anchor the light in every part of me, and then allow the light to expand and radiate to the subtle bodies and aura, and to the living earth and to the cosmos. On some days, in some meditations, the image of Mother Mary comes to my mind, or the image of Jesus, and I sit in silence feeling their love. After these ideations, I sit quietly in silence for some time, and then I blow out each of my candles, always saying "Aum" before each light goes out.

When doing this Brain Illumination Meditation, I am bringing light into my brain while also practicing relaxed but precise breathing. Pranayama, the practice of controlled breathing exercises, was created to help increase the flow of the life-giving force - prana. During my meditation I use the method of breathing I learned from Leonard Orr. With this powerful circular breathing technique, the feeling of prana filling the body can be exciting. For some who may have difficulties letting go, the feeling can even be overwhelming.

In both the morning and evening I practice one form of the Fire Breath pranayama exercise - a rapid breathing only through the nostrils. On the exhale I contract my stomach muscles for a forceful release of air. The fire breath quickly gives a lot of energy, and as I am visualizing light entering deeply into me during the strong inhalation, my entire being feels elevated and free, as if ready for flight.

Fire gives a metaphor to the fire breath pranayama, but candlelight and fire ceremonies utilize and honor the power of fire itself. Just next to the puja table, there is a sunken area of the living room we call the Kiva. Kiva is a native American word for a subterranean ceremonial space, always with a fire pit. Our fireplace sits on one side of the Kiva, and on many days, and often on special occasions, I perform a sacred fire ceremony. These ceremonies have their origins in venerable old traditions, but I often add my own form or interpretation to the ceremony. Sometimes it is the addition of some new scientific or philosophical concept. Sometimes it is only a small reminder of the modern idea that all these traditions share a common search for unity with the Divine.

Before I even see my puja table in the morning, before I even enter the room where my puja table sits, I have already spent nearly two hours in preparation for the day. When I wake up in the morning, I'm immediately here, fully awake in the moment, all sleep has vanished. I go in the bathroom and clean myself. I start by cleaning my tongue with a tongue scraper. I brush my teeth, and then with a dry body brush I go over my entire body. I started this brushing habit when I was fifteen years old. The brushing cleans away old skin and impurities, and stimulates the healthy skin cells.

I then dress myself, and at a small shrine in my bedroom, actually in the morning and evening as well, I do a short ceremony, a meditation to center myself. Then, I start each morning by drinking warm water. I am saying "Aum" all through the day - a short blessing I offer before many actions. With water, I use the power of my mind's intention to create more than a blessing. I create a small program. I program the water with a concept, in a way similar to a computer programmer giving instructions to an operating system. In my mind I say, "I program the molecules of this water with love, light and detoxification." When I think these words I visualize the molecules changing.

When I take a bath every morning, I do the same programming. I developed this daily bathing practice from an intuitive understanding of the importance of our relationship to water. This was some years before hearing Leonard Orr's compelling philosophy concerning water, which borrows its main idea from the Hindu practice of ritual bathing. I saw the scientific evidence of this relationship in the work of the Japanese scientist Masaru Emoto. His experiments, and his magnificent microscopic photographs of frozen water crystals, clearly show the effects of consciousness on water.

I am fortunate at this time in my life to live near Mt. Shasta where every week I fill up glass bottles of water from a small spring that is the headwaters of the Sacramento River. Many people every day hold their water bottles under this generous stream that pours out from the rocks and earth. I use only glass bottles because most if not all the plastic bottles give off some amount of chemical particles into the water. I store the bottles for the week in a cool dark place as I use them up.

As I drive to this spring with empty bottles in the back of the car, I always pass a small road that leads to a giant bottling plant. Large corporations have discovered the increasing value of pure water, and there are now divisions in the community over the value of selling Mt. Shasta's water. Ecological and ethical concerns suggest letting Mother Earth keep her fragile promise to maintain the flow of water into the Sacramento Valley. Our friends at the Mount Shasta Bioregional Ecology Center work every day, like community organizations in many places, in the struggle to keep our priorities in balance.

I drink a lot of water during the day, often with a few drops of fresh squeezed lime juice. The lime helps to neutralize acid in the body, and it tastes so nice in the process. Following the schedule of my digestive system, I help my intestines to continue their work on yesterday's food by only having cleansing liquids in the morning. First I have water, then fresh squeezed orange juice, and some time later I have apple juice made from a centrifugal juicer. Around lunch time I make a blender drink of carrots, beets, celery and ginger. I usually eat my first solid food of the day between one and three in the afternoon. The pure juices give me vitamins and energy, but just as importantly, they work well with my body's morning digestion - cleaning out my system so it can begin fresh on the new solid food I take each day. Even with this helpful morning practice, I also periodically fast, and use special herbal preparations for cleansing my body. About an hour before dinner I have a protein drink made with a banana and Blue Green Algae from Klamath Falls, Oregon.

I take dinner between seven and eight o'clock. From the theory and practice of cleaning and cooking I experienced during three years of professional training in school, I learned a lot about basic necessity. I have a very efficient and practiced routine for cleaning all parts of my home, and the same care and understanding goes into how I cook. Heating oil to the right temperature depending on what you are cooking, or knowing which potatoes to use for mashed as opposed to fried, or how to cut vegetables so that they cook evenly, or how to combine four simple ingredients to make a tasty dressing - all these skills are thoroughly in me, like for most experienced housewives, as natural and easy to manage as riding a bike.

I usually don't like to eat after eight in the evening. This gives my body a full half a day to spend on digestion without any interruptions. When I introduced this diet to Rasa in 1992, after two months of not eating at night, having only juice in the morning, and eating my light cooking for lunch and dinner, he lost forty pounds. As I write this, many years later, he has never regained that weight, and he says that a simple changing of his patterns made all the difference.

Every morning I exercise and practice yoga. Many years ago I read a little book called the *Ancient Secret of the Fountain of Youth*, by Peter Kelder. It describes six yogic exercises, what he calls the

Five Tibetans, and a sixth practice that is for people who wish to transcend their sexuality. These yogic exercises are simple but very effective.

I then run on a treadmill for fifteen or twenty minutes. Before I got the treadmill I would run circles around the small pyramid in the back yard. I would make forty to fifty laps around the pyramid, and the deer were always fascinated. They like to run too, but I think they were always trying to figure out why I kept going only in circles.

These daily cycles of cleaning and centering are all a part of my meditation. Even though I describe an elaborate ritual for my sitting meditation, and my puja table requires a lot of attention, the actual entrance I make into a blissful state could be done anywhere, and in an instant. I often offer a blessing during the day as a way of expressing the unity of all things. It may be a ceremony as simple as closing my eyes for a moment and silently saying Aum. I love that simple ritual, but I also love the ceremonial elegance of Lakshmi, Goddess of abundance. I love the splendor of sitting before so many candles with so many images of divine energy around me. I love all the pomp and reverence, but I also love the simple Aum. The reason I can love both extremes of expression is that neither one is really important. Without any actions, words or thoughts, I can experience the unity of all things.

I have had many teachers over the years, and they have all brought me step by step to greater realizations. Usually I don't follow teachers, but I may follow their teachings. The teachings carry an inherent wisdom. The teachers may or may not carry that wisdom in their lives. For me, a spiritual teacher who demonstrates the teachings radiates love and light in action.

When I sat at my puja table with the thought, "The spiritual teachers are coming to you," I immediately thought of a conversation I had the week before. My friend Uma came for a visit with her three children Diami, Chekpa, and Whope. Sitting on the porch, Uma told me about a new spiritual teacher, a powerful woman, with very modern teachings. My first impulse was to tell her that I was not interested in a spiritual teacher. She said that this European born Indian teacher was the disciple of a great Indian guru, and the guru had sent her to the west to teach.

I had the thought, "The spiritual teachers are coming to you," Uma's words came back to me, and I reached for the telephone to make a reservation at a spiritual event with this new teacher to be held in Asbury Park, New Jersey. This was Sunday, September 9, 2001. On September tenth I flew from California to Massachusetts. Before the end of the next day, every airport in America was closed. America was under attack.

The Indian spiritual teacher would be offering a three day event at a hotel on the Atlantic shore, just south of New York City. The event started on the fourteenth, but Rasa and I planned to drive down the night before. On September thirteenth we drove south and through the top of Manhattan to get to New Jersey. We slowly drove by steel-eyed policemen who made all the cars on the interstate highway passing through Manhattan slow down through police barricades. The whole lower part of the city was in smoke. Most of the rest of the trip you could still see New York smoldering in the distance. When the Indian teacher, Mataji, arrived at the hotel we were with a group of devotees in front waiting to greet her. I came up to this smiling radiant woman and she took my head in her hands, I put my arms around her and I felt that I was connected to a beautiful being.

I had never sought a guru. I have had profound connections to many teachers, both personally and through their teachings, but never with the traditional Hindu concept of guru. I hungered for divine wisdom and transformation, and in my mind I had doubts about the guru relationship. I didn't want to lose my independence on the path to total freedom. I knew I had to surrender on the spiritual path, but I didn't want to give my power away. Was this the ego afraid to lose its power? Did my heart long for a great teacher?

I was very impressed on that first meeting in New Jersey. I was impressed by the teacher, but I was equally impressed by the deep respect offered to her by her devotees. The path of Bhakti, devotion to the divine, can take the form of any human relationship. We can be devoted to a lover, a parent or a friend. Devotion to a teacher is known as guru-bhakti. All forms of bhakti honor not the other's ego or personality, but the divine that resides within us all. I admired the devotion of Mataji's followers, and their surrendering love to their teacher, but even with that auspicious meeting, I still resisted the idea of taking Mataji as a guru.

Because we arrived the night before the beginning of the three day event, we sat in with a group of about thirty people for a private audience (what the Hindus call Darshan) with Mataji in her hotel suite. When I entered the room I took a place near the back on the sofa. Mataji pointed to me and then pointed down in front of her, asking me to sit in front. This was an informal gathering, Mataji conversing lightly with this small group. In between, she was always talking on the cell phone, talking to people who could not fly and were driving to the event from across the country. She gave advice to the drivers, giving them loving energy and telling them to stay awake!

The next morning the event started. I didn't know any rules or protocols for a retreat with such a notable teacher. I was standing outside the main meeting hall with a tape recording of a beautiful Hindu chant performed in honor of Mataji's guru in India. I wanted to give her this tape as a gift. I found out later that the protocol required that everyone be seated before Mataji enters. I was waiting at the doorway when she turned around the corner. As soon as she saw me, she yelled loudly, "Go back in the hall!" I was shocked by a reaction that looked like anger to me. I went back to the hall and took my place. Inside I was feeling some confusion, a little out of center. Over the next hours Mataji sat in a large hall of Americans who were three days before violently attacked and still in shock.

Mataji's spiritual message centered on love in action. Three days after 9/11, she used this message in an effort to bring the people in the room to a level of compassion and forgiveness. Her talk was passionate, intelligent and uplifting, but I always thought a spiritual teacher demonstrating the model of a spiritual teaching would express loving kindness, patience and understanding from the heart. Why, at times, was this spiritual teacher so angry?

After some hours Mataji looked all the way to the back of the hall at me and said, "What did you want?" I said, "I just wanted to give you a tape recording of a chant made for your guru." Mataji said nothing more. When the next pause came, I was out in the hall and still feeling out of my center. I didn't understand what had happened. I felt as if my Inner Child was in fear. Lizzy, someone close to Mataji, then came up to me and said, "Don't be sad. Mataji's love is unconditional."

After the event in New Jersey, I sent Mataji an e-mail and explained with respect that I was sorry for breaking the protocol. Still, for quite a while my Inner Child was troubled by that event, and I didn't see her again until two years later. Bastian, who had became deeply connected to Mataji, went to many of her events in this time. Then in 2003, Mataji gave a talk in the East West Bookstore in Mountain View, California. I spontaneously decided to go. The whole time sitting in front of her tears were running down my face. As a child, when I did something wrong, and my mother punished me, I always cried. I never cried right away, but always some time later, after turning and turning in my thoughts. In my mind, sitting in the East West Bookstore, I felt as if I were sitting in front of my mother. In this moment I felt my feelings turning. Something inside of me was awakening.

On Mataji's fiftieth birthday there was a wonderful huge celebration at a hotel in Huntington Beach, California. A special Yagna (a traditional Hindu fire ceremony) was held to honor Mataji. I didn't have the money for travel and to attend this event, but just before the event I sold a painting that provided more money than was needed for the cost of the whole trip. Bastian and I drove to

Mataji's celebration with the cheerful thought that suddenly having the money was an auspicious sign.

I saw Mataji again in 2003 in Marin County at an event she sponsored. A spiritual teacher, who I will just call The Teacher, was the main guest speaker at the event. After a short while listening to The Teacher, in his manner and crass jokes, I sensed that he was more disrespectful than reverent for an audience looking for a higher vibration. I got up and left the hall in the middle of his presentation. There were others who also left the room. When the pause in the program came I decided with Bastian to leave the event. Some weeks later we were surprised to receive a call from Mataji who was in Bordeaux, France. She asked why we left the event. I explained my feelings and described how I thought there was no heart in his teaching. She listened carefully to my words. We talked for some time more. The conversation moved away from the subject of The Teacher, and in the end she told me to come and speak further with her at the next one of her events. After I hung up the phone, I began to think about this telephone call from Mataji. I had the sense again she could have been my mother, this time asking about something in my life that disturbed me.

Mataji's new spiritual-humanitarian organization held a regular schedule of events, and Mataji had begun to invite various progressive thinkers and experts to offer new spiritual insights. The events were becoming larger and larger over time, with more and more people attending over a series of several days to a week. Often the events were expensive to attend and held at resort hotels, and Bastian and I wondered sometimes about all the people who may not be able to afford to attend these events. We even wondered how we could afford it. We made the decision that going on vacations for two weeks out of every year would probably cost the same, and so we attended the events as often as we could.

The next time I saw Mataji was in 2006, in Vale, Colorado. I still felt some resistance towards this revered teacher, but the last day of the event, May 14th, was my sixty-fourth birthday, and as was the tradition, I was very excited to walk up to the podium to Mataji to receive a special blessing. Bastian had purchased a flower garland to give to her. She would then bless the flowers and place them over my head and on my shoulders, as was the Hindu tradition. I was so moved by the sacred elegance of this simple ancient ceremony. In my excitement, I nearly didn't hear anything, but I felt the love and light in the moment.

In my morning meditation many times after the Vail event, I envisioned my Merkaba, the mystical vehicle, a perfect geometric form, gold on the outside and pink inside, and I beamed myself as a hummingbird to Mataji. The hummingbird always came back in bliss. The *Ma* in Mataji refers to the universal mother. In the Hindu tradition, this title signifies an embodiment of the divine female form. As I came to understand this ideal form, and my own conflicts with motherhood, my spiritual connection to Mataji began to evolve.

The next time I saw her was October 2006 in Palm Springs, California. The city's convention center and the adjoining hotel was transformed for the seven day retreat into a temple for the Higher Self. Starseed had been invited to perform every day at the event. People came for lectures, presentations, singing bhajans, participating in discourses by Mataji, but mostly for the bliss of Darshan, a Sanskrit word that literally means, *to see with reverence and devotion.* Devotees see the light of truth in the words and actions of the guru. Mataji encouraged all to see the divinity in everyone - not as an abstract concept, but in every graceful action and kind gesture. Over days of a large group continually offering graceful gestures of kindness to one another, gradually there builds a powerful energy field. You can see a glow in people's eyes. Their bodies appear light, their movements relaxed. Several times every day all would enter a large hall with a large sacred geometric structure, mesmerizing spiritual art on easels before all the walls, a large white podium in front with bouquets of fresh flowers, and large speakers on all sides so that every word from every presenter, and all the music would resonate clearly whether one sat in the rows of chairs or sat in lotus posture in a semi-circle around the podium. Mataji would enter this loving environment each day as if she were the embodiment of Lakshmi, gracefully walking up the long aisle, in a traditional Hindu ceremonial manner, smiling and offering her palms together in the traditional Namaste. Everyone returned the salutation, offering their palms together in that natural pose of praise. In the West we pray with hands together. In the East the same gesture is used as a greeting that honors the divinity within us all.

At this event I had a strong transformation. After some days, I realized that the pain of my Inner Child who was so hurt, was triggered by Mataji, but I could clearly see how it came from my childhood, with my mother. I felt that the resistance, the disappointment, the anger just disappeared. I just surrendered. I had seen Mataji as a mother figure, mixing up that image with my troubled history. I could finally see through the illusions and layers of motherhood, and I could surrender to the source within myself, the divine mother within me.

Hundreds of people gathered for each day of the week long retreat, and each day Bastian, Rasa and I, as Starseed, sat on oriental carpets, closed our eyes in silent preparation, and then played as people all around us sat in meditation. We always receive whatever energy an audience brings into a performance, and at this event, the radiant energy in the hall inspired us to play with great devotion. On the last day of the event, unexpectedly to us, Mataji asked us each up to the podium to receive a special honor in thanks for our playing. I was called first, and in my gratitude to Mataji for her help in my transformation, I was excited just to be able to thank her. When I came to her, she unfolded the wrapping of a gift for me. She said, "This is very special." She told me that her guru had given her this gift for her to wear when she went *out to the world*. It was a red silk jacket covered with gold embroidery. She told me that she gave this to me for my puja, my devotion, and I was overwhelmed. I told her of the great transformation I had in the last days experienced. I told her my Inner Child had been hurt, and that pain once had been triggered by her in 2001. I said that I told Bastian at the time that Mataji was very tough, wonderful, but tough. She laughed to hear that. She called Bastian to the podium and showered him with praise and gratitude and gave him several gifts, among them, a Murti. Mataji gave a Murti to each of us. In the Hindu tradition, a Murti is a statue, that when blessed by a Brahmin priest or a guru, becomes an energized manifestation of the Divine. Mataji looked at Bastian and me, and said that we were an example of what is special about couples that is unique in the creation. We were both smiling, excited in the moment, but as I sat down I realized that I really didn't know what she meant. Was she referring to the two of us sharing a spiritual path?

When Rasa received his gifts from Mataji, she gave him several gifts, as she had done with Bastian and me, but then she looked to him and said, "Thank you. Thank you for your love. Thank you for sitting here every day and playing for us. Thank you for allowing the sound of God to take us back into our very true nature. I'm grateful. Namaste."

Mataji had given us each a garland of enormous roses and carnations. We stood together as the hall applauded, and then as Bastian and Rasa returned to their instruments, I stopped, turned and walked back to Mataji. I said softly, "Mataji, would you please grant me one wish?" Mataji immediately said, "Uh-huh," agreeing, but looking at me with some amusement. I rubbed the back of my hand with my fingers and said, "I would like to have that smell from you on my hand." Many Indian gurus are known to have siddhis or spiritual powers. I had not heard anything about Mataji having special yogic abilities, but some days before, I saw her rub her fingers on the back of a woman's hand. The woman smelled her hand and smiled in bliss. I went up to the woman later and asked to smell her hand, and I inhaled a sweet soft fragrance unfamiliar to me.

Mataji laughed loudly when I whispered my request to her. She asked me to repeat the request into the microphone. I did, and she said, "Tough guru doesn't do that!" I said, "Oh yes! Tough gurus do everything they want!" She immediately took my hand and rubbed it with her fingers. I smelled the back of my hand. There was the fragrance! I cried out, "Yoo-Hoo!" The hall erupted in joyous laughter. As soon as I took in that wondrous smell, my face relaxed into a beautiful blissful smile. Mataji turned to Norma, the Master of Ceremonies for the event, and said "Look at this. Did you see this? Suddenly she becomes younger!" Norma said, "She looks like fourteen years old!" In that moment full with Shakti, all unease had disappeared. I was as free and full of love like a young girl. And now, here I was. Smiling in bliss.

I always wondered after that, *how did she do this? Did she have the power to manifest that smell?* I still don't know. Modern science has a limited understanding of the seemingly limitless potential of the quantum zero field, so influenced by consciousness. Did Mataji's consciousness and intentions produce this smell? I really don't know.

The spiritual teacher can act like a catalyst and help bring out what is needed for a person's next step in spiritual development. After six days being in Palm Springs I experienced a great resolution of many past events in my life. I understood Mataji's role in this transformation. I was extremely grateful for her participation. I was even mesmerized by the whole remarkable phenomenon. I was like many of the devotees who had the ego adjusted by the example of the guru. I wanted to express my gratitude, but even though the transformation was real within me, I still felt something missing. I realized that when attending Mataji's events, I was always putting an effort into being devotional. I was always trying to participate in all the aspects of the events, the singing, presentations, the lectures, the smiling pleasant talk during meals, but I was always trying. My devotion appeared to be an act coming from the mind.

I was at first attracted to Mataji because of her teachings. Her teaching for me was global. This I first heard in New Jersey, in 2001. She is herself Eastern and Western, having Indian parentage and born in the West. She embraces religious philosophies from both, and as a modern planetary representative, presents within her philosophy the most current cultural, social and scientific realms. In her intensive retreat sessions she swiftly moves from ancient concepts to modern marvels, weaving the known of old and new into a fabric of marvelous possible nows.

I believe this description of Mataji, but in that first meeting in 2001, I asked the question, "Why, at times, was this spiritual teacher so angry?" I never found a clear answer to that question, but continued to feel uncomfortable with that emotional tone. While clarifying some idea in a lecture, Mataji would suddenly loudly call someone by name, and give them a stern, sometimes threatening instruction, like, "If you don't stop thinking, then you should leave the room!" I never liked this disturbance at a spiritual gathering. Why single out one person with such harsh words in the middle of hundreds of people on a spiritual quest for compassion? Why bring us to the level of grade school? We are not in a worldly school. We are in a spiritual school where we work with subtle energy. When we are all in a meditative calm, this strong emotional act becomes a disturbing energy that stays for some time in the room. Yes, I know that we should not be attached, and we should let go in that moment to the distraction, but why do we need the distraction? I can imagine that people might observe Mataji's occasional harsh tone, and think that a certain devotee might need this kind of harsh lesson. I usually thought there was probably a better place and time to so intimately enlighten a person about their difficulties on the path.

Many Eastern teachers speak about enlightenment. In Eastern philosophy many levels of enlightenment are described, from brief glimpses and feelings of bliss, to total liberation, fully being one with the light, experiencing everything as one. In the simplest sense, any time light enters the consciousness, we are enlightened. Any time we let go of our attachments, physical or mental, we feel lighter. This is an enlightenment. Once we see how simple enlightenment can be, we can develop the techniques and practices that allow us to experience this bliss at will, from now to now.

I realized through experience over many years how the regular practice of ritual builds its own special energy in a space. As I daily use the center of my house, sitting at my puja table, and as visitors sit in front of this alter, we all give into the space the energy of our spiritual intention. In honor of Mataji and to help further the teachings she offered, Bastian and I dedicated one day every two weeks to opening up this sacred space for a meditation gathering. We named the gathering in this space The Temple of Oneness, and advertised the temple in our Mt. Shasta community. Over an hour and a half we would meditate, sing bhajans (sacred chants), and we would often listen to or watch some of the recorded teachings from Mataji. We offered these temple gatherings for two years. At some point during this time, to my great surprise, I found I was losing interest in the teachings. Even more of a surprise to me, I soon felt that I was not really inspired by the teacher anymore. I was really only interested in my work to integrate my experience with this spiritual teacher into a meaningful lesson. I realized that whoever the teacher may be, it is always the student who must do the learning. The concept of the Brain Illumination technique I received from Mataji was new to me, that we could consciously direct light and intention into the specific parts of the brain. I am very grateful that I did learn this from my experience with Mataji, but I felt it was not necessary to create a temple in order to bring this and other ideas to the community. I realized that if I wanted to tell someone in my community about Brain Illumination, I could simply tell them, or tell them to buy the DVD. I didn't need the formality of a temple to pass on a good idea. But Bastian and I built a temple, and in devotion to the teacher, we tried to make it work. We received many emails from a hierarchy of devotees about how to run the temple. We were asked to file reports on our progress and participate in telephone conferences on how to improve participation in Mataj's regional centers. This is all a reasonable request when trying to build a humanitarian organization. In devotion to Mataji, we were eager to help, but with my free spontaneous mind, I couldn't follow the rules. I originally loved the idea of building a temple. I was naively in love with the idea, and had few thoughts about the connection to an organization.

It is easy to become attached to a teacher. In the Hindu tradition the teacher is greatly honored. The spiritual teacher is sometimes lavishly honored. At Mataji's events devotees would eagerly buy photographs of the teacher, radiant in the style of Lakshmi, the

Goddess of Abundance. I too bought the photographs, to honor the teacher, and to have the compassionate eyes of the teacher around me in my life, offering the promise of guidance. I learned about the humility of reverence for a teacher with Mataji, but after three years I began to feel the reverence was misplaced. I had always felt the power of my spiritual progress came from a simple understanding. Simply, *I Am*. When I Am, I am one with the great teacher of the Higher Self. It is this teacher that throughout my life gave me clear messages of truth from my heart. I realized with a clear message from my heart that I would choose to leave Mataji. I would leave the community that grew around her. I would return to the spiritual practice that let me experience truth in any moment with the simple spoken word "aum."

Any master in any field in Indian culture who can help you focus on a teaching can be called a guru. Spiritual gurus can help bring into focus the Self's relationship to the universe, but the purpose of having a guru is not having a guru. We can't possess even the greatest of teachers. We can only use the teachings to let go of attachments so we can find our own way to higher truth.

For me it was not easy to let go of my attachment to Mataji. I honored her as a teacher throughout her rise in popularity. In the years since I met her in 2001, when she was an unknown Indian teacher creating her first impressions in America, her followers had increased greatly in number and the organization around her had grown. After receiving honors in India, and new titles from Indian spiritual organizations, her appearances in public became more elaborate, more formal, and with more rules.

I followed the habit of attending the large and small community gatherings, sitting for hours in large halls listening to Mataji and the many teachers who added their own voices. I had grown into the habits of Mataji's spiritual community, but never accepted the social rules created to help devotees conform to the advice from the teacher. As a free thinker, always examining any teaching in the light of new information and understandings in the moment, I have always walked in and out of rules. Rules don't always allow the free thinker to wander freely. I found myself sitting in these large halls and thinking, "What am I doing here?" But the ego always has ways to excuse any attachment. The ego says, "I'm not devotional enough. I don't want to surrender, I should just stay seated." Yes, I want to surrender. I want to surrender to my Higher Self, my I Am. But sitting in a large hall full of devotees, the ego wants to be included. The ego wants to play the devotee game.

I liked the idea of being a member of a vibrant spiritual community. I was genuinely excited about the first day of each event, staying in a nice hotel, meeting interesting new people, first entering the large hall decorated to create a high spiritual vibration. During the events themselves, I always found moments of stillness in devotion. Sometimes I had realizations about myself. Most of the event's activities, however, I had very little interest in. To be a good member of the community, I participated, but in time I could not understand the need for so much social interaction. I understood that the ego is challenged in extreme environments, and people on such a journey may need some careful guidance, but I was wondering why I needed to do so much to find the divine stillness within? These week long events were called *Intensives*. I understand the need for intensive experiences, but I was finding that in between the few moments in each event where I would have a spiritual realization, I was mostly being distracted by the shopping, the consumerism. There was a gift shop at every event where one could buy spiritual paraphernalia, and every one probably ended up there once a day, to buy a CD from a presenter, or buy a photograph or book from Mataji, or Indian clothes, or a statue of a deity. I have no problem with some materialism in a material world. I liked buying CDs or DVDs from presenters, or buying books with good information. I like buying nice clothes, but I was feeling myself become more than just a consumer at the gift shop. I consumed a week of lectures, songs, meditation techniques, advice, and with it all the rules that defined the proper protocol. Why did I do this? I first asked myself this question two years before I found the answer. I continued to attend long events, and continued to get very little from the experiences. But I seduced myself in my guru experience. I knew that I would have to challenge myself, confront unpleasant parts of myself. I wanted to fully devote myself to that task. I thought attending long events that I did not enjoy was part of the path of devotion. I thought listening to information, most of it I already knew from past experience, was required because I needed to politely, respectfully be attentive to the messages from the guru. I thought full participation was the act of devotion I was seeking.

One evening I was sitting in my living room looking at my puja table that throughout my life had evolved according to where I lived, sometimes large and grand, sometimes only with a candle and what I call a small traveling Buddha. Now I was looking at my puja table, and at all the rooms in my house, and everywhere I looked I saw photographs of Mataji, in frames, in calendars, on postcards. I thought, why do I need all these personal representations of Mataji's spirit? I know many people who are very devoted to their gurus. Some are great consumers of spiritual goods and artifacts, others are more modest in their devotion. I think many of them have received great benefits from their devotion to their gurus. I too received a great benefit with the help of a guru, but in my spiritual effort, I confused devotion with honoring. I thought devotion to the guru was the spiritual path, when I should have been honoring the guru, and giving my devotion to the path. Honoring the guru was part of my spiritual path, but like a devotee addicted to any glance from the guru, I found myself looking for evidence that the guru approved of my efforts. I found myself devoted to the guru's idea of how I should be enlightened. I found myself devoted to another person, when I should have been devoted to my Higher Self.

I suddenly felt a deep longing for liberation from my attachments. I thought about the many photographs of Mataji, and the photographs of other gurus and teachers in my house. In entering the guru experience, I had enthusiastically entered a worship of teachers. I have always honored the icons of the world's major religions. I have statues and paintings of Jesus, Mother Mary, Buddha, Shiva and others, but these historical figures have become concepts for me. They represent compassion, mercy, wisdom and spiritual power. I have no interest in the personalities of these great personages. I do not worship the actual Jesus or the actual Buddha. I am devoted to their teachings. When I went to one of Mataji's events, like most devotees, I wanted contact with the teacher. I wanted her to notice me, and when that was not happening, I wanted to be like all the other devotees - pleasant and devout. But this is not me. I like to be pleasant, but I also love to speak my mind, and sometimes cry out in defense of a great idea, or against a great injustice. I like to be devout, but after three years of trying to please the guru, trying to follow the organization's rules, trying to fit into a spiritual community and spending so much money in the process, finally I saw the immediate need to stop the drama, stop the acting, stop the ego's clever schemes. Finally I had to stop looking for truth outside of my own God-given nature.

I created a ritual. I sat at my puja table, half of the photographs of personal teachers in the house sitting in frames before me. I looked to each of the teachers and offered my gratitude. In my thoughts I said, *I have grown from your teaching. I have allowed new knowledge to enter my consciousness. My personality has become a better vehicle for the great spirit that resides within me. I now put all personalities aside and bow down to that great spirit within us all.*

I then went and collected all the photographs of gurus and teachers in the house and put them in boxes. Some I later gave to friends. Others I gave to one of Mataji's center leaders in a distant city. I then completely transformed my puja table, returning it to my older style that honors only the spirit of the universal truths.

Then I created a fire ritual. As in the Hindu tradition of Shiva's fire ceremony, I honored the God of transformation in my Self by burning off my attachments to the personal form of the teacher. As the fire burned and I chanted I felt a great weight lifting. Sitting before the fireplace, tending the logs and burning embers, I was conscious of my body's movements, but my spirit felt as free as the dancing flames. I began to sing, "I Am Free! I Am Free! I Am Free!"

When I look back, my life has been wonderfully transformative, and continues to be. With all my going in and out of my Self, I am much more often in my center. I am still transforming, but being more and more in balance, I can transform with greater awareness. I am conscious of acting with my heart. This compassion that arises through the heart heals the little fearful child in me who finally understands the transformative power of love.

Chapter 20

Opening my Heart

The moment you have in your heart
this extraordinary thing called love
and feel the depth, the delight, the ecstasy of it,
you will discover that for you the world is transformed.
                                                    - Jiddu Krishnamurti

Through the opening of my heart I experienced a wonderful healing process. All the experiences of my past sit like information in a computer, influencing my every action. The healing energy of the heart clears past programming, and I am from now to now able to reconnect to all and everyone in my life with a new pure loving intention.

Since my mother died in the year 2000, I have thought a lot about our relationship throughout my life. I realized that through all my times of turmoil she was always there, sometimes sharing the trials, but always accepting me with an unending love. She was a very compassionate soul. Like anyone's mother, she was not always understanding her children, especially me. I was not always an easy child to understand. I could be sweet, and even naively innocent with an open heart, but I usually wanted my way, when I knew what I wanted. I could easily act like a little devil. But throughout my adult life she was always there and ready to make me a cup of very fresh tasty coffee as we would sit and talk *über Gott und die Welt.*

In the last years, as I was visiting my mother, I began to watch her very closely. As a young adult, I was, in dress and manner, thought and action, as different from my mother as I could be. Children have to leave the nest, sometimes rebelliously, but always to create their unique personalities. Usually, either earlier or later in life, women unconsciously tend to act more and more like their mothers. I would sit with my mother, and look to see if I had fallen into any unconscious patterns simply because they were old and familiar patterns, and not my own patterns, but borrowed from my mother.

Throughout the first fifty years of my life I was surrounded by women and men, but I had very few female friends. My deep connection to Claudia R. began as conversations with our faces pressed up against the bars of our prison cells, holding our tiny mirrors through the bars to see at least a smile or a sympathetic frown. My step-daughter Ulrike, Joachim's daughter, is both a daughter and a friend. Ulrike's intelligence and curiosity as a child grew into a thirst for knowledge and understanding. In the 1970s we explored our experiences, feelings and ideas in hours of introspective talk. Many of those conversations took place as we traveled on journeys through countries in Europe, as well as in India. With Bernadette Kearney in Ireland, I found a friend who had a firm understanding of both the routines of daily life, as well as the dreams of metaphysics and transformation. Our conversations would wander joyfully in many directions. With many women, I felt our conversations went nowhere, only round and round in circles of gossip and superficial observations. With men, I enjoyed the intellectual journey. I felt like our conversations were going somewhere. Men usually don't like to gossip. They usually don't like to think deeply about how their feelings influence their actions. They prefer to express their emotions in the thrill of an adventure. They are usually uncomfortable talking about the emotions of our personal relationships. Then I figured it out. As I began to see how I suffered under the power of a male pattern the men themselves seldom saw, I saw that most women seemingly suffered in the same way. After centuries of subservience, we only had the small things to talk about. Like any oppressed class, we had our radical thoughts and radical thinkers, but the thoughts were often hidden after years of suppression, and the radical thinkers, in some cases, were burned at the stake. Even with the radical news from the feminist movement, only a minority of women were capable of discovering, or even then admitting, how deeply their lives were interwoven with the injustice they felt powerless to confront. But within the gossip and talk of little details, women carried the wisdom of caring for the family and home. In the little details, often neurotically discussed, a deep understanding of the importance of human relationships survived. With fear and uncertainty mixed with hard work and compassion, women have through the centuries held the world together. The men who return to the security of their homes every night usually think that security is provided by them. Women know instinctively the importance of cooperation, love and peace.

I always knew I had a tremendous power within me, but I poured that energy into looking good. I became masterful at playing the game required by the dominant male pattern. As my true Self began to emerge above the fog of my confusion, I began to look around me, and everywhere I saw the same fog, and everywhere within the fog I could see the faint lights of women's souls struggling on. Sometimes, I see another head lifted out of the fog. It is not easy to rise above the confusion, and because I see the path for so many women is so hard and often painful, I have comfort that I am not alone. That comfort is the compassion all women feel for other women when they rise above the fog.

Within this healing process, my heart came to my children. I had long felt both guilt and shame over leaving both my children in the care of their fathers. I will forever be thankful to Beatrice and Liesel for being the mothers to my children so lovingly. Even though I could feel at the time that this would be best for them, the deep pain of that separation was always with me.

At the time, I didn't understand how the struggles within my own psychology influenced my feelings and actions. From early childhood, I had closed my heart as a defense against the abuse I endured. I developed a fear of closeness, as my experience so deeply connected intimacy with danger. I wondered if I could even be a mother when I was first pregnant. I felt so closed off from sharing a simple kind embrace with a man, how could I show love to a child? And yet, I love my children with an unquestioning heart. The universal female aspect that gives birth to life inherently knows compassion. While writing this book, so deeply looking into my life, I saw the effects of the stark patterns I had developed, and how they melted away when I expressed the love I felt for my children. That universal love of mother for child can be called an instinct, but that definition does not fairly describe that powerful force.

Years ago I spoke to my son Ralf. I chose my words for him consciously as I explained why he grew up living with his father from seven years old on. I told him that throughout his entire life I loved him with all my heart, and I was always with him even when the circumstances of my life made my physical presence impossible. Ralf told me not to worry. He said, "I have always been happy having two mothers!" I know that he also grew in confidence through the actions of his father. Rolf had always been a kind and steady roll model for Ralf. In 1999 Ralf flew from Dusseldorf to New York City. Rasa and I picked him up from the airport and together we drove wide-eyed through the valleys between giant buildings in Manhattan, enjoying exciting New York. The next morning we took the long elevator ride to the top of the World Trade Center. We stood on the observation deck together looking down into the busy city streets, and then across the harbor and bridges and over the Atlantic to Germany where all our past history stood invisible in the distance.

Twenty years ago Claudia Susanna and I traveled, just the two of us, for a holiday in Corsica. Just recently Claudia Susanna stayed with me at my house in California. This was the first time in all those years where we were again alone together without children, husbands, friends. We talked long and deeply and felt the love and respect we had for one another. We knew that all was well, and would be.

We sat every morning on the porch having coffee, and every time our wild deer friend Eva would come by to greet us. We have a ridiculous chaotic video of Claudia Susanna and me sitting on the porch with a large female deer and her three baby fawns. Eva is standing in front of our small table. I am stroking her long neck, scratching her behind the ears, and all the time the babies are looking around, sometimes pulling some milk out of Eva, but always running in and out and around her. Claudia Susanna and I are just laughing and laughing.

I have had two fathers in my life. Both of them were named Walter. My German birthfather, Walter Jermutus, lost when I was two, only stays in my memory as some words of description from my mother, and as images in a handful of photographs. In one photo he poses in his officer's uniform - a striking thoughtful expression on his face. In the other photos he is standing with other soldiers in a foxhole in Russia, mountains of snow everywhere around them.

Walter Kendra, my Polish step-father, refugee from the Nazis, protected my mother from the Russian soldiers at the end of the war. I have great appreciation for the steadfast generosity he has lovingly continued over the years to give to my mother, to me and to my sister and brothers.

As I write this memoir, my three brothers have all passed on. Before my brother Günther died, I spoke with him often on the phone. When he was in his final days, he slipped into a coma. I called the hospital in Germany during this time and asked the doctor to let me talk to Günther. The doctor said, "No, I'm sorry, but your brother is in a coma." I told him, "You may think I am completely crazy, but I believe that he will understand me." The doctor immediately agreed, and said that he had recently read in a medical journal about cases where they believed that was possible. The doctor then put the phone up to Günther's ear. I told my brother that he was in a process to die, that he had nothing to fear, and he was surrounded by all of our love. I told him that he had lived a good life, and that now he could let go. The next day he passed away.

My sister Rita, an unfailingly compassionate soul, has become the jewel in the family since my mother passed on. Rita has cooked for and looked after my step-father, now eighty-seven but still in good health, and in many of the ways of my mother, she has kept the family close together. Her home, a very *gemütliches* (cozy) home is the center for birthdays, anniversaries, Christmas, and any other family gathering. She has, over their entire lives, also kept close ties to Ralf and Claudia Susanna.

With Bastian's mother Gisela, I began a relationship under the most trying of circumstances for a mother-in-law. Her son fell in love with a woman in prison. Over the years we have built a kind and loving harmony between us. I usually call her once a week - bringing our homes in California and Berlin together - sharing family news, and often talking about new ideas and views in spirituality.

My younger brother Klaus' wife Brigitte, still lives in Wesel and lives in my heart always as a kind presence when my life was so chaotic. I recently spoke to Brigitte on the phone, and we performed a small healing ritual. Last year her doctors discovered she had cancer. She has been undergoing chemotherapy treatment. I suggested that she also go to the chapel in Kevelar and offer a prayer to Mother Mary. She told me quickly that she had already done that, many times. After that, on the phone, we had our small ritual. I told her not to think during the ritual, simply believe in the power of prayer. There are so many cases of remission from cancer that doctors can not explain. Some doctors are willing to admit the importance of a patient's own state of mind and heart, and how that state affects the path of illness. Belief in the help of Mother Mary is only one way of tuning one's consciousness towards health. Every thought we have will have an effect on the entire being. Praying to any holy being in any tradition can have the same positive results.

I love rituals. I spontaneously create rituals, as well as repeat, like the saying of "Aum," a familiar ritual again and again. When created with one's heart, a ritual can connect the heart to other spirits and to the entire universe. On my property in Lake Shastina I have many trees. These are mostly pine trees that protect the property from the lake's strong winds, and provide a small forest that makes the deer and other woodland creatures feel safe. In the late spring the pine trees produce an enormous amount of pure cadmium yellow pollen. On a windy day the pollen flies and swirls in the air in waves like transparent silken curtains. On a calm day I will hold a large bowl under the lowest limbs of a tree, and collect ounces of pollen just by shaking a branch. That rich yellow color then becomes part of a painting in the future.

One day I walked around the property, offering my love and gratitude to all the trees. I went to each of the largest trees, walked slowly around the tree, and offered my appreciation. When we first moved here, we cleaned the dead branches out of our mini forest. We raked a lot of the old pine needles, and in time, more small creatures, rabbits, possums, raccoons, and others came through the woods. When I appreciate any being, either plant or animal, it is only a part of my compassion for every being on the planet. We can offer our thanks to small parts of the creation when we create rituals in the material world. It may seem like we can as individuals only make small gestures to change or improve the world, but all these acts of love resonate beyond.

I learned a special ritual from my friend Fumi, who is half American and half Japanese, and the director of the The World Peace Prayer Society. The ritual comes from the peace organization Byakko Shinko Kai in Japan. Reiko, a Japanese friend of Fumi's, tested Rasa and me at one of the initiation points. Reiko visited us in Massachusetts. She stood in my studio, as a Japanese master, and performed a powerful mudra, a sacred hand movement that seemed to emanate from her whole being. Rasa and I then performed our parts in the ritual under her watchful eye. The ritual includes the recitation of mantras, and a series of hand and body movements. After we completed these tasks, we began the drawing of the yantras - precisely designed mandalas, or circles. The yantra is considered to be sacred architecture, usually drawn or painted. It is seen as a geometric channel for cosmic truths. For the next stage of the ritual we would draw two yantras on special paper we received from Japan. In a mandala of one hundred and five concentric circles, spaced very tightly together, we would write within the circles, starting from the center, in very tiny letters, two Japanese mantras, one for each yantra. One mantra was *Ware Soku Kami Nari - I Am A Divine Being*. The other was *Jinrui Soku Kami Nari - Humanity is Divine*. As I wrote each mantra I followed a required breathing pattern. The space between the lines in the mandala was so tight that the writing had to be incredibly small. The instructions for how to write were meticulous, and as I finished the first few circles I began to see the evenly spaced words fade into a whirling pattern. After the eleventh ring in the mandala, after reciting this mantra again and again as I wrote, I began to feel the effect of this concentrated effort. I used special micro-pointed pens, also from Japan, to fit my tiny letters into the tiny space, changing colors intermittently after filling in large parts of the circles. In the end, after weeks of writing, I had finished my yantras. I then photographed them, and as requested by Byakko Shinko Kai, they now are stored in their archives in Japan along with the photographs of many other yantras from around the world. This was an exercise to help me experience through ritual the divinity within us all. During the days of learning the mudras and mantras, and completing the yantras, I was continually reminding myself of our shared divinity.

Of all of the spiritual traditions, I find I am most strongly attracted to Tibetan Buddhism. The Tibetan Dzogchen teachings describe the astounding nature of existence with a profound simplicity. In reading Dzogchen literature, I am laughing again and again at myself and all the world as I read about the deceptive psychological games of the ego, and the struggle to let go of illusion. These teachings are given with such humor and compassion. A delightful Dzogchen teacher, Lama Lena, often visits Mt. Shasta. Once she sat in front of a group of people who were all listening intently to her teachings. To illustrate the illusion that separates us from the formless state of pure consciousness, she suddenly said, "Don't read the word on this sign," and then she held up a large sign that said "boat" in bold letters. She slowly moved the sign from left to right so everyone in the room could have a good look at it. For the people in the room, the boat was inescapable. How quick the conditioned mind reacts!

Some years ago, through the help of Lama Wangdor Rinpoche, I began to sponsor a young Tibetan refugee living in India. Her name is Tashi Dolma, and she fled Tibet with her mother and siblings. She is an earnest student and so grateful for help in her schooling. Through her many letters to me, I can see in her compassionate words, her great devotion to the teachings of the Buddha, to life, learning, the love of family, and the deep traditions and beliefs of Tibet. I saw the fall of the Third Reich, and then the fall of the Berlin Wall and the Soviet Empire. It is long past time for the end of all imperial nightmares. One day I hope the occupation of Tibet will end, and all Tibetan refugees will be able to return to their homeland in peace.

Many people have written about the transformative words and ideas of a great teacher. I believe they do transform. My understanding of reality has been magnified and clarified by many great teachings. This has all been a part of my healing process - the long process of healing the wounds of karma.

I began my healing process instinctively, in much the same way my body heals a wound. Unconsciously, I began with an outer covering of guilt and denial, like a scab on a wound - a way, in the moment, to relieve my pain. When I was able, years later, I acquired the tools to heal the wound itself. I say tools because I realized, as I became more aware of the different levels of my self, I had to use different methods to reach the different levels. Most especially through Zaida, I was able to work on the physical and emotional issues, and some of the mental patterns. With yogic breathing I could flood my being with prana, and loosen the hard connections wired into my consciousness. With Brain Illumination I could direct that healing energy to my amygdala. The amygdala connects our conscious thoughts with the regions of the brain that control our emotions. With a conscious heart, I could flood the amygdala with compassion and light, a powerful antidote to illness that modern medicine has yet to fully acknowledge.

In healing the frightened child within me, I washed away old patterns built into my brain. With this cleansing came Shakti. Shakti, the Hindu's female counterpart to Lord Shiva God of transformation, is actually the energy of Shiva's power. I needed to burn off the hard shell of resistance I built to protect the frightened little child within me, and I needed to find compassion in myself to melt those walls around me. These are walls of the ego built as a protection against overpowering forces. These walls can serve a useful purpose for a frightened child, but the adult me, free of the old walls, can reach both in and out. I can reach more deeply within my being, and reach more effectively out to other beings. Free of the walls, I can freely receive. I can receive love, without the memory of being exploited. The melting of barriers in myself frees my Shakti, and I can give and take with greater strength and wisdom.

In exploring ancient wisdom and modern discoveries I have looked to find a harmonious recipe for conscious evolution. This could also be called learning to lose one's gravity. My deepest understanding of this path always comes through finding a deep stillness within. Sitting at a puja table or by a stream in nature, it doesn't matter how or where one does this. Of course there are many meditation techniques to quiet the mind. Many teachers, however, point out that the stillness is always available, and it is not the length of practice or the particular technique used, it is the intention of the individual that brings results.

Through stillness one feels more deeply, and can then connect more easily to the heart.

Once during my evening meditation I was thinking about our connection to the universe. I opened my journal and wrote the following:

An - Aus - an - aus

Aus dem Nichts ensprengt Alles.

Das ganze Universum
Die gesamte Kreation bin Ich – ist in Mir
Reines Bewusstsein

On – Off – on – off
Out of Nothing springs Everything
The entire Universe
I Am One with the whole Creation
Pure Consciousness

I wrote these words with the inspiration to invoke the experience of being one with All, through a mystical doorway best described by quantum physics. One of the many astounding revelations from the study of the quantum world, the world of the most small, is that the experimenter's consciousness influences the outcome of the experiment. At the Stanford Research Institute experiments were conducted where thoughts from outside a sealed laboratory influenced the actions of a computer in the lab. This may mean reality comes into existence anew in every moment, arising out of the stillness in the Zero-Point Field, and like for the scientist in the quantum laboratory, our experience of every moment is influenced by our presence in that moment. The power of our intention can influence the form of every moment. These modern ideas may help to explain some of the concepts behind the Brain Illumination Meditation, and other similar systems.

I have always been in love with new ideas, and when I feel with my heart that the new idea or technique resonates within me, I usually spring into the new idea with all my energy. Sometimes I later find the new and exciting idea was not as exciting and useful as I originally thought, but I am also very quick to let go, and usually even a disappointing experience teaches something I need to know – perhaps only that I need to learn to be more discerning.

These new ideas have taken many forms. My fascination with

DNA has introduced me to various scientific and esoteric views and techniques. Both Bastian and I received training in the nascent field of DNA Activation - a form of visualization meditation. Visualizations use the power of the mind to construct idealized realities. Whether this kind of focusing actually changes this or other dimensions of reality, we will learn as more and more people experiment.

In one focusing exercise, part of my ritual from the Japanese Byakko Shinko Kai, I was instructed to declare that the next 70,000 people I saw were all divine beings. With every person I saw I would say, in my thoughts, the mantra *Jinrui Soku Kami Nari - Humanity is Divine.* Everywhere I went, I would see people, and to each one I would remind myself with the mantra that they were divine, and then I would count them, until I reached 70,000. 70,000 is a lot to count, but the large number only made me more eager to get started. To accomplish this task, I bought a small mechanical counter, the kind you hold in your hand and press with your thumb for each new number. It's a joyful exercise to continually look at everyone as divine. I see someone, think the mantra, then click the button. I was instructed not to count divine beings while driving, and there were a few other helpful suggestions, but very quickly I didn't care about where I was, I was simply observing everyone in the best possible light, and clicking away. No one seemed to mind. Reaching 70,000 took several weeks - some days more active than others. I was very busy when flying from Massachusetts to California where I was in several crowded lines at airports. Some people asked me who I worked for, and why I was counting. I would turn to them, acknowledge them as a divine being, click the button, and then simply say, "I'm counting divine beings. Everyone's included!"

When most of our lives we walk through the day with the non-stop chatter of our thoughts jumping from subject to subject, the simple act of controlling our thoughts holds enormous power. A musician practices scales over and over, and soon becomes more fluid in moving from note to note when actually playing a tune. This is a common method for teaching the brain a new way to behave.

The brain even cooperates by creating any newly needed brain cells and neural networks. In teaching my brain to quickly see every person as a manifestation of the divine, I gradually become more fluid in expressing that same intention when I'm not simply counting, but out in the world interacting.

Through both visual art and music, an abstract freedom directs the sights and sounds I create, but like any artist, I am grounded by years of study, practice and experimentation - a gradual learning process of what works, and what does not. I love giving this same attention to every part of life. Mantras and visualizations help to focus my mind. Various practices, like yoga, massage, muscle toning, breathing exercises help to keep the body fit. But all these ideas and techniques work together as mind/body practices enhancing the entire being. Leonard Orr's simple connected breathing technique completely changed and improved my health on several levels - not just the physical parts of the body effected by the respiratory system. All these experiments and proven methods I've tried are all simply ways of healing, reprogramming, and activating the human vehicle.

Some years ago I read a small book on Toning, the practice of free vocal expression without guidelines or forethought. You just open your mouth and make the first sound that comes out. Of course you find out that the sound that comes out, supposedly free of intention, actually expresses the joy as well as tension in that moment of toning. Try singing right now without planning or even thinking of what it is you are going to sing. Be loud, be soft, be dissonant, be harmonious, be uninhibited. Just use your vocal chords to express yourself in the moment. It is always interesting to test this little known art.

I have always loved to sing, and as I became more clear and confidant in my Self, I have returned to the love of singing I had as a child. For many years I chanted the Hindu mantra Om Namah Shivaya. Starting in 1997 I began to regularly sing mantras using words and melodies I spontaneously composed. With Bastian playing synthesizers, we have recorded most of these chants. I begin these chants with a preparation similar to my meditation, with awareness and devotion. We usually have one recording of a chant playing in the hall when people come in to our Starseed concerts. Like the praise for the Hindu deity in the Om Namah Shivaya mantra, my mantras use short phrases in German and English to express in my daily languages my praise for the Divine.

This chant for the opening of my heart was spontaneously composed and recorded in German in the summer of 2000,

Invocation

Ich rufe die Öffnung meines Herzens herbei

Ich bitte mein Höchstes Selbst zu mir zu kommen

Und mich in das Feld der reinen Liebe zu tragen

Lehre mich die Geheimnisse des Herzens

Lass mich von Herzen handeln

Lass mich von Herzen sprechen

Lass mich von Herzen verstehen

Und zeige mir Deine Wege

Oh Herz, öffne Dich mir und bring mir Frieden

Aum

Invocation

I call forth the opening of my heart

I ask my Higher Self to come to me

To bring me into the field of pure love

Teach me the secrets of the heart

Let me act from the heart

Let me speak from the heart

Let me understand from the heart

And show me your ways

Oh heart, open to me and bring me peace

Aum

I am listening in the last year a lot to O. S. Arun, a master of the art of devotional singing. Music, especially singing, I believe, enters us and can change our consciousness faster than almost any other art. In Indian music philosophy the voice is considered the first and most expressive instrument. All other string, wind or percussive instruments are emulating the voice. When I hear O. S. Arun sing, I feel the devotion in his being radiating out through the sound waves of his voice. My whole being experiences the power of his devotion, and in sympathetic response I float on a wave of bliss. The Indian drums accompany him, using their infectious patterns to help lift his melody and text even higher. The chorus that sings the kirtan repetition of the chant, sound as if they are all in ecstasy, like Gopis following Lord Krishna in blissful adoration.

Kirtan, also known as Bhajan singing, is a call and response form of music where beautiful descriptions of the Goddesses and Gods are repeated over and over. When singing in full devotion to the deities there is no thinking. The ego can disappear, and when you are in a room with others singing with you, and their egos disappear, a tremendous energy is created with everyone's Higher Self free to be in total devotion. Our hearts open in the experience of unity with the divine. In recent years kirtan has become more and more popular in the West. Snatam Kaur, Krishna Das, Jai Uttal and others travel widely and lead halls full of Western people in a sacred Indian art. The beauty of the lyrics and music and the joy of devotion combine to lift people away from dogma and ideas, away from thinking altogether. In devotional song we can bring our inner experience of bliss into exquisite material form as our voices vibrate through the air, and these sacred syllables resonate through the universe.

I have recently been listening to an amazingly devotional recording from a Dutch singer named Hein Braat chanting Hindu scripture. His rich baritone voice vibrates my entire being with the sound of those ancient words. Many years ago Hein Braat had a great curiosity about Yoga and Eastern Philosophy, but he found he had no interest in sitting in uncomfortable positions, or sitting alone inside his mind for long periods, or even studying any of the ancient texts. What he did find fascinating was the art of chanting. He studied Sanskrit pronunciation and practiced the most sacred Hindu mantras and chants. I have listened over and over many times to one track of Hein Braat's recording of two important Hindu mantras. He sings the *Maha Mrityunjaya* mantra. The text beautifully addresses the three-eyed Lord Shiva, who permeates existence like a wonderful fragrance and nourishes all life. Shiva is asked to grant us immortality - *may we be liberated from death as easily as the fruit falls from the vine.*

My transformations play out in many forms. The burning of emotional passions, the drama of rational creations, the wondrous clear moments of perfect stillness - the cycles of events turning, evolving ever higher in an upwards spinning spiral. In all the stages of my adult life, I have expressed myself in my paintings. In the last decade or so of strong transformation, my painting has in many ways changed, and yet in some ways my artistic path has not changed at all.

My preparation before painting has not changed significantly. I still carefully choose my theme, and the theme influences my choice of materials and the size of the canvas or silk. I still meditate before I start painting my free abstract expression, and I still use the special mantra I created many years ago while in prison.

I have described how I responded in my art to America - big, modern and fast America. That response was an expression of my America, the America I have discovered, but my transformation was opening my heart at the same time I was taking in so many impressions of this energetic foreign land. A lot was happening simultaneously within me and all around me. I would prepare for painting with familiar motions, but my set and setting, you could say, my being and my environment was entirely new. I have experienced many aspects of America. I have compassion for its problems and I am delighted by its diversity and creative hunger for change and everything new. To this inner and outer dynamic, my art has also responded. My most recent series was entitled *Gratitude*. When you endure a great trial, such as most of our transformations are, you may come to the end and cry, "Thank God!" Maybe you are thankful just to be through the ordeal, but with an open heart you can also be thankful for the divinely inspired process that makes the transformation possible.

I began my career in art as an Abstract Impressionist painter. My impressions of nature, usually landscapes, became abstract forms on the canvas. Years later, through my inner journeys to my Self, I became an Abstract Expressionist painter. My abstract forms became an expression of my inner Self's experiences. What I call an expression of my inner Self, others have described as intuition, or insight, or an expression of the sub-conscious. Over time, I came to know this inner me as my Higher Self, that me that is one with everything, filled with compassion, and dedicated to actions that uplift and heal. That understanding has brought a new focus to my art. In recent years I realize that I have become what I call a Trans-Expressionist artist. In the meditative state I enter when I paint, the ego follows the energy of my Higher Self. My Higher Self lives totally in the moment. Unlike the ego, it does not filter or interpret information. My Higher Self communicates a healing compassionate message that describes the ongoing process of my transformation as an artist, in the moment, from now to now, as the brush moves across the canvas.

I write a lot in these pages about my transformation and the opening of my heart, but I am still on my journey. I know I am always learning and transforming and moving further and further into higher and higher levels of awareness.

I write a lot in these pages about the struggles I have overcome in my journey, but the struggles are not the goal. The details in my life and the number of years I have been *on the path* are the chapters of my story, they are not the main character. The "I" I talk about, the Higher Self I am - this Me has always been here, no matter how far I journey. There's the anecdote of the disciple who asks the guru, "How can I improve my meditation?" The guru asks, "How long have you been meditating?" The disciple says "I have been dedicated in practicing my meditation every day for thirty-five years." "Thirty-five years!" the guru cries, "What are you doing here? You should already be enlightened!" Many masters have talked about how there is a thin veil between our everyday consciousness, and enlightenment. In any instant we could simply move the veil. In any instant we could let go of all attachment and simply be. The disciple in the story was perhaps happy in her life because years of meditation can help calm the busy human mind, but there is a difference between the happiness of the three dimensional world, and the joy of enlightenment.

Happiness comes from many things, but always things. Bliss, or what in Sanskrit is called *ananda*, comes through the heart and lets me feel that sacred energy the Greeks called *agape*, or *divine love*.

The Hindus and Buddhists say that in each lifetime we work out past karma. We correct the mistakes we made in the past, while we try not to make more in the present. The Hindus and Buddhists are not content, however, to simply toil in ignorance lifetime after lifetime. Karma literally means action. The Karma we build up is simply the results of our actions. When these results are the product of the ego's actions, they call the results samskaras, or impressions left on the conscious mind and subconscious when any ego action is performed. When our actions are performed with the highest love, these mental constructions from the ego are not created. We do not become further burdened by the weight of heavy impressions. Actions from the Higher Self radiate from the heart and produce light, waves of light carrying the energy of cosmic love.

I was born in a Western Christian nation, and raised in a Christian family. I went to church, but as a child I was mostly interested in singing the hymns. As an adult, I do not have an interest in most of the organized forms of religion. I believe in the Mercy of Mother Mary, the Love and Forgiveness of Jesus, and the Devotion of Mary Magdalene. These are models that resonate with me.

I have learned about spirituality from both Eastern and Western traditions. Each has its own ability to connect a devoted seeker to higher truth. I have followed many teachings in my life, but my goal is not to be a student. I must act with the wisdom of a teaching. It doesn't matter whether it is described as Eastern or Western, Hindu or Christian. Labels divide the world. Wisdom unites us.

In 1998 I visited my mother and I had the feeling I would never see her again in this life. This was a little over a year before she died, and it was the last time I saw her. Bastian and I took my mother to the most famous Catholic pilgrimage site in Germany, the Chapel of Mercy in Kevelar, only an hour drive from my home town. I sat with my mother in the chapel and I prayed that she would have a good passing. In this place where centuries ago a poor farmer had a vision of the Mother Mary, I was asking for mercy for my mother. As I sat in a Catholic chapel with my German mother, I was content to see the forms of my family's religion and culture as innocent as the clothing one wears in this region, simply our way of being in the world. The church, the religion, and the culture may look different from land to land, but the hunger for higher truth is universal. We all have the same hearts and minds that must make sense of a confusing world. As religion grows, its message is often diluted by the rules created to bring order to a congregation of unruly egos. Often, the people with the strongest egos determine the path of the religion, while the original inspiration for the religion becomes lost, or distorted to allow for human desires. For this reason, I seldom trust the organizations that grow around great ideas. I look instead to the ideas themselves, and the actions taken to bring those great ideas to light. I may study the guidance of teachers from east and west, but for me the greatest teacher is life itself. We always have both good and poor examples of all the teachings. It can sometimes be hard to know the difference. I can only know the truth of a teaching through my own actions, and the transformations they create. With compassion and pure intention, these transformations lead to the conscious evolution of my Self and all around me.

I am a housewife. On one level this statement is still true. It is more accurate to say, I am an artistic multi-dimensional being, infinity in the shell of a body. With this consciousness, all of my care

315

for the house and family becomes the practice of consciously living my life from now to now, in service to all existence, offering every action with love.

Chapter 21

Niwo

Buddhism has the characteristics of what would be expected in a cosmic religion for the future: it transcends a personal God, avoids dogmas and theology; it covers both the natural and spiritual, and it is based on a religious sense aspiring from the experience of all things, natural and spiritual, as a meaningful unity.

- Albert Einstein

I began my life in great turmoil, always feeling that the only thing I could depend on were my own resources, my own sense of self. That seemed to me to be the only reality I could trust. Over time, as I grew more self reflective, I began to see the ego as a *lower self*, and the confident, spontaneous, compassionate *me* as a reflection of my *Higher Self*. I have struggled throughout my life to come to my Higher Self, to find my Higher Self, to be true to my Higher Self. I saw this Higher Self as the part of me that is connected to the Divine, unburdened by karma, beyond the programming of family and culture - a pure me. But when I think of all the times I felt I was truly in touch with this Higher Self, it was those moments of perfect stillness - where there were no thoughts of anything, and without thoughts - there was no me. No desires or attachments - not even the conception of a Higher Self. This was odd. When I was finally *in touch with my Higher Self*, I found it didn't exist.

What did exist was an awareness of an endless space of luminous energy, and every time I emerged from this space, I brought with me a tremendous feeling of wellbeing. I can only describe it as love. I began to see a formula. When I let go of my self, end the control of the ego, and even let go of a conception of a Higher Self, I disappear into the luminous energy, and then return to my self empowered by that luminous energy. What a miraculous experience!

I suppose I could be happy just to dip in and out of that wondrous experience every day, and I could be quite blissful and content, but it doesn't work that way. This transformation occurs after I have let go of all attachment to my self. That means that all those things that are important to the ego dissolve - all desires, all attachments. That's a lot of stuff to suddenly not have. What an incredible lightness of being! There is no busy ego grabbing my attention! But as a result, my attention is free to look beyond my self, and as a being filled with love who looks clearly at the world, I can not help but turn that love into compassion.

Epilogue

I know that every woman has her own story, and that my story is simply one of many - neither greater nor lesser of a life. I know that a lot of women have suffered far more than me, and suffer still. In my story, light overcomes the darkness. There's a joyous transformation. A story with joy is a story that women need to hear from other women. There is an uplifting spiritual theme in this story, but I think that in the telling of any meaningful story, spirits can be elevated. I am fascinated with the elevation of spirit - the raising of consciousness. I believe that fascination helped to create the joyous transformation.

Philosopher Ken Wilber would probably consider many of my experiences on the spiritual path to be part of *The Great Search* - his term for all our efforts at seeking oneness with God, or seeking enlightenment. Using the language of Buddhist philosophy, he describes enlightenment in terms of recognizing the *ever present awareness* - the pure consciousness that is not our thoughts, but our own awareness that observes our seemingly endless stream of thoughts, and our seemingly endless searching for spiritual enlightenment. We are already aware, Wilber argues. The awareness is ever present. There is no need to search for what is always here. He concludes that all of these efforts of The Great Search can be best described as "profoundly useless."

My Great Search ended in *Niwo* - perfect stillness. An abbreviation of *nirgendwo*, the German word for nowhere, Niwo (pronounced in English as *nee-voh*) is a peculiar word that popped into my mind when a woman once asked me about what technique I used in my meditation. She wondered if perhaps I was repeating a mantra, or visualizing another reality. I have repeated mantras and visualized other realities, but in my simplest meditation, I do nothing. I told her I simply let my thoughts come and go.

She thought about that for a moment. I could see her thinking about her thoughts. She sighed, and then asked me, "Where can I go to get away from my thoughts?" I replied with a word I had never before heard, *Niwo*. Nowhere. Perfect stillness.

Those extraordinary moments of perfect stillness - I have experienced them, but I have also experienced the ordinary moments of painful reflection on the errors I've made in my life, and the regret for the pain I may have caused others. As I examine myself, and choose to improve myself, I move forward, but I see behind me my mistakes. These usually have been my missteps as I move too quickly through the world. Sometimes in my speedy thoughts and actions I have had no patience for anyone who would challenge my thoughts or impede my actions. In those moments, my swift emotions can lead me to harsh misjudgments. When I realize my harshness, I can only condemn those actions of mine, and forgive myself for being so ignorant. In the blind ignorance of my youth I followed unconscious imprints and programs and searched for security in the arms of men - men who simultaneously fascinated and frightened me. In the blind naivete of my great spiritual search I spent most of my time looking for what I already possessed. While forgiving myself for any lack of intelligent thought or behavior, I have turned my missteps into opportunities, and I see this discernment of truth as the best chance I have to consciously evolve and express myself with wisdom and compassion.

My passion for higher consciousness has led me to write this book, and I wish that women who read this book and see something of themselves in the story may find some comfort or enlightenment.

Higher consciousness lets me experience an indescribable beauty. I see reflections of that beauty in daily life. I am attracted to beauty in all facets of life - in nature, in art, in the human form and human ingenuity, and most especially in the beauty of an intelligent mind where you look in the person's eyes and see clarity and compassion.

Aum.

Photo Gallery

My aunt, father and mother in Wesel - 1936

My mother (left) and me in my Godmother's arms
walking home after my baptism in Göttelfingen- 1942

My mother and me in Lüdertz - 1944

Wesel after the Allied bombing - 1945

My family and me (far right) - 1954

My boyfriend Rolf in his air force uniform
with my brothers Günter (left) and Walter - 1959

On my wedding day with Rolf - 1959

Rita and Ralf in Wesel - 1963

Bergen aan Zee, Holland - 1969

With Claudia Susanna on the terrace
at Breiter Weg, Wesel - 1973

Joachim's daughter's Ulrike and Klaudia, Wesel - 1970

At Breiter Weg, Wesel - 1974

At Breiter Weg, Wesel - 1976

My mother and me in front of Rock Cleopatra - 1976

Joachim in Ireland - 1978

Ulrike and me in India - 1978

With Claudia Susanna and Ralf, Wesel - 1980

Archibald in Ireland - 1981

At Rasa's wedding - 1982

With Timothy Leary, Hamburg - 1982

With Bastian, Berlin - 1984

Photograph from my exhibition while *on leave*
from prison - published in the *Bild Zeitung Berlin,
the highest circulation newspaper in Europe* - 1984

My sister Rita, Klaus Rosenthal,
and others at Claudia Susanna's wedding - 1989

My mother and sister - 1990

Claudia Susanna, Klaus and Demian, Berlin - 1992

Demian, Berlin - 1992

My mother and my son, Ralf - 1997

In Los Angeles - 1998

Rasa and Bastian, Mountain View - 1998

Painting *The Sixth Tibetan*,
Northampton - 2001

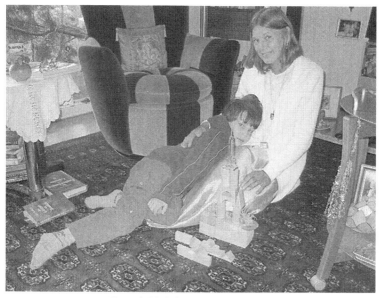

Cosma's birthday, Lake Shastina - 2002

Lake Shastina, California - 2003

343

Painting in my studio, Northampton - 2004

Bastian and me hiking on Mt. Shasta - 2005

Sitting with friends in the pyramid, Lake Shastina - 2008

Starseed in concert at Tara's Refuge, Mt. Shasta - 2005

Demian and I greet a wild deer friend, Lake Shastina - 2006

With Bastian and our dear deer friend Eva - 2009

With Rasa, Lake Shastina - 2009

With Sharon, Lake Shastina - 2009

Bastian, Purusha, me, Joanna Cherry, Karen Rogers and
Eric Berglund at Bastian's birthday party, Lake Shastina - 2009

With Eva, Lake Shastina - 2010

With Rasa and Bastian at Lake Shastina - 2009

Skyping with Claudia Susanna from Northampton to Berlin - 2010

Marlis at Starseed Gallery
www.starseedgallery.net

Starseed Music:
www.starseedmusic.net

Deer in the Yard:
www.pelorian.com/deer.html

Made in the USA
Charleston, SC
22 October 2015